China's New Social Fabric

edited
by

Godwin C. Chu
Francis L.K. Hsu

Kegan Paul International
London, Boston and Melbourne
in association with
The East-West Center
Honolulu

First published in 1983
by Kegan Paul International
39 Store Street, London WC1E 7DD
9 Park Street, Boston, Mass. 02108, USA and
296 Beaconsfield Parade, Middle Park,
Melbourne, 3206, Australia

Printed in Great Britain by
The Thetford Press Ltd., Thetford, Norfolk

Library of Congress Cataloging in Publication Data

Main entry under title:
China's new social fabric.
Includes index.
Contents: Societal integration and communication in China
Godwin C. Chu—Communication in China's mass mobilization campaigns
Charles P. Cell
Participation, communication, and political integration
Victor C. Falkenheim—[etc.]
1. China—Social conditions—1949-1976—Addresses, essays lectures.
2. China—Social conditions—1976- —Addresses, essays, lectures.
3. Social interaction—China—Addresses, essays, lectures.
I. Chu, Godwin C.,
1927- . II. Hsu, Francis L. K., 1909-
HN733.5.C44   1983   306′ .0951   83-4401

ISBN 0-7103-0050-6

TABLE OF CONTENTS

Preface   v

I INTRODUCTION   1

1   **Societal Integration and Communication in China**   3
     Godwin C. Chu

II MASS-LEADER RELATIONS   23

2   **Communication in China's Mass Mobilization Campaigns**   25
     Charles P. Cell

3   **Participation, Communication, and Political Integration**   47
     Victor C. Falkenheim

4   **The Mass Line and Leader-Mass Relations and Communication
     in Basic-Level Rural Communities**   63
     Marc Blecher

III COORDINATION AND INTEREST ARTICULATION   87

5   **Communication from the Party Center: The Transmission Process
     for Central Committee Documents**   89
     Kenneth G. Lieberthal

6   **Goal Structure and Coordination in China's Rural Local
     Administration**   119
     Steven B. Butler

7   **Peasant Interest Articulation and Work Teams in Rural China:
     1962-1974**   143
     John P. Burns

IV CONFLICT RESOLUTION 173

8 **Mass Media and Conflict Resolution: An Analysis of Letters to the Editor** 175
Godwin C. Chu and *Leonard L. Chu*

9 **Horizontal Mobilization and Communication for Conflict Resolution: The Tachai Case** 225
Mitch Meisner

V EPILOGUE 249

10 **Integration in China: The Post-Mao Years** 251
Godwin C. Chu and *Francis L.K. Hsu*

Contributors 287

Index 289

PREFACE

China has undergone some tumultuous changes in the last three decades, yet Chinese society has not only stayed intact, but has made progress. The pace at which the country has reunited following the death of Chairman Mao Tse-tung has taken the outside world by surprise. What are the integrative forces in contemporary China that have held the society together during the course of its revolutionary transformation?

To discuss that question, a group of scholars gathered at the East-West Center in January 1979 for a conference on Communication and Societal Integration in China. Coming from such disciplines as anthropology, communication, history, political science, and sociology, they examined various aspects of the Chinese social system for clues.

What they found is a new Chinese social fabric that in part has its roots in China's traditional social and cultural foundations. Drawing its strength from the local communities, the Chinese system is integrated through an intricate web of communication channels mostly laid down since the founding of the People's Republic in 1949. The downfall of the radicals after the death of Mao has altered the policy regarding the interim objectives of the system, but not its basic structural processes.

Many developing societies are today looking for a way out of their quagmire of scarce resources and low productivity. Their common dilemma is between hanging too close to the status quo and heedlessly tearing up their basic social institutions in the name of change and progress. China's experience in the last thirty years, both its success and its setbacks, might be of interest to at least some of them.

The Chinese experience could be relevant to highly industrialized countries as well. Even in affluent societies there are pockets of scarcity and extreme need that require correction. All too often the tendency is to seek a solution by pumping in more money, while neglecting other tasks, such as communication, which may play a vital role in generating the desire for self-help.

It is difficult to acknowledge adequately the advice and suggestions offered by many of our colleagues. We would particularly like to express our thanks to A. Doak Barnett for his advice during the planning of this conference when he spent 1976–1977 at the East-West Center as a Senior Fellow. A note of appreciation is due our editorial consultants, Victoria Nelson and Linley Chapman, for their valuable assistance in preparing this manuscript.

Funds for the conference and this publication were provided by the East-West Center, with a supplementary grant from the U.S. Office of Education administered through the East Asian Studies program of the University of Hawaii.

The views and interpretations, however, are entirely those of the individual contributors and are not necessarily shared by the funding agencies.

Godwin C. Chu
Francis L. K. Hsu

Honolulu, Hawaii
December 1981

I. Introduction

Societal integration is a structural process that permits an optimal or minimal fulfillment of the basic functional requisites of a social system. By analyzing a number of historical periods during which Chinese society came close to disintegration, Godwin Chu proposes a paradigm of functional requisites that the structure of the village community fulfilled in traditional China. The weakness of this old system, however, lay in its feeble lines of communication between center and periphery.

China under communism has retained and strengthened the integrative features in local communities. What distinguishes the China of today from that of the past, Chu suggests, is an extensive communication network that incorporates the local communities into a national entity. How this communication network operates at various levels to achieve national coordination and resolve conflicts during the process of China's societal transformation is the main theme binding the chapters of this volume.

Societal Integration and Communication in China

Godwin C. Chu

A remarkable characteristic of Chinese society has been the resilient stability that has run through a cyclical pattern of decline and resurgence lasting nearly three thousand years. Many times, the Chinese social system has edged toward the brink of disintegration after the initial prosperity of a new dynasty. But somehow, following a chaotic upheaval that might have ruined a nation of lesser stamina, a tattered Chinese society has always managed to pull itself together. Integrative forces begin to congregate. Order and stability are gradually restored.

Contemporary China provides the latest illustration of this ingrained process of recovery and reintegration that has characterized the Chinese system. During the clouded years of the Cultural Revolution, China presented to the outside world a spectacle of systemic disorder, even breakdown. Yet today, not quite a generation later, China has not only repossessed itself but felt sufficiently reassured to embark on four comprehensive programs of modernization. Where lies the inner strength that generates this kind of integrative force in China?

To answer this question, we can examine some of the historical periods during which the forces of integration were temporarily paralyzed and the perils of disintegration seemed particularly imminent. Of many such instances, we shall discuss five periods in Chinese history that share considerable similarities.

Disintegration in Chinese History

The first period we shall consider was one of turmoil following the death of Shih Huang Ti of the Ch'in Dynasty (221–207 B.C.). When two low-ranking soldiers, Chen Sheng and Wu Kuang, started an uprising with a small band of followers and no weapons more formidable than wooden sticks, the whole country was ready to respond with an upswelling revolt. The second was the Ch'ih-mei ("Red Eyebrows") movement during the brief reign of Wang Mang (A.D. 9–23). Conditions were so unbearable that hundreds of thousands of peasants, their eyebrows painted red as a symbol of defiance, joined the rebels and fought determinedly for years. Almost the same patterns were repeated in the Huang-chin ("Yellow Turbans") movement (A.D. 184–192) that preceded the Three Kingdoms. Fifteen centuries and many similar peasant uprisings later, the wild looting and massacres by Chang Hsien-chung and Li Tzu-ch'eng brought the tottering Ming Dynasty (A.D. 1368–1644) to an end.[1] One may add here the episode of the T'ai-p'ing Rebellion (A.D. 1851–1864). Although Hung Hsiu-ch'uan initiated the movement with a few ideological fragments borrowed from Christianity,[2] and there was undoubtedly an element of racial hatred against the Manchu rulers, the movement gained its strength largely from widespread peasant discontent.

With the exception of the T'ai-p'ing Rebellion, each of these peasant movements brought down the preceding empire. Although the Ch'ing Dynasty survived the T'ai-p'ing rebels for half a century, it never recovered from the damage inflicted during the fifteen years of ravage. Subsequent foreign intrusions merely hastened its demise.

All these periods of massive unrest have some characteristics in common. In each case, practically every component of the Chinese system fell apart. While each rebellion had its own unique elements, in general the initial pressure came from a deteriorated allocative system. Because of corruption, wanton waste, or gross mismanagement in the government, sometimes compounded by population pressure, the distribution of material rewards fell to such a low point that not only was task performance no longer rewarding, but minimum subsistence became impossible. This was usually the result of a nonresponsive decision-making process at all government levels that ignored the barest necessities of individual survival. Gradually, faith in the major social institutions for upholding core values dissipated or, worse still, the popular acceptance of the values themselves became temporarily eroded. Conflicts between the peasants and the government accumulated and were magnified. Whatever communication existed between the center and the peripheries broke down. When attempts to resolve conflicts by normative means failed, even a minor incident could set off a popular revolt. The social system began to disintegrate.

From an examination of these five historical events, we can see what systemic functional requisites must be fulfilled to maintain societal integration. In any social system there are certain essential tasks of production that require cooperation in a context of competition. They are necessary for the physical well-being of the system's members. At all levels, decisions have to be made with regard to the use of labor and material resources to carry out the task performance function. A somewhat equitable allocative system must exist to distribute material rewards and social recognition. These functions are vital to the maintenance of the system itself as a requisite. We shall refer to task

4

performance and system maintenance as two primary goals of the system.

In pursuing the primary goals, the system generates two secondary goals as a means of achieving them. First there must be general acceptance of certain fundamental societal goals and basic norms to regulate task performance as well as distribution of rewards. Because the goals and norms are supported by cultural values and beliefs, it is important that the majority members of the system accept a common core of these values and beliefs. The acceptance of goals, norms, values, and beliefs is achieved through socialization, the process through which the cultural heritage of the system is carried on. Secondly, because the pursuit of task performance and system maintenance generally gives rise to tension and conflict, there must be ways of reducing tension and resolving conflict. When disputes arise, as they inevitably do, there must be socially acknowledged processes for settling them.

A culturally patterned, complex flow of communication, vertical as well as horizontal, holds the system together in such a way that the functional requisites are maintained and both individual needs and group survival are fulfilled (see Figure 1). A social system thus consists of a network of relations that are mediated through communication and oriented toward the fulfillment of these systemic functional requisites. Societal integration is a structural process that permits an optimal or minimal functional fulfillment, defined in terms of both physical and sociocultural environments.[3]

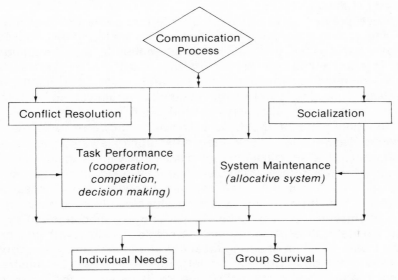

Figure 1
Communication and the Social System

Societal Integration in Traditional China

From this analysis, we suggest that societal integration functions at two levels that complement each other. There must be political integration to establish effective administrative control over the territories so that law and order will prevail. In traditional China, this was achieved when a new dynasty established itself after conquering or uniting the other contending forces. But beyond political integration, there must be social integration at the local level, to maintain the basic institutions in a viable state so that the systemic functional requisites can be fulfilled.[4] The resilience of traditional Chinese society, as we shall see, lies in its communal foundation of social integration.

Political integration in China at the national level is generally traced back to Emperor Shih Huang Ti of the Ch'in Dynasty. After his conquest of the six other kingdoms in China, the emperor took several important measures. He abolished the feudal system that had carved the nation into many semiautonomous political entities and placed the country under a unified administrative structure consisting of provinces (*chun*) and counties (*hsien*). He streamlined the diverse transportation systems of the formerly separate kingdoms and introduced a uniform written language. These measures were successful in quickly restoring order to China after prolonged warfare, largely because underlying the different political regimes of the Warring States period (403–221 B.C.) was a common sociocultural institution begun in the early years of the Chou Dynasty (1066–771 B.C.).

Much praised by Confucius (552–479 B.C.), this was a communal foundation built upon the clan system, which the founders of the Chou Dynasty had codified in order to strengthen their family-based imperial rule. This communal organization (*hsiang*) had its administrators whose duties included maintenance of law and order, dissemination of directives from the government, education, mutual help and social welfare, military and labor services, and taxation.

The backbone of the local community, however, was the clan networks. Task-related cooperation, allocation of rewards, resolution of local conflict, and socialization took place largely in the institution of kin relations, for which the Chou rulers had developed elaborate rites and rules. The predominantly rural communities were more or less self-contained miniature social systems with close-knit communication within themselves. They were held together by a political-administrative structure that maintained only marginal points of contact with grassroots areas. It was a system of strong local ties and loose centralized control.

How traditional Chinese society functioned can be illustrated, almost in a quasi-experimental setting, by its paralysis and restoration, all within the century following its unification under the Ch'in Dynasty. With his many military ventures in remote lands, his consolidation of the

Great Wall, and his lavish taste in gigantic palaces, Shih Huang Ti managed to deplete the national resources within his reign of twelve years. Taxation under his rule climbed to thirty times as much as in the previous generation. He drafted hundreds of thousands of peasants for military service and construction; he sent, for example, some 700,000 peasants to build a tomb for himself at Li-shan. Many died of exhaustion. Even though the emperor held a tight, centralized control till the day he died, his wasteful spending and repressive measures nearly destroyed the local communal foundation. His empire collapsed three years after his death.

The founding emperors of the Han Dynasty that succeeded him apparently recognized this shortcoming and adopted a completely different approach after the country had been politically unified. Generally known as the "Rule of Huang Lao,"[5] this was governing by nonaction which restored the vitality of the local communities by reducing taxes and levies and letting the people rest and recover. Meanwhile, law and order were strictly enforced. The Han government did not undertake major national programs of economic reconstruction during that period. It simply removed the interferences and excessive demands of the previous administration and let the local communal institutions resume their role of societal stabilizers. The results were quick and effective. The forty years during the reigns of Emperor Wen (179–156 B.C.) and Emperor Ching (156–140 B.C.), after the imperial Han family had worked out its internal succession problems, was one of the most prosperous periods in Chinese history. In the villages the barns were filled to the brim with grain. In the national treasury, the coins remained untallied and unused for so long that the strings rotted.

This cyclical pattern of *i-chih i-luan* (chaos and order) has been repeated time and again in Chinese history, compounded on several occasions by invasions from northern barbarians. Before a dynasty collapsed, its local communal foundation first began to erode. Chaos followed. Then a new political order was established that allowed the local communities to recuperate and even prosper, until another round of administratively induced chaos gradually set in. The Ming Dynasty, perhaps the most repressive rule of Han origin, again came close to destroying the local communal structure by its heavy taxation and corrupt administration. The country suffered more than ten years of devastating plunder by hungry peasants who had been driven to join the rebels Chang Hsien-chung and Li Tzu-ch'eng. The tragic end of the dynasty came when its last emperor hanged himself after the rebels had stormed his capital.

The Ch'ing Dynasty (A.D. 1644–1911) followed. After nearly a century of relative order and prosperity, the traditional Chinese social system faced its most crucial test—the impact of Western civilization. In the previous two thousand years, the forces of societal disruption had largely been internal, originating from a structural weakness that exposed the local communities to excessive demands from corrupt bureaucrats, and through them a degenerate imperial house. When these demands were alleviated, usually not until after the endurance of the peasants had been stretched beyond its limits, the local communities were able to recover, often with amazing results. Throughout its history China had suffered many alien invasions, mostly from neighboring tribes in the north and, less frequently, the northwest, which either admired the Chinese culture and were eventually assimilated or, like the Mongols, retreated into their own nomadic territories. The impact of the West was different. The intruders were from an entirely different cultural background and possessed superior technology.

The Westerners came, moreover, at a time when China was at a particularly aggravating point of administrative disorder, with corruption reaching unprecedented dimensions. For instance, when the case of Prime Minister Ho Shen was finally exposed, it was found that he had amassed a personal wealth estimated at 800 million taels of silver. The malaise was prevalent throughout the country. The popular saying among officials then was: "With a three-year term as a clean magistrate, you collect 100,000 taels of silver." In contrast, the Chinese peasants lived in misery. As much as half of the crop went to the landlord as rent. Out of the remaining half, the tenant had to pay various production expenses. Furthermore, the price of rice was usually kept low at the time of harvest. Out of ten peasant families, not even two or three could make ends meet.[6]

Yet the tax collectors pursued the peasants relentlessly. This was what Tseng Kuo-fan, the scholar-statesman who eventually put down the T'ai-p'ing Rebellion, wrote:

> While the price of rice has dropped by 50 percent because of the new exchange rate for coins and silver, local governments pursue their tax collection with vigor. Tax collectors are sent out to chase delinquent taxpayers day and night. They are arrested and brought into the court, and given severe corporal punishment that spreads blood and flesh all over the courtroom. The more difficulties the people have about paying taxes, the more relentlessly the tax collectors chase them. If a person himself cannot pay the tax, his more wealthy kinsmen are arrested and required to pay. Sometimes, even other relatives and neighbors are held in custody until the tax is paid. Our people indeed live in misery.[7]

Tseng was one of the few officials who cared enough to tell the truth. Most officials were more concerned with their own position because the truth might be disturbing to their superiors. Lung Chi-jui, a

8

contemporary of Tseng, wrote to a friend about the widespread unrest that was consistently ignored by the government:

> Most governors do not want to assume any responsibility. They usually find it advantageous to cover up the real situation. If there are one or two subordinates who want to take action, they usually end up being reprimanded for not reading the mind of the governor correctly.... The governors are doing this partly because it is the wish of the prime minister not to disturb the emperor.... The national treasury has only limited funds, which they say should not be wasted for trivial matters.[8]

Communication between the central administration and local organizations was thus practically nonexistent. The situation was aggravated by the pressure of a growing population, which had expanded from about 143 million in 1741 to more than 432 million in 1851.[9] Chinese society was on the verge of a breakdown. But because of grossly inadequate communication built into the system, the imperial court in Peking did not know. This was the context in which the T'ai-p'ing Rebellion broke out in the mid-nineteenth century.

While the situation China faced in the nineteenth century was complex, the fundamental difference from previous crises was the threat from Western powers. Ever since British gunboats bombarded China in 1840–1841 to protect Britain's lucrative opium trade, China had been engulfed in a century of humiliating warfare, first with the West and then with Japan. Because of this, the situation confronting China by and large called for a national response rather than communal regeneration. Because of the loose communication linkages between center and peripheries, however, Chinese society was incapable of concerted national action. Dr. Sun Yat-sen's revolution in 1911, riding the crest of popular unrest, brought the Ch'ing Dynasty to an end, but it lacked the organizational ability to mobilize the people and resolve the issues left by the Manchu rulers. The next decades saw many petty battles among the warlords who had taken over much of China, periodic natural calamities and famines that were compounded in some regions by incredibly heavy taxation,[10] repeated invasions by the Japanese accompanied by unrestrained massacre that ended only with World War II, and the victory of the Chinese Communists in their civil war with the Nationalists. This was the state of near disintegration when Chairman Mao Tse-tung founded the People's Republic in October 1949.

This brief historical sketch, inadequate though it is, suggests a few tentative observations about integration in traditional China. Clan relations at the local community level were the warp and the weft of China's social fabric.[11] The systemic functional requisites were fulfilled largely in the local community, and through that fulfillment the traditional Chinese system derived support for political integration. The latter was maintained through a national bureaucratic structure symbolized in the person of the emperor and buttressed by a written legal code and the cultural value of submission to authority.[12] This system, which drew strength from the local communities, functioned best with minimal interference from the central administration. The Chinese bureaucracy was characterized by a high degree of *jen-chih* (personalized rule), the effectiveness of which waxed and waned depending on the integrity and ability of the emperor and his ministers. The system had a major flaw. It was weak in stable institutional mechanisms (other than Confucian-inspired self-discipline and personal integrity) that could effectively reward efficiency and prevent abuse of authority.[13] When the abuses reached a point where the systemic functional requisites could no longer be fulfilled at the community level, social integration began to erode. Political integration, deprived of communal support, soon collapsed.

Under that system, communication was close and frequent only within the local communities, and lateral communication among them was generally limited to nearby geographic areas. Downward vertical communication moved only to carry demands for taxes and military or labor services. A serious gap in the traditional Chinese social system was an almost total lack of institutionalized channels for upward communication. This was epitomized by the popular saying, "The emperor is as remote as the heaven"—that is, totally unreachable. These structural weaknesses—the lack of lateral and upward communications—were most seriously manifested in the absence of institutionalized mechanisms for either the articulation of interest or the resolution of conflict on a national scale. The former was expressed in occasional outbursts of peasant violence; the latter was frequently played out in imperial court conspiracies.

Because the strength of the system lay in the local communities as stabilizing building blocks, the system itself was able to remain largely unscathed despite the many changes of dynasties. Government by nonaction, ironically, was not detrimental but rather beneficial to the functioning of the local communities as long as the demands on the population were not excessive. The relatively low degree of political integration, however, made it difficult for China to undertake major tasks that would require a national effort, such as large-scale economic development or concerted endeavors toward sociopolitical reform in order to meet the threat of Western colonization. Following the collapse of the Manchu Dynasty, the situation was further aggravated by the warlords' plundering, but especially by the destruction wrought during the prolonged Japanese invasion after 1937. When the Communist Party emerged in 1949 as the victor of the civil war, China was in a state of both political and social disintegration.

Integration and Change

With its overwhelming military strength, the Chinese Communist Party quickly restored political integration to the country. Veteran Party leaders who had survived the Long March and outlived the ordeals of Yenan took over the central administration and the provinces. In just a year, the Party had the whole country under effective control. Nearly a century of turmoil, which had begun with the Opium War, ended with the establishment of the People's Republic in Peking.

The situation in which Chairman Mao found himself in 1949 was not entirely unlike the one faced by the founding emperors of the Han Dynasty. At last the country had been unified. Internal strife had ended, and external exploitation by European imperialists had ceased. Should Mao follow the policy of Emperor Wen and Emperor Ching, and let the Chinese peasants rest and prosper? During the brief spell of a year or two following the Rural Land Reform, the peasants did begin to show signs of prosperity after they had acquired land. But the ideology and goals of Mao were far from the nonaction philosophy of Huang Lao. The speedy recovery of the rural economy was brought about largely as the result of the radical measures of the Land Reform, in which lands were summarily expropriated from landlords. Mao did not stop. He wanted continuous change. He proceeded with more action programs because his objectives were not merely to introduce a new order to end a century of sociopolitical chaos, but to do this in a way that would bring about a radical societal transformation. The task therefore was not just to provide a new foundation for political integration so that the old institutions could be regenerated, but rather to restructure Chinese society by weaving a new social fabric out of conflict. The old institutions would be replaced with new ones that could fulfill the same systemic functional requisites in a revolutionary manner. Mao wanted both integration and structural transformation.

How is the dual purpose of radical change and societal integration achieved in China?

A central driving force has been the Party, which has provided a high measure of political integration during the last thirty years. There have been power struggles and purges throughout this period. But except for the total chaos during the initial stage of the Cultural Revolution, from the summer of 1966 to the spring of 1967 when the Party apparatus was paralyzed by the internal fight for power, these spasmodic upheavals have changed the personnel and policies, but not the structure and basic functions of the Party. The dominance of the Party as a force to mold a revolutionary Chinese society has continued.

In the past, a dynasty began to fall apart when the allocative system ceased to provide for the minimum needs of individuals. The roots of cyclical disintegration in Chinese history thus lie in the collapse of the

11

allocative system. In the People's Republic of China, the allocative system has remained largely intact, even during the three years of natural calamities and famine from 1959 to 1961. This was mainly the result of major structural changes in production relations implemented in the 1950s. Two reform measures in that period redressed some of the inequities in the traditional Chinese allocative system. The Rural Land Reform of 1950–1952 took land away from the landlords and redistributed it among the peasants, thus ending a perennial source of discontent among the Chinese rural population. Eventually the peasants were reorganized into collectives, first in the Agricultural Cooperatives of 1953–1956, and finally in the People's Communes of 1958.[14] The resolution of the Sixth Plenary Session of the Party's Central Committee, convened in June 1981, acknowledged the Agricultural Cooperative movement and the People's Commune movement to be two of the mistakes made by Mao. The former was implemented in haste, while the latter exhibited the error of extreme leftism.[15] Corrective measures were taken in 1959–1961, after the initial disaster of the Commune movement, to reduce the degree of collectivism and restore private plots and rural open markets.[16] The communes have continued to experience management problems and bureaucratic abuse. Fundamental reforms were being tried in 1981.[17] On the whole, however, the reforms of the early 1950s enabled the Chinese peasants to receive a more equitable share of the fruits of their labor than ever before, even though this share was at times rather marginal to their material needs.

In the cities, the *Wu Fan* (Five Antis) movement in 1952 and the subsequent Joint Public-Private Management of 1955–1956 had similar effects on urban workers.[18] The state expropriated industries and businesses. As state employees, workers can count on limited but stable wages. Both the communes and the urban factories have had their share of difficulties, especially with regard to work incentives. Over the years the Party leadership has been vacillating between overreliance on symbolic incentives on the one hand, such as production rallies, red banners, and honor rolls, and limited encouragement of individual material incentives on the other.[19] The trend after the Gang of Four has been to lean cautiously toward the latter. By and large, those early structural changes did minimize, though not totally remove, the potential threat to societal integration in China bred of an unjust allocative system.

These changes were achieved by communication campaigns, which combined the powers of persuasion and group pressure. The implementation of the Rural Land Reform provides an apt example. Mao achieved his objective of rural transformation by the skillful use of communication in a group setting, taking advantage of deep-rooted peasant grievances. First, through public announcements in the media and the dispatch of rural work teams to the villages, he sent a clear message to the peasants: The perennial situation of inequity that had existed in their villages was about to change. The Party was going to take land away from the landlords and redistribute it to the peasants. This stage was important because unless the peasants saw their situation as changeable, no change would be feasible.

At this point, the peasants were still unorganized and unconvinced. Using emotional appeals, members of the rural work team visited individual peasant families and asked them to "spit bitter water," that is, tell about their past grievances. Through such emotional arousal a class distinction began to emerge—*us* the oppressed peasants against *them* the landlords. This was the beginning of new group formation.

Next, the peasants were called together and the suggestion was made that they organize themselves into peasant associations. This step was made more readily acceptable to the peasants because of their familiarity with various clan-related associations in traditional China. The final step was to engage the newly formed peasant associations in concrete actions, in the form of mass rally and class struggle against the landlords. At the rally, emotion-laden accusations and demands for action against the landlords were presented by a select few, to be followed by confiscation of the landlords' properties and redistribution of land.[20]

Over the years the Party has waged other campaigns of an ideological nature. Some were intended for periodic cleansings of corruption and bureaucratism among Party cadres, such as the *San Fan* (Three Antis) movement in 1951, shortly after the Communist victory, and the *Ssu-ch'ing* (Four Clean-ups) movement of 1964. Others, such as the Antirightist movement of 1957, were directed at the intellectuals. How communication has been used in some of the major ideological campaigns has been analyzed by Baum and Teiwes, Chu, Liu, and Yu, among others.[21] These campaigns, while effective in achieving their immediate objectives, paid the price of demoralizing the Party's rank and file and alienating the intellectuals. The resolution of the Sixth Plenary Session considered the Antirightist movement and the Four Clean-ups movement to have gone too far. These movements are judged to be among the mistakes made by Mao. The Party's new leadership has recently vowed not to wage such ideological campaigns any more. The campaigns in the early 1950s, however, served the vital function of bringing about structural change in the allocative system and establishing new relations between the masses and the elite. They are of historic significance. In Chapter 2, Charles Cell examines the processes and techniques of these campaigns, especially the earlier ones.

Such mass-elite relations are important because they provide a new structural framework within which task-oriented cooperation and competition at the grassroots level can take place. Marc Blecher, in Chapter 4, details the close and intimate relations that exist between production team leaders and commune members in the countryside.

Bureaucratic abuse apparently still exists, as Blecher has documented on the basis of reports in the official Chinese media. Viewed in historical perspective, for example, in comparison to what Tseng Kuo-fan found during the Ch'ing Dynasty, these cases of abuse by authority, which were openly criticized, could be considered exceptions that prove the general pattern of more or less egalitarian local relationships among China's rural population.

At the national level, the relations between the ruling Party and the mass of people are now both close and complex. China's failure in the historical past was due partly to lack of a decision-making system that was responsive to the needs of the people. As Falkenheim explains in Chapter 3, the Party's objective is not merely to respond, but rather, to lead the citizens in a drive toward revolutionary change. This task requires both direction and feedback, and has met with considerable difficulty because of fluctuating policy guidelines in the last thirty years. Nevertheless, the Party has been actively interested in popular sentiments and reactions, if only for gauging the prevailing mood in order to expand the basis of grassroots support. The retreat from the initial excesses of the People's Commune movement bears out the point that if a policy is found totally unacceptable, the Party is not reluctant to back down and modify its decisions.[22] The candid assessment by the Party's new leadership of mistakes committed in the past, including those made by Mao himself, provides a telling example.

Underlying these processes of task-oriented relations at the local level and decision making at the national level is a crisscross network of communication channels serving the functions of information and coordination. A major institutionalized means of communication by which the Party regularly informs the Chinese citizens of important decisions and enlists their support is the Central Committee Documents, often disseminated down to the lowest units in the administrative structure. In Chapter 5, Kenneth Lieberthal looks into two important documents, one on the death of Lin Piao and the other on the campaign to criticize Lin Piao and Confucius, to illustrate the dissemination process.

The more concrete problems of administrative coordination involved in task-oriented cooperation and competition are examined in Chapter 6 by Steven Butler, using China's agricultural mechanization movement as a case study. Many practical difficulties are documented. In terms of societal integration, the important point is not that there are difficulties—there always will be—but that communication channels exist for airing and eventually resolving these difficulties.

A unique means of communication that can bypass the bureaucratic cobweb is the work team, or *kung tso tui*, which has played an active role in many campaigns since the land reform movement. John Burns has shown in Chapter 7 that while carrying out its primary tasks of

14

investigating corruption and promoting production, the work team can receive and transmit demands of the peasants, thus serving as a channel for the articulation of grassroots interest.

All social systems contain sources of conflict. In a system that is undergoing major changes, conflict is likely to be magnified because these changes usually disrupt the status quo and aggravate the jostling for power and positions. In China, conflict is of even greater significance because it is more than a byproduct of structural tension and social change. In Mao's philosophy, conflict was to be deliberately employed as an active mechanism for exposing contradictions in the system, to be followed by conflict resolution and structural change. This follows his motto, *Pu-p'o, pu-li* (If [you] do not destroy, [you] do not establish). Conflict among groups of distinctive class consciousness was believed to be capable of releasing from the oppressed class the latent energy that could alter the existing social structure and eventually achieve the goal of socialist transformation.

Indeed, this pattern can be discerned in most of the early campaigns directed at structural change. In the Rural Land Reform, conflict was aroused between the peasants and the landlords. In the Five Antis movement and that of Joint Public-Private Management, workers were pitched against owners and management. In the Cultural Revolution, the radical faction under Mao adroitly activated the students and organized them into the Red Guards to challenge the Party bureaucrats. The disruption caused by the Red Guards paved the way for the takeover of power by the coalition of the radical group and Lin Piao. Even in campaigns without a manifest theme of class struggle, such as the Agricultural Cooperative movement and the People's Commune movement, the Party found it instrumental to point to the counterrevolutionaries as negative reference groups for rallying the support of the peasants. These campaigns illustrate how the Party seized upon a certain latent conflict in the social system and used it as a stimulant for initiating changes in the social structure.

To achieve a degree of integration, particularly after each structural change, the system must allow for conflict resolution by providing the citizens with normative channels for expressing their side of the issues. One such channel in China is the letters-to-the-editor columns in the *People's Daily* and other newspapers. In Chapter 8 Godwin Chu and Leonard Chu analyze the letters published in the official *People's Daily* over a twelve-year period, covering 1967–1968 during the Cultural Revolution and 1976–1978 in the aftermath of the arrest of the Gang of Four. They show that through this channel the central leadership orients itself toward the divergent views and conflictual issues at the grassroots level, and sometimes adopts policy modifications.

Resolution of local conflicts used to be mediated through the clan networks and handled by the landed gentry. It now follows a different route, in which the peasants play an influential role in the context of the new mass-elite relations. Although the celebrated Tachai brigade has been recently exposed as a fraud, the rise of its leader Ch'en Yung-kuei during the early days, before he caught the eyes of Mao, shows the way in which a local cadre appealed to indigenous peasant support in countering bureaucratic power during a period of political conflict. In Chapter 9, using a wide range of materials, some recently made available, Mitch Meisner analyzes the local conflict resolution process in the early days of Tachai.

Communication Strategies

When we look back at events in China during the last three decades, we are struck by two salient features in the Party's strategies for structural change and societal integration. First, while the Party has vigorously sought to remove the vestiges of the traditional past, it has not failed to recognize the strength Chinese society derives from its grassroots foundation, the local communities. Over the years, the Party has taken measures to modify and to consolidate this foundation, which now operates in the sociopolitical context of the People's Communes. The road from the landlord-dominated Chinese villages to the communes has been a tortuous one, marked by violence, conflict, enthusiasm, frustration, and adaptation on the part of the Chinese peasants. The experiences of the last few years, since the downfall of the Gang, have demonstrated clearly that the commune's old model of high collectivism was counterproductive and largely responsible for the low income of the peasants. Steps have been taken, particularly since 1980, to provide more individual incentives, which Godwin Chu and Francis Hsu have discussed in detail in Chapter 10. The results have been a substantial improvement of the standard of living in the rural countryside. However, the point should not be lost that, even though some of the more radical measures in the late 1960s and early 1970s seemed to defy the limits of human endurance, the current commune structure combining egalitarian local leadership and individual productivity in the context of small groups would not have been possible without the initial changes. Now that the communes have survived these trials and errors, they have become the new foundations of contemporary Chinese society. Whether or not they will be given a new name in the future would appear to be immaterial. The communes have been and will remain a cornerstone of stability in China.

Secondly, because the Party has been striving for a degree of integration during the continuous process of change, contradictory as the two ends may seem, the traditional approach of nonaction has been rejected. In the face of foreign encroachment and a drastically altered international environment, simply for survival there must be coordinated national efforts to mobilize the Chinese people for development and modernization. Some of the action programs, such as the land reform, have been instrumental in shaping the contours of the new Chinese society. Others have proved either ill conceived or implemented in haste, such as the initial rush to organize the communes. The most disruptive has been the Cultural Revolution, for which Mao is held mainly responsible.[23] To many Chinese, both inside and outside the Party, life during those years was so painful that the period is now referred to as the "ten years of calamities." If these agonizing experiences have any redeeming feature, it is possibly that they indirectly united the Chinese people, intellectuals and others, against the excesses of extreme leftism. Equally important, those campaigns provided concrete behavioral embodiments for the skeleton of China's communication networks. Because the campaigns required active participation, the people in China physically came to use the channels of communication extensively, thereby giving them a life of their own. In other words, the campaigns were not only made possible by the use of the communication networks, but conversely contributed to the institutionalization of those networks.

The specific manner in which the communication channels have been used by the Party leadership to maintain societal integration in the process of change is the main topic of this volume. It is our thesis that while the basis of societal integration in traditional China lay in its communal foundation, the Party leadership has gone a step further by bringing the local communities into a closely coordinated national system, linked by multiple communication channels through continuous action-oriented change programs. In this volume, we shall not delve into the socialization process, or rather, the Party's organized efforts to change the Chinese culture. That topic has been thoroughly discussed elsewhere.[24] The effectiveness of those ideological communication campaigns has been found to be below the Party's expectations. Nor shall we analyze the allocative system, except to note the impact of structural change on the distribution of rewards and document the latest changes in the communes. The main body of this volume examines selected issues related to two other questions basic to societal integration as previously outlined in Figure 1:

1. In what ways are communication channels used in China to correlate and coordinate the various groups in task performance with respect to societal goals and means of achieving these goals?
2. In what ways are communication channels used to manage latent tension and to resolve manifest conflicts among various component groups in the system with respect to resource allocation as well as goals and means?

Since the purge of the Gang of Four, these questions have taken on renewed significance as the country moves away from radicalism and mass movements toward stability and management efficiency. The return to a more pragmatic policy orientation was initially slow, and began to gather momentum after 1979. The earliest signs of rural prosperity facilitated by changes in the communes seem to have strengthened the basis of social integration in the local communities. Political integration at the national level has reached a new height following the Party's Sixth Plenary Session, which reached agreement on the assessment of Mao. The system inherited by the Party's new leadership seems to be hampered by considerable inertia, however. While the Gang and their high-echelon supporters have been removed from the Party, millions of middle- and lower-level cadres, who were brought into the system by the radical groups while the Gang was in power, have stayed in their respective positions. Their enthusiasm for the new policy is yet to be fully demonstrated. In 1981, there were indications that some segments of the military leadership had second thoughts about the liberal trend in literature that for a time seemed to surge ahead as part of the modernization drive. It is still too early to tell how far the pragmatic trend will go before it is restrained by a radical counter movement, improbable as it may seem, or by a fragmentation of Party leadership, which is unlikely though not totally inconceivable. Effective use of the communication channels can minimize the perils of internal discord and promote stability and integration as China proceeds toward its goals of modernization.

NOTES

1. J. B. Parsons, "The Culmination of a Chinese Peasant Rebellion: Chang Hsien-chung in Szechuan 1644–46," *Journal of Asian Studies* 16 (1957):387–400.

2. See Vincent Y.C. Shih, *The T'ai-p'ing Ideology* (Seattle: University of Washington Press, 1967); Franz Michael, *The T'ai-p'ing Rebellion*, Seattle: University of Washington Press, 1966); also Eugene P. Boardman, *Christian Influence upon the Ideology of the T'ai-p'ing Rebellion, 1851–1864* (Madison: University of Wisconsin Press, 1952).

3. The notion that integration is a structural process in which the fundamental functional requisites are fulfilled is implicit in Durkheim's concept of "organic solidarity," which "involves definite relations bound together in a system of different specialized functions." For his discussion of organic solidarity versus mechanical solidarity, see Emile Durkheim, *Division of Labor in Society*, trans. George Simpson (Glencoe, IL: Free Press, 1947), pp. 129–131. The systemic approach presented here is based largely on Talcott Parsons, *The Social System* (Glencoe, IL: Free Press, 1951).

4. The concept of integration has been used in largely similar ways by others. Olsen refers to functional integration versus normative integration. The former is akin to the functional approach adopted here, while the latter refers to the reaffirmation of common social norms and values. Liu, in discussing national integration in China, identifies two stages—penetration and identification. Penetration refers to the process by which the central government reaches regions that hitherto were autonomous politically and culturally. It is essentially a process of political integration. Identification refers to the process by which "the media gradually diffuse a set of common norms, values, and symbols among the population, especially the youth, so that identification, vertically between the ruler and the ruled and horizontally among citizens and groups, can be established." Liu's identification stage is similar to Olsen's normative integration. Both are treated as value acceptance, to be achieved through socialization processes, in my conceptualization. The distinction between political integration and social integration made here is parallel to Sheridan's concepts of territorial integration and social integration. Both are essential to the general societal integration as a structural state in which basic functional requisites are met. See Marvin E. Olsen, *The Process of Social Organization* (New York: Holt, Rinehart and Winston, 1968); Alan P.L. Liu, *Communications and National Integration in Communist China* (Berkeley: University of California Press, 1971), pp. 2–3; and James E. Sheridan, *China in Disintegration—The Republican Era in Chinese History 1912–1949* (New York: Free Press, 1975), pp. 5–26. Deutsch has used the concept of integration primarily to refer to the emergence of national entity, which is essential to political integration. See Karl W. Deutsch, *Nationalism and Social Communication: An Enquiry into the Foundation of Nationality*, 2nd ed. (Cambridge, MA: MIT Press, 1966). These concepts are incorporated into a systemic scheme in my conceptualization.

5. *Huang Lao chih-chih*, or "Rule of Huang Lao," refers to the philosophy of the legendary Huang Ti and Lao-tze, which advocates a government by nonaction as the most appropriate government system for the Chinese.

6. This situation was described by Chang Chien sometime before the T'ai-p'ing Rebellion broke out. See Huang Ta-shou, *Chung-kuo chin-tai shih* [History of Contemporary China], vol. 1 (Taipei, Taiwan: Ta-chung-kuo Publisher, 1953), p. 355.

7. Ibid. The date of this document, as yet unascertained, was probably during the period of the T'ai-p'ing Rebellion.

8. Ibid., p. 358.

9. Ibid., p. 353.

10. In Szechwan Province, for instance, taxes through 1971 had already been collected by 1933; in another district, a sum eleven times the annual tax was collected between October 1931 and March 1933. See Jean Chesneux, *Peasant Revolts in China, 1840-1949*, trans. C. A. Curwen (New York: W. W. Norton & Co., 1973), p. 79.

11. For an analysis of the Chinese clan structure, see Morton H. Fried, *Fabric of Chinese Society* (New York: Octagon Books, 1969), particularly pp. 68–98; for a description of a Chinese village prior to the Communist revolution, see Isabel Crook and David Crook, *Revolution in a Chinese Village—Ten Mile Inn* (London: Routledge & Kegan Paul, 1959), pp. 18–30. For an analytical view of Chinese clan structure in comparison with the social structures of India and America, see Francis L.K. Hsu, *Clan, Caste and Club* (Princeton, NJ: Van Nostrand, 1963).

12. For the Chinese cultural value of submission to authority, see Francis L. K. Hsu, *Under the Ancestors' Shadow* (Stanford, CA: Stanford University Press, 1971).

13. The government of imperial China had a position known as *yu shih*. Somewhat like ombudsmen, these officials had the responsibility of preventing the abuse of power by directly reporting the misdeeds of officials to the emperor. With the exception of the Manchu Dynasty, each dynasty had its models of courageous *yu shih* who were not afraid to speak out against powerful ministers. On the whole, however, the *yu shih* system was ineffective because *yu shih* acted as individuals without institutional support.

14. The process of structural change from the Rural Land Reform to the People's Commune movement has been analyzed by Godwin Chu. See Chu, *Radical Change through Communication in Mao's China* (Honolulu: University Press of Hawaii, 1977), pp. 35–60, 187–214.

15. "A Resolution on Certain Historical Questions of the Party since the Founding of the Nation," unanimously passed by the Sixth Plenary Session of the Eleventh Central Committee of the Chinese Communist Party on 27 June 1981, published in the *People's Daily*, 1 July 1981.

16. See Chu, *Radical Change*, pp. 187–214.

17. For a description of the Chinese commune system and some of its management problems before 1976, see William L. Parish, "Communist Agricultural Organization: China—Team, Brigade, or Commune?" in *Problems of Communism* 25 (March–April 1976):51–65. For recent changes in the communes, see Chapter 10 in this volume.

18. See Chu, *Radical Change*, pp. 35–60.

19. For a more detailed analysis, see Chu, *Radical Change*, pp. 88–134.

20. See Chu, *Radical Change*, pp. 35–60.

21. See Richard Baum and Frederick C. Teiwes, *Ssu-Ch'ing: The Socialist Education Movement of 1962-1966* (Berkeley: Center for Chinese Studies, University of California, 1968); Chu, *Radical Change*; Alan P.L. Liu, *Communications and National Integration in Communist China* (Berkeley: University of California Press, 1971); Frederick T.C. Yu, *Mass Persuasion in Communist China* (New York: Frederick A. Praeger, 1964).

22. Chu, *Radical Change*, pp. 187–214.

23. "A Resolution on Certain Historical Questions of the Party since the Founding of the Nation."

24. Godwin C. Chu and Francis L.K. Hsu, eds., *Moving a Mountain: Cultural Change in China* (Honolulu: University Press of Hawaii, 1979).

II. Mass-Leader Relations

The goal of the Chinese Communist Party leadership is not to maintain the status quo but to achieve social transformation and development through the resolution of conflict. The ultimate end is a new form of societal integration. This objective requires both the coordination of individual citizens and mass participation on a national scale in what is known as the "mass line" approach.

Charles Cell details the intensive and intricate communication strategies the Party has used to solicit information for policy guidance, to explain to the people what needs to be done and why, to enlist their active participation and, finally, to evaluate the results. The diverse communication strategies, from mass media to group meetings and to *tatzupao* (now defunct), are typically embodied in a campaign, the latest example of which is the current movement for Four Modernizations, which condemns bureaucratism and waste.

Both social change and integration are to be achieved in China by involving the mass of the people in continuing action programs directed toward socialist development.

The communication strategies that Cell has analyzed move primarily from the top leadership to the citizenry. The elite-mass integration envisioned in the mass line model calls for flow of communication from the bottom up as well. This feedback flow, Victor Falkenheim believes, is essential to articulating demands from the grass roots and reconciling contradictions between party goals and the aspirations of the citizenry. It promotes congruency between Party policy and mass interest.

Falkenheim argues, however, that ideological and organizational constraints operated to create a disparity between the mass line ideals and political practices. This disparity apparently reached sizable dimensions in the years when the radical group was in power, a period from which he derives most of his data. On the other hand, Falkenheim does not think these constraints have done irreparable damage. Systemic safeguards exist that tend to minimize their consequences so that loss of vital information to the policymakers is minimal. He further cites recent official statements to indicate that the new Party leadership is aware of the situation and is taking steps to correct it.

To the extent that mass-elite communication becomes more stable and the channels of communication less constrained, Falkenheim suggests, the result may be both a better harvest of information and more responsive policy.

At the grassroots level itself, as Marc Blecher demonstrates in Chapter 4, there is close intragroup communication between local leaders and the peasants that comes close to mass line ideals. It is primarily through informal channels in the villages, not formal channels,

23

that commune members and their team leaders work out their production plans and cooperative use of resources.

Local solidarity, which Blecher calls "communion," is built on a foundation of equality and intimacy, made possible by structural changes in rural China since the early 1950s, which has allowed commune members to choose their leaders from among peers. Through genuine feedback from the commune members, not just formalistic expressions, local leaders are able to gauge the unexpressed mood of the masses as well as interpret and reformulate their expressed views. Although abuse of authority exists, Blecher considers the mass line in its local implementation to be a creative and potentially powerful approach to revolutionary leadership.

2

Communication in China's Mass Mobilization Campaigns

Charles P. Cell

Alan Liu in his book *Communications and National Integration in Communist China* has noted the centrality of the campaign in the communications process.

> Of all the means of communication between the leaders and the led in Communist China, mass campaigns were perhaps the most reflective of the Communist Party's strategy of national development.[1]

Many writers have attested to the importance of the campaign in the national life of China.[2] Others, mostly from firsthand experience, have provided us with detailed and often graphic accounts of the communication process at work in a single campaign. Still others have discussed the communication process in the campaign.[3] None, however, have attempted to examine systematically the range of communicative options that have been used in the campaign process. That is the central purpose of this chapter. Secondarily, the use of these communicative techniques will be illustrated through reference to case studies.[4] First, however, the role of communication and the campaign must be placed in the context of China's overall developmental strategy.

Communication, the Campaign, and China's Developmental Strategy

At the core of China's developmental goals has been the commitment to decreasing inequality. In terms of both spreading material resources more equally among all sectors of the population and promoting greater popular participation in the political process at base-level institutions, the Chinese leadership has emphasized the use of campaigns as the major means for pursuing their goals.[5] At the same time, this has brought them into conflict not only with traditional values and beliefs,[6] but also with certain classes and groups within the society

25

(e.g., landlords, Kuomintang supporters, "capitalist roaders"). These conflicts or contradictions provide the basic legitimation for campaigns, especially struggle campaigns. Contrary to the views of some writers,[7] the goal of a campaign is to resolve contradictions or conflict rather than to create them. Of course, while the struggles and communication between opposing sides in a campaign work their way through the campaign process, additional conflicts may come to the surface between opposing forces, such as between landlords and peasants or between workers and those labeled "capitalist roaders." The intent of a campaign, however, is ultimately to resolve the contradiction in order to move to a higher stage of development; that is, to progress further down the road to socialism and communism.

When the contradiction is not resolved, such as during the Great Leap Forward (that is, when the campaign is left with more unfulfilled goals and problems or shortcomings than accomplishments or achievements), dissatisfaction and alienation can emerge not only in those deemed to be part of the enemy groups or classes (which is normal in a struggle campaign), but in the masses as well. This inhibits the integrative function, in contrast to campaigns where most goals are realized and the majority of the population responds with support and satisfaction to the new programs and institutions generated. New conflicts or contradictions arise as old ones are resolved, but this is not due to the nature of conflict within the campaign, but rather, as Marx, Mao, and others have noted, to the inherent nature of materialist dialectics themselves.

Although integration is for the leaders and the society a beneficial outcome, the most important aim of the campaign as an institution is not merely the integration of society, which is basically a social control function designed ultimately to serve the leadership at the expense of the population. Rather, the fundamental goal of campaigns in China has been that of social change, the changing of cultural and social patterns, political and economic institutions, so that more people will benefit more equally. A leadership bent on stability and maintenance of the status quo and the institutionalization of existing inequalities would have little interest in the use of campaigns, which require ideological commitments based on persuasion in order to mobilize the population.[8] This objective can only be accomplished if the people feel they will benefit from their commitments to mobilization. What are the roles of communication in the campaign process?

To be successful, the communicative techniques of a campaign must emphasize change, commitment, persuasion, and ultimately, involvement, rather than control, maintenance, and integrative functions. Thus, the following discussion of these techniques must be understood in light of their emphasis on change in contrast to control.

Communication Techniques of the Campaign

The range of communicative techniques used in campaigns is enormous. While most of the options will be mentioned here, it is impossible to be certain that all have been accounted for. It does appear, however, that these techniques generally take one of two forms. Either they tend to emphasize the imparting of information about a campaign and the efforts of the leadership to mobilize the population, or they directly involve the population communicating among themselves as they participate in the campaign. These two options correspond to the communication process from top down and bottom up, respectively. Let us examine each set of communicative alternatives.[9]

Informational Communication

Techniques used for informational communication can be further subdivided into three basic categories: media communication, display communication, and meetings.

Media. A wide range of written materials is used to promote campaigns, with newspaper articles and editorials among the most common. "Campaigns usually begin with a series of articles and editorials in newspapers."[10] Of equal if not more importance as a means of communication are radio broadcasts which, via the widespread presence of receivers and the loudspeakers present in virtually every village, can reach the people directly from the outside.[11] However, the newspapers probably penetrate more deeply into the consciousness of the population. While it is easy to turn a deaf ear to the radio loudspeaker, it is more difficult to ignore newspapers that are read, considered, and discussed in small groups. In addition, pamphlets and books are often used to provide information about campaigns. Most campaigns issue pamphlets to a specific province or other geographical area, stating the goals of the campaign along with relevant directives and a description of means to be used.

These means of communication appear in multiple forms to carry out the campaign. Songs, poems, cartoons, short stories, stories of people sacrificing their lives to carry out the campaign, along with statements by national and provincial leaders, are among the content of the printed and wireless media. Some are long, others short, the shortest being the slogan, which is used in virtually every campaign.

Display. Banners and posters are perhaps the most common forms of display communication. They will often contain the same messages as media forms, but are distinguished by their continuing presence throughout a campaign in villages, neighborhoods, and homes. They are used during parades, draped over entrances to production and institutional units, and displayed on stages as a backdrop for meetings and rallies. Slogans play an important role in establishing the tone of a campaign by directing the people to the most useful types of change required to meet the campaign's goals.

Much more substantial but far less common in the communicative process of a campaign is the role of exhibits, especially photographs and handicrafts. These are usually employed at later stages of a campaign to communicate successful examples of change and to reinforce positive patterns for continued activity. (They are not to be confused with major exhibits such as the Rent Collection Courtyard, which was developed after a campaign, in part to commemorate it.)

Meetings. All meetings involve the participation of the people, but, depending on the type of meeting, the audience can be more passive or active. This section deals with the former type, where the neighborhood or village is called together to receive information about a campaign and to encourage or heighten its participation in it.

At the outset of virtually every campaign, there is a mobilization meeting.

> [Mobilization meetings], an essential part of the process of putting politics in command, [are] for the cadres to make clear to the people the whys and wherefores of proposals to put forward what must be done to implement them. . . .[12]

First a mobilization speech would be made.[13] The mobilization speech becomes yet another way to communicate the need for change by explaining the goals of a campaign. For the countryside or the urban factory or institutional unit, it is often the first personal contact the people have with a campaign, and often becomes the first direct effort to mobilize them. In the context of group gatherings, other means are used to mobilize the people, including film shows, slide shows, drama troupes, and dance groups, as well as plays and skits. These communicative forms are often performed by propaganda teams that are organized either on an occasional basis, such as students from a university,[14] or on a permanent professional basis to tour neighborhoods, institutions, and villages.

Finally, during most campaigns, group or individual targets are identified as the key group, behavior, or manner of thinking that needs to be changed. The target may be a group or class of people, or a way of thinking or acting.[15] Group targets have included landlords, capitalists, bureaucrats, intellectuals, or cadres, depending on the campaign. These targets are either "enemies" of the people, or people thought to be basically good but in need of some reform—depending on whether the principal contradiction to be resolved by the campaign is antagonistic or nonantagonistic. Paralleling these targets are ideological targets— erroneous ways of thought or behavior. These range from the evils of bureaucracy, corruption, and waste (the central targets of the Three-

Antis campaign), to more diffuse, "go-slow" attitudes toward various campaigns such as the cooperatives or communization. Although the process of dealing with these targets involves substantial participation by the people, their identification at this point is merely the process of the leaders communicating to the people what type of group or behavior is to be the central focus of change. It is then the major task of the people to identify who the individuals or groups are and what type of action constitutes undesirable behavior. Participation then begins in the effort to change.

Let us now turn to the techniques of communication used to obtain the participation of the people in a campaign.

Mass Participation Communication

Media. Undoubtedly the most widespread means of communication is the involvement of the people in the mass media. This includes the frequent use during campaigns of letters and essays, written by individuals or groups, printed in newspapers or read on radios to promote the campaign and state their support for it.[16] Related to these activities sometimes is the establishment of local ad hoc newspapers, of which the Red Guard papers were the most famous and widespread example. Short of this extreme are uses of blackboard bulletins and big-character posters. The *tatzupao*, until they were banned in early 1980, were undoubtedly an important and common means whereby practically anyone could capture the attention of coworkers, friends, and neighbors.

Although outwardly less important, nonetheless significant is the wearing of badges and pins. In some campaigns, Mao badges or other types of pins were used to promote the campaign. During the Cultural Revolution, there was even something of a competition to produce the most creative or biggest pin. One of the largest was a handmade effort by a kindergarten girl. Measuring nearly six inches in diameter, it covered at least a quarter of her chest!

General Activities. More significant in terms of evidence of involvement in a campaign is a whole range of activities including pledges to work harder to promote the campaign; competitions, individual or collective, to promote production; and donations of spare time or material goods to support the campaign. Not all of these may be perceived as acts of traditional communication; but when there is a publicized donation of goods or energy or a competition with prizes, rewards, and publicity, communicative messages are being imparted about model behavior. The same is true of special mention of the participation of youth, minority, or women's groups, particularly in the latter two cases, where such mention is often tied to exhortations about the need to further equalize the status of minorities and women.

In terms of truly extended involvement of the population, there was probably no communicative means more important for carrying out a campaign than *hsia fang*. Not only were new ideas brought in from the outside to the villages and work places, but equally important was the impact on the individuals sent there as well as on the coworkers left behind. Those who were sent into the villages and work places were given an extremely strong message about the importance of communicating with peasants and others at local levels, about learning from and understanding the consciousness of the vast majority of the population. There was perhaps no communicative technique more forceful than this for changing patterns of behavior and thought. Even for those coworkers not sent down, the message was clear. In the early years of the 1950s, when being sent to the lower levels was often seen as punishment for improper behavior or thinking, this act communicated to others not sent down: If they were involved in this kind of thinking or behavior, the message was that they, too, could be sent down.[17] In later years (the 1960s and 1970s), when *hsia fang* became a virtually universal process, whether temporary or permanent, for certain groups such as cadres and youth, the message was very forcefully communicated: The need to learn from, understand, and accept peasants and others at the local level was an inescapable requirement for service to society and individual promotion within it.

Meetings. So far, the meetings relating to informational communication we have examined involved passive rather than active participation by the masses. We now turn to a dozen or so different types of meetings that serve primarily to involve the people directly in the communication process of a campaign.

There is probably nothing more pervasive than the Communist use of meetings to foster communication and mobilization.[18] Even by 1948, peasants seemed to be aware of this. In the twenty years or so before the arrival of the Communists in Long Bow village, there had not been a single village meeting. The landlords used the tactic of "divide and rule," preferring to minimize group communication. In the few months after the Communists arrived, meetings had become so common that the peasants began to complain:

> "Your mother's. . . ." said Yuan-lung [an old peasant]. "Another meeting! Will there ever be an end to meetings?" And he hummed a little jingle that he had heard that day from the disgruntled Li Ho-jen, "Under the Nationalists too many taxes; under the Communists too many meetings."[19]

> Study meetings . . . are by far the most prevalent and frequent [type of meeting].[20]

Study and discussion of current events or of local work and activities tend to be organized around small, formalized study groups of ten to twenty people each. They are usually based in a member's primary unit of activity during the day (e.g., factory, agricultural work group, government office, school, or neighborhood if the member is retired or a housewife).

Study group meetings are constantly occurring, sometimes even on a regular schedule.[21] As with many of these communicative means, however, they occur more frequently during a campaign,[22] when their use often begins right after the mobilization meeting. Their immediate purpose is to increase mass understanding and commitment to the campaign mobilization effort about to begin. Of course, these meetings tend to continue throughout a campaign as a means to obtain feedback on the participants' attitudes toward it. Indeed, campaigns seem to heighten the importance of small groups in inducing individual change, in contrast to noncampaign periods, when study groups appear to perform mainly a maintenance function.[23]

Perhaps the most common type of meeting is criticism/self-criticism. Although these meetings may occur in larger group settings, they are as likely to be a part of the small group meeting. During a campaign, they generally occur in relation to a target who is among the masses, that is, who has not been classified as an enemy or bad element. During rectification campaigns, for example, the focus is usually on cadres and how they can improve their workstyle. Cadres are expected to criticize themselves first, but if their criticism seems unsatisfactory to the people attending the meeting, those people are expected to make their own criticism. Of course, as Hinton so graphically shows, peasants were often reluctant to come forward to communicate their real feelings, especially when the first rectification was carried out in Long Bow village.

During the larger campaigns, this process sometimes became relatively intense, even to the point where a unit's ordinary work was eclipsed.

A struggle meeting involved more serious errors, usually committed by targets labeled as the enemy—such as landlords, rightists, and people with capitalist tendencies. Although these targets might have been redeemable and able to later join the ranks of the masses, their errors were considered to be of sufficient magnitude that they had to undergo an extended period of thorough criticism, self-examination, and denunciation that sometimes culminated in forms of physical abuse, usually unsanctioned by the campaign's guidelines. In this context, the communication process was intense and mass participation was relatively high.

When, however, a target's errors were so serious that an early return to the ranks of the masses was not foreseen, there was sometimes an accusation meeting. This was essentially a denunciation of the target through a portrayal of the target's crimes by the victims themselves, a very graphic form of communication. Sometimes, for the most serious cases, this was done in preparation for a public trial where the masses were again asked to present evidence of the target's crimes.[24] These types of meetings, almost always involving the whole institution or village, were relatively common during Agrarian Reform in the effort to expose and eliminate the most brutal landlords, if they had not already fled. Clearly, the sufferings of the peasants at the hands of these people contributed greatly to the level of emotional involvement and intense communication.

A special type of meeting was held when the target or enemy was not present. These condemnation meetings were held to denounce bad forces such as American imperialism during the Korean War and Japanese militarism during the effort in 1960 to oppose the American-Japanese security treaty. These meetings have also been used to denounce important persons who have become enemies, such as Liu Shao-ch'i and the Gang of Four. The masses were mobilized to condemn these targets in absentia.

In theory, these various types of meetings were seen as distinct stages on a continuum of escalation depending on the severity of the error—that is, criticism/self-criticism, struggle, condemnation, accusation, public trial. In reality, however, the distinctions were not always clear. The masses sometimes became the target of struggle; the enemy groups or classes were occasionally just criticized. Although this sometimes occurred because of improper cadre guidance, it also occurred because it was often rather hard to determine just what constitutes an act of criticism as distinct from an act of struggle. For example, peasants who felt a fellow peasant or cadre had committed a rather serious error might offer rather harsh criticisms, but the same peasants might not put much emotion into "struggling" a landlord who had not been that brutal toward them.

Other types of meetings may combine both the negative and the positive. The "recall bitterness, think sweetness" meeting encouraged the masses to think of the hard times before liberation and compare them with the present, improved conditions.[25] These meetings were used at times to communicate the need for extra sacrifices.

Still other meetings are called during campaigns to select work models, that is, people or groups who have made exemplary contributions to the work of the campaign. They are often selected because of their high activist commitment to the campaign. The concept of a model, of course, implies communication of a message of the ideal behavior to be exemplified. As far back as 1945, Mao described the qualities of good work models:

You possess three good qualities and play three roles. First, the role of initiator. That is, you have made surprising efforts and many innovations and your work has become an example for people in general, raised the standard of workmanship and inspired others to learn from you. Secondly, the role of the backbone. Most of you are not cadres yet, but you have formed the backbone, the nucleus of the masses; with you it is easier to push forward our work. . . . Thirdly, the role of a link. You are a link between the leadership above and the masses below, and it is through you that the opinions of the masses are transmitted upwards and those of the leadership downwards.[26]

Obviously, Mao was clearly aware of the important, communicable role that work models can and do play in moving Chinese society toward its goals.

Collective models might constitute a small work group or a whole team, often nominated by an entire factory or brigade, and reported to higher levels along with a leadership recommendation. At various points, additional selections may be made for county, provincial, or national models.

There was . . . a "mobile red flag" awarded every month to one of the companies. As to the model workers, their photos—taken by the commune photographer—were posted at the foot of the Tower of Heroic Ambition, with a brief account of their accomplishments in work, study and physical training; and all were called on to follow their example.[27]

Here we can see how two means—models and photographic displays—are combined to communicate exemplary behavior.

Among the most symbolic of communicative events are rallies, demonstrations, and parades, which occur at all levels of society, although three distinct levels are considered here: local (village to district or commune), regional (county to major city or provincial capital), and national (in Peking, usually in Tien-an-men Square). These events are usually aimed at mobilizing participation as well as communicating successes in a campaign. For example, during Agrarian Reform, land deeds burned at local rallies communicated the end of exploitation by the landlords as well as the achievements involved in land expropriation.

This broad range of communicative activities demonstrates almost without exception that the communication means available during campaigns vary from those available outside of campaigns. For example, study groups are ongoing and occur at all times, not just during a campaign. But their frequency is much greater during campaigns. Even more obvious is the intensity of communication during campaigns, especially those that are larger and involve higher levels of mobilization. Campaigns bring problems and contradictions to the fore, and often imply intense conflict, such as that between a peasant and a landlord or, during the Cultural Revolution, between a worker who feels he or she has been abused and a cadre. Emotions are aroused, hatreds are much closer to the surface. The personal stakes on both sides are very high. The communication process becomes much more intense under these conditions. Moreover, the use of communicative means during a campaign tends often to follow a pattern. At each stage, different means tend to be emphasized over others.

The Process of Communication during Campaigns

Although no precise number of labels is officially given, most campaigns appear to go through four stages: policy formulation, information dissemination, mass participation, and summation and evaluation. The communicative means just described tend to be concentrated in the second and third phases of the campaign—those that are the most public and for which more information is available.

Policy Formulation

Someone—often Mao himself—would first suggest that a particular contradiction existed, requiring a mobilization campaign to resolve it. Such a conclusion would normally be based on the enormous amount of reporting that goes on from one system level to another. This kind of communication is largely written and often open to public scrutiny. Former cadres who have been interviewed readily describe the significant proportion of time spent on writing, reading, summarizing, and transmitting reports. From this process of communication, Mao and other leaders were made aware of problems, such as the difficulties experienced in the cooperative campaign in agriculture in 1954 and early 1955, and contradictions relating to agricultural organization and production in the mid-1960s. When the contradictions were deemed important enough by the leadership, proposals were drafted and circulated for a mass mobilization campaign to resolve them. For example, on 31 July 1955, Mao made a speech to Party secretaries attacking the slow pace of cooperativization in the countryside and calling for greater mobilization efforts.

There is no assurance at this point, however, that the campaign will be adopted. Often opposition emerges, requiring that the proposed campaign be discussed and debated. This process is generally more verbal, often occurring within Party gatherings, although occasionally open to groups of cadres or the population at large. For example, it was not until October 1955 that Mao's speech of 31 July was published, signaling his victory and the beginning of the campaign for Higher-Level Cooperatives.

Although the Cultural Revolution did not begin its more public phases until May or even June 1966, as far back as January 1965 Mao had come to the conclusion, based on the statements and actions of Liu

Shao-ch'i and his supporters, that they would have to be removed.[28] Some of the most revealing of these differences surfaced in the directives of the Socialist Education campaign, with the often contradictory positions centered around the role of work teams. While this first phase was less public and therefore might seem less important, it was, in fact, of crucial importance in the formulation of policy, in communicating the need for the campaign, and in mobilizing support for it.

Implementation: Information Dissemination

A public statement is usually made to announce a campaign. The statement may consist of a special report, a special combined editorial in the *People's Daily* and *Red Flag*, and/or radio broadcasts. These statements are often communicated to local institutions via a mobilization meeting. Posters sometimes played a role. The opening public salvos of the Cultural Revolution, for example, were apparently the posting of *tatzupao* at Peking University.[29] At this point, the need for mobilization and participation is communicated to the population by the use of many of the means described earlier. While different campaigns have used different means, the general pattern suggests that the more intense the campaign (that is, the greater the level of mobilization), the greater the number of communication means and the more often they will be used.[30] While informational communication tends to predominate in the early stages of a campaign, the stage of implementation continues concurrently as the third stage begins to pick up.

Implementation: Mass Participation

At this stage, the campaign swings into full gear, emphasizing maximum participation by the population. Public communication between leaders and led and especially among the population itself reaches its peak. The means of mass participation communication described earlier come fully into play and become relatively intense, depending on the magnitude of the campaign. Papers, letters, and articles are written about individuals and groups to promote the campaign. The Cultural Revolution, for example, saw an enormous rise in popular media communications, especially in the form of the now-famous Red Guard newspapers. Groups of all types—such as production, study, labor brigades to assist other units—are formed or given renewed emphasis as a direct means of promoting mass participation in the campaign. Finally, the enormous range of meetings described earlier usually increases in intensity and frequency.

Summation and Evaluation

This phase begins as the more visible phases of a campaign begin to reduce in frequency and scope. Although some summarization and evaluation do occur throughout the participatory stages of the campaign—to monitor its progress and make suggestions for changes—toward the end the evaluation/summation process is most important. On the basis of reports and other communications received, the decision is made on when to halt or decrease the intensity of the campaign, with a view to bringing it to an end. Although most campaigns tended to be relatively successful (that is, accomplish their goals or basically resolve the principal contradiction), this would not be a foregone conclusion. In some cases, such as the Great Leap Forward, the consensus would be reached that the campaign was basically not successful, and reasons would then have to be determined (there was sharp disagreement in this particular case among the leadership[31]). Then, a decision must be made on whether to delay further attempts to resolve the contradiction or move ahead with a new campaign. Even more common is the situation where, in the process of resolving one contradiction, others may occur. The captured and now-published Lien Chiang documents are a well-illustrated example of how a campaign (in this case, the Four Clean-ups or Socialist Education campaign) can lead to the development of more problems or contradictions.[32] Another example occurs when the errors of cadres in carrying out the campaign may lead to a rectification campaign.[33] Hinton's book presents an excellent illustration of this process.[34]

Communication in the Mobilization Process

In examining the means of communication during mobilization, we have just barely scratched the surface of the process, which is much more graphic than the bare-bones description presented earlier.

Communication in the mobilization process is not a simple task. People cannot be automatically convinced of the use of a few communicative techniques alone, nor can they be convinced just because a cause may be to their benefit. Baum indicates how difficult it was to mobilize the peasants, especially during the early stages of the Socialist Education campaign.[35] This was largely due to the work style of the cadres and contradictory directives from the Party center.[36] Hinton, in his portrayal of Long Bow village, for example, relates that when the Communists first came and began to prepare for Agrarian Reform, some peasants even argued that it was right for landlords to own the land and engage the peasantry in tenancy arrangements.[37]

The mobilization/communication process spreads like waves on the surface of a pond. A small group of activists who understand the campaign and its importance must be found to take the lead; in the case of Long Bow, to speak out first.[38] Sometimes no one can be found to start the process. Even if they can see the potential benefit, people may hold back. On at least two occasions, the peasants of Long Bow held back when the Communist leadership tried to persuade them to come forward, to speak out. At one point they feared the return of the Kuomintang. They would suffer from having said too much against the landlords. At another point, when four erring cadres who had been arrested by an outside work team for wrongdoings were released and allowed to return to the village unpunished for lack of evidence against them, the peasants backed off, feeling that cadres were protected but that they, the peasants, would suffer if they spoke out.[39]

The old system had not changed; their comments, at least, reflected those fears:

"What's the use of speaking out? The old cadres mount the horse as if nothing had happened." "Yu-lai has returned and he is the same as ever." "It is better to work hard at production and let those meet who want to meet." "We are gloomy because our opinions are no use at all."[40]

Getting people to set aside these basic, honest fears and join the communication process in a campaign is a complex task that has required years of commitment, persuasion, and mobilization. Certainly one critical element in whatever success and achievements have been won has been the constant exhortation of the cadre leadership to be "responsive" to the masses, to engage in, and openly accept, criticism/self-criticism. In a 14 November 1950 *People's Daily* editorial on the work of cadres to establish power in urban areas, this approach was stressed:

When conducting a . . . campaign . . . attention should be given to the gathering of opinion of the masses on the work of the government and on the style of work of the cadres. During conferences, when attempts are made on the parts of the representatives to criticize and examine the work of the government and the style of the work of the cadres, they should be accepted with the utmost modesty. It is up to all responsible personnel to carry out criticism and self-criticism in the most responsible, sincere and candid manner so as to increase the masses' confidence in the people's government, improve the relationship between the masses and the cadres, improve our work and conquer the obnoxious inclination for bureaucratism and orderism.[41]

This could not be a forced process: cooperation was of the essence. *"No progress can be made unless the individual is willing to cooperate."*[42]

For the Chinese population in 1949, this process was not easy to understand. Having come through two wars in the previous decade and borne the suffering that accompanied them, particularly at the hands of landlords and the Japanese, they were understandably more interested in food, clothing, and shelter than in the process of communication via criticism/self-criticism.

In the midst of a Rectification campaign in 1948 in Long Bow village, an old woman peasant tried to extract more material goods from the suspended village head, Chun-hsi:

> "Two or three pieces of clothing! That's not enough," snorted Old Lady Wang, all primed for further battle.
>
> But Old Tui-Chin, the bachelor peasant, who was more and more emerging, by virtue of his extreme objectivity, as spokesman for the northern group, disagreed. "We don't want the things, our aim is to get him to admit his mistakes and speak the truth."
>
> At this, Old Lady Wang spat furiously on the ground. "Who can eat self-criticism?" she asked.[43]

Some understood the meaning of criticism/self-criticism, others had yet to do so.[44] Still, the peasants did not fully comprehend the intricacies of the mobilization process, and became so worked up about the suspended village head that they urged that he be sent to a people's court to be tried. Here the leading cadre stepped in; the peasants had gone too far:

> The people's court is for serious cases that we cannot solve ourselves. As for Chun-hsi, his case is big, but not, in my opinion, big enough for that. Suppose you punish him severely? Are his crimes as big as those of others? Then what will you do with the others? Their punishment must be even more severe. I think it would be better to compare records. Let's balance his crimes against those of others. Let's consider his attitude. Did he speak frankly?[45]

Not an easy task, by any means. How to mobilize the peasants (and workers), to communicate to them the significance of their actions so that they will be willing to participate yet not carry things to an extreme? The cadres of Long Bow often had to search for the intricately fine line separating success from failure in the mobilization process.[46] They obviously did not always succeed.

If the process of correctly mobilizing through criticism/self-criticism was difficult, even more so was the task of correctly carrying out struggle, given the animosities and emotions the target of struggle often generated.

38

In the context of Maoist political behavior . . . "struggle" is a formally defined process in which the target, usually a political offender, is subjected to charge after charge with ever increasing intensity until he admits his guilt. Yet the purpose of the struggle process is more than just punitive. Rather it is intended to provide the target with a starting point from which to begin actual political and ideological remoulding. Similarly, those who attack are also expected to learn as they do so and thereby to improve their own political and ideological competence. Struggle [is the] . . . acting upon a person or the environment in order to effect a basic change and realize a specific objective.[47]

Thus, when the Communists spoke of the elimination of a class such as the landlords, they did not necessarily mean physical elimination. Often they were referring to the transformation of people and whole groups so that the target person, class, or problem (i.e., contradiction) would no longer exist.[48] Mao in his own famous self-criticism noted how once he became a student he began to feel himself superior to workers or peasants. Only after living with peasants and workers and going through what is often a painful process of tempering, struggle, and criticism is it possible to transform oneself from one class to another.[49] When transformation is accomplished with an entire class, then the elimination of the class is considered complete.

The transformation process would not be easy, either for individuals or for the social environment as a whole. The campaign would be the vehicle, with mobilization the guiding strategy. Within this process, two of the watchwords were to be *criticism/self-criticism* and *struggle*.[50]

Mao was certainly aware that this process would fail if pushed too far too fast. His exhortation was unmistakably clear: If you wanted to undergo transformation, "*you* must make up *your* mind" to do so. Hinton has reinforced this by arguing that "no progress can be made unless the individual is willing to cooperate."[51] Certainly the Party and others would do all they could to persuade, to channel, to provide the setting for a commitment to mobilization and change. But to use terror or coercion was to fail:

The Chinese Communist leaders emphatically deny the utility of terror for long-range leadership purposes and recognize that its use, however guarded, must give way to methods of persuasion to induce support. In effect, the initiation of violence on any enlarged scale even to resolve agricultural crises and unrest is an admission of leadership failure and a retreat into reaction.[52]

In marked contrast, the Russian Communist leaders seem to have all too often set aside the harder path of mobilization and fallen back on coercive measures to induce change.[53] This should not obscure the fact that even in China, particularly during struggle campaigns, coercion was often used because of pressure from the top to carry out the campaign rapidly, from errors of local cadres, and/or from emotions aroused in the intensity of communication at the peak of some campaigns.

In specific terms, the commitment to persuasion often meant slowing the process of socialist transformation. For example, during the campaign to establish Mutual Aid teams, cadres were admonished in a Party Central Committee directive not to push reluctant peasants too fast:

> Even in a village where the overwhelming majority of peasants have joined the Mutual Aid teams or cooperatives and where only a very small minority of peasants remain individual farmers, the attitude of respecting and uniting such a minority should be adopted.[54]

What did this mean in practical terms? In Long Bow in 1948, it meant that for a number of weeks the peasants simply withdrew from the formal communication process and would not come to meetings. There were no more material goods to be divided (the "fruits of struggle"), only ideological matters to discuss. Besides, they had spring planting to do. Why should they go to meetings? As Hinton relates, one peasant said to his friend when he called for him for the evening's meeting after a hard day in the field, "I'm tired, I'm going to bed early. I don't want to go to any meeting. Can anyone arrest me for that?" Indeed, the peasants knew that, unlike in the old society, "coercion and beatings were absolutely forbidden."[55] Those who used them on the masses would be called to account for their improper work style.

And so to the process of persuasion yet another watchword was added: *patience*. As Edgar Snow said of Mao, "although he distrusts long periods of stability and is never satisfied with the pace of change ... he is practical and capable of great patience in achieving a goal."[56]

A county Party secretary talked about patience in almost monotonous terms in describing the task of assigning class status, a task that could be easily generalized to the communication process in a mobilization campaign.

> We must explain, discuss, report, evaluate, classify, post results; explain, discuss, and report—again and again. This is very troublesome, very difficult, very time consuming.[57]

It is easier to be impatient, as a work team cadre in Long Bow admitted one day in 1948:

> I am discouraged. Ten years ago when I began to work as a cadre, people said, "When the Japanese are defeated, then the Revolution will succeed." But the Japanese have surrendered and war continued. Now ten years have passed. It is too slow. Where is the industry we dreamed about?[58]

In the village I visited in 1972, I was told that the proper implementation of the communication process—only the use of persuasion and patience—cost the village three long years in the effort to transform the land. The story, related by the Party secretary of the brigade, is worth retelling because it reflects his perception of how difficult the communication and mobilization process is. The alternatives were stark—waiting three years or coercion:

> Before 1956, in the period of preliminary cooperatives, the work of transforming slopes into terraced fields could not earnestly begin. The ownership of the land was still private. It was most inconvenient to transform the land, to convert the slopes into terraced fields.
>
> In the spring of 1953 we did attempt the transformation of slopes into terraced fields, but the class enemy made trouble. The class enemy incited some peasants. "Now you have transformed your land. If you withdraw from the cooperative and go alone, you will be better off." These people were taken in by the class enemy and withdrew from the cooperative. This caused difficulties on our part in transforming the slopes. Members of the cooperative said it was useless to transform the slopes. "If one slope is transformed into terraced fields, and that family withdraws from the cooperative, what is the use of doing that?"
>
> So, actually, the work of transforming the slopes began only in 1956. In 1956 we established an advanced cooperative. The land was owned collectively, so it was very easy to decide which slopes should be transformed. . . . However, three years had passed in our ten-year plan [to transform the land].[59]

This certainly is not an isolated example. Participant-observer studies of villages in China since 1949 all note at least one if not several instances of recalcitrant peasants who did not want to join a cooperative or participate in other aspects of the communication process of the mobilization campaign.[60]

In summary, what can be said of the communication process? The least is that the process is fraught with difficulties and failure. The most is that, given the social conditions of China in 1949 and the scope and breadth of the changes attempted since then through the campaigns, the effort to change Chinese people, to transform them in attitudes and behavior by means of these communicative techniques and the mobilization process has unquestionably been one of the greatest social efforts in the history of humankind. Hard reality, however, undoubtedly lies between. Communication via mass mobilization is an intricate process. It is perhaps relatively easy to see and to measure on the surface but relatively hard to capture and to share as it bumps its way along, meeting this problem here, that roadblock over there, facing frustration around the corner, temporary setbacks at the next turn, all the while trying to keep moving with patience and persuasion, to avoid the breakdown into failure and coercion. Yet given the enormous changes in China's social structure, levels of popular commitment and involvement, and the massive material improvements in the daily lives of the Chinese people, it is hard to question the fact that substantial benefits have been realized from the use of communicative techniques in the mobilization campaign.[61]

NOTES

1. Alan P.L. Liu, *Communications and National Integration in Communist China* (Berkeley: University of California Press, 1971), p. 87.

2. E.g., Gordon A. Bennett, *Yundong: Mass Campaigns in Chinese Communist Leadership,* University of California at Berkeley Center for Chinese Studies China Research Monographs, 1976, p. 15; James R. Townsend, *Political Participation in Communist China* (Berkeley: University of California Press, 1967), p. 185; John Gardner, "The *Wu Fan* Campaign in Shanghai: A Study in the Consolidation of Urban Control," in *Chinese Communist Parties in Action*, ed. A. Doak Barnett (Seattle: University of Washington Press, 1969), p. 477; A. Doak Barnett, *Communist China: The Early Years, 1949–1955* (New York: Praeger, 1964), p. 135; and Charles P. Cell, *Revolution at Work: Mobilization Campaigns in China* (New York: Academic Press, 1977), p. 6.

3. Liu, *Communications and National Integration*; Frederick T.C. Yu, "Campaigns, Communication and Development in Communist China," in *Communication and Change in Developing Countries*, ed. Daniel Lerner and Wilbur Schramm (Honolulu: East-West Center, 1967), pp. 195–215; and Godwin C. Chu, *Radical Change through Communication in Mao's China* (Honolulu: The University Press of Hawaii, 1977).

4. Material in this chapter is based on research reported in the author's book *Revolution at Work*.

5. Preliminary evidence suggests that under the current leadership of Hua and Teng, China's goals may be shifting from those of the Maoist era.

6. Chu, *Radical Change*, p. 3.

7. E.g., Richard Solomon, *Mao's Revolution and the Chinese Political Culture* (Berkeley: University of California Press, 1971), pp. 37, 254; G. William Skinner and Edwin Winkler, "Compliance Succession in Rural Communist China," in *A Sociological Reader on Complex Organizations*, ed. Amitai Etzioni, 2nd ed. (New York: Holt, Rinehart and Winston, 1969), pp. 410–438; and Alexander Eckstein, "Economic Fluctuations in Communist China's Domestic Development," in *China in Crisis*, ed. Ho Ping-ti and Tang Tsou (Chicago: University of Chicago Press, 1968), pp. 691–729.

8. Cell, *Revolution at Work*, p. 93.

9. It is important to realize that most of these communicative techniques also occur in China outside the campaign setting. The discussion here, however, will be confined to the context of the campaign.

10. Marriet Mills, "Thought Reform: Ideological Remoulding in China," *Atlantic Monthly* 204 (December 1959):71–77.

11. Chu, *Radical Change*, p. 300.

12. C. S. Chen and Charles P. Ridley, eds., *Rural People's Communes in Lien-Chaing: Documents Concerning Communes in Lien-Chaing County, Fukien Province, 1962–63*, Hoover Institution Publication no. 83, Stanford, CA, p. 124.

13. Isabel Crook and David Crook, *The First Years of Yangyi Commune* (London: Routledge & Kegan Paul, 1966), p. 223.

14. Cell, *Revolution at Work*, pp. 91–92.

15. Mills, "Thought Reform," p. 75; Yu, "Campaigns," p. 204.

16. Chu, *Radical Change*, pp. 238–241.

17. Rensselaer W. Lee, "The *Hsia Fang* System: Marxism and Modernization," *China Quarterly* 28 (October–December 1966):40–62.

18. Fu-sheng Mu, *The Wilting of the Hundred Flowers: The Chinese Intelligentsia under Mao* (New York: Praeger, 1962), p. 153.

19. William Hinton, *Fanshen: A Documentary of Revolution in a Chinese Village* (New York: Vintage Books, 1968), p. 222.

20. Mu, *Wilting of the Hundred Flowers*, p. 154.

21. Ibid., pp. 154–155.

22. Martin K. Whyte, *Small Groups and Political Rituals in Communist China* (Berkeley: University of California Press, 1974), p. 213.

23. Ibid., p. 232.

24. Mu, *Wilting of the Hundred Flowers*, pp. 153, 160–161.

25. Ibid., p. 153; Whyte, *Small Groups*, p. 298.

26. Peking Review, 12 January 1962, p. 17; see also Jack Chen, *The New Earth: How the Peasants in One Chinese County Solved the Problem of Poverty* (Peking: New World, 1957), p. 125.

27. Crook and Crook, *First Years of Yangyi*, p. 84.

28. Stuart R. Schram, "Mao Tse-tung and Liu Shao-chi: 1939–1969," *Asian Survey* 12 (1968):275–293.

29. For a discussion of the importance of *tatzupao*, see Chu, *Radical Change*, pp. 232–238.

30. Cell, *Revolution at Work*, p. 105.

31. Schram, "Mao Tse-tung and Liu Shao-chi."

32. Chen and Ridley, *Rural People's Communes in Lien-Chaing*.

33. Cell, *Revolution at Work*, p. 72.

34. Hinton, *Fanshen*.

35. Richard Baum, *Prelude to Revolution: Mao, the Party and the Peasant Question, 1962–1966* (New York: Columbia University Press, 1975), p. 77.

36. Ibid., p. 81.

37. Hinton, *Fanshen*, p. 129.

38. Ibid., p. 115.

39. Ibid., pp. 419–421. For a similar discussion, see also C. K. Yang, *Chinese Communist Society: The Family and the Village* (Cambridge, MA: MIT Press, 1965), p. 139.

40. Hinton, *Fanshen*, p. 423.

41. *People's Daily*, 14 November 1950, quoted in *Survey of China Mainland Press*, 15 November 1959, p. 8.

42. Hinton, *Fanshen*, p. 388; emphasis added.

43. Ibid., p. 338.

44. For a discussion of this problem, see also Townsend, *Political Participation*, p. 202.

45. Hinton, *Fanshen*, p. 339.

46. Ibid., p. 335.

47. Gordon A. Bennett and Ronald Montaperto, *Red Guard: The Political Biography of Dai Hsiao-ai* (Garden City, NY: Doubleday, 1971), p. 36.

48. Liu Shao-ch'i, "On the Party's Mass Line," in *On the Party, A Report to the Seventh People's Congress of the CCP*. [Reprinted in *People's China*, 1 July 1950.]

49. Mao Tse-tung, *Selected Works of Mao Tse-tung*, 4 vols. (Peking, Foreign Languages Press, 1967), 3:73.

50. Franz Schurmann, *Ideology and Organization in Communist China*, rev. ed. (Berkeley: University of California Press, 1968), p. xlii.

51. Hinton, *Fanshen*, p. 388.

52. John W. Lewis, *Leadership in Communist China* (Ithaca, NY: Cornell University Press, 1963), p. 5.

53. Thomas P. Bernstein, "Leadership and Mass Mobilization in the Soviet and Chinese Collectivization Campaigns of 1929–30 and 1955–56: A Comparison," *China Quarterly* 31 (July–September 1967):1–47; John Rue, *Mao Tse-tung in Opposition* (Stanford, CA: Stanford University Press, 1966).

54. In *People's China*, 1 July 1953, p. 13.

55. Hinton, *Fanshen*, p. 431.

56. Edgar Snow, *The Long Revolution* (New York: Random House, 1972), p. 187.

57. Hinton, *Fanshen*, p. 411.

58. Ibid., p. 444.

59. Transcribed from recorded tapes of the introductory session at Sandstone Hollow Brigade, Tsunhua County, Hopei Province, 28 March 1972; edited for clarity and grammar.

60. See, e.g., Chen, *The New Earth*, pp. 107–111; Crook and Crook, *First Years of Yangyi*, pp. 9–10; and Jan Myrdal, *Report from a Chinese Village* (New York: Signet Books, 1966), pp. 145–149.

61. Cell, *Revolution at Work*, pp. 173–174.

3

Participation, Communication, and Political Integration

Victor C. Falkenheim

Integration perspectives at first blush seem ill suited to the analysis of Chinese politics and society, particularly in the last decade. Specifically, their functionalist underpinnings and system-maintenance biases would appear to clash with the very logic of a revolutionary society whose approach to development has been predicated on conflict as the basis of progress.[1] Yet much of Chinese political practice can also be seen as preoccupied with the fruitful management of conflict and its transformation into more potent forms of social cooperation and unity. The leadership's current urgent stress on "stability and unity" can be seen in this light as an effort to translate the conflictual legacy of the Cultural Revolution into a new unity on goals and methods.

My principal concern in this chapter is to explore the relationship between rates of citizen political participation and the quality of political and social integration.[2] Specifically, I will seek to assess the validity of the view articulated by integration theorists and shared by some Chinese writers that the development and maintenance of effective input channels for demand articulation significantly shape the quality of vertical ("elite-mass") integration.[3]

Participation will be defined as "activity by private citizens designed to influence government decision making,"[4] while integration, for conceptual purposes, will be treated as a dependent variable, definable and measurable on three interdependent dimensions: the level of diffuse system support; regime or elite legitimacy; and degree of specific normative or policy consensus.[5] Given the difficulties of measuring levels of participation and integration and isolating participation from the other integrative factors, this study will not attempt to formulate or empirically test hypotheses regarding the linkage between participation and integration.

Instead, the chapter has three aims: first, to abstract briefly, from "mass line" theory, core Chinese views on the integrative role of participation and communication; second, to describe and assess the effectiveness of the channels of communication made available to citizens in the post–Cultural Revolution period (primarily on the basis of interview data); third, to explain the disparity that emerges between mass-line ideals and the reality of severely constrained participation in the past decade, assessing the implications of that disparity both for prospects of unity and integration in China, and for integration theory in general.

I will suggest that to the Chinese leaders, integration is an instrumental not an ultimate goal. Consequently, the level of integration sought at any given time will determine the quality and frequency of mass inputs rather than vice versa. Frequently, the leadership will not only tolerate but anticipate low levels of support, and will seek, temporarily at least, deliberately to block input channels by appropriate political cues. This is an approach to integration that stresses the long-term importance of effective and responsive policy and reflects the primacy of substantive conceptions of legitimacy (output) over procedural conceptions of legitimacy.[6] I will also argue that this emphasis is understood by a citizenry well schooled in the centralist reality of mass-line politics.

Integration and Participation in Mass-Line Perspective

There is no difficulty in inputting a long-standing concern with integration to the Chinese leadership, if one accepts a rough equation between the concept of integration and the Chinese term *t'uan chieh* (unity). While the two terms are not precisely analogous, *t'uan chieh* in Party usage, implying an authentic goal consensus—a qualitative connotation absent from the concept "integration"—they are close enough for analytical purposes. Certainly, there can be no question regarding the importance accorded unity in Chinese Communist Party writings. A matter of urgent concern to the Party on strategic grounds before 1949, it has received continued stress since, reflecting both the postulated identity of long-term state interests with popular interests, and the pragmatic insistence on the importance of mass support to the successful implementation of a broad range of ambitious development programs.

Chinese theory and practice regarding the problems of forging a unified mass movement have been best summarized in writings on the mass line.[7] In mass-line theory, unity does not exist naturally but has to be achieved painstakingly. The often-proclaimed unity of the 95 percent of the population designated as the revolutionary masses is at best nominal, and conceals significant conflicts and differences in terms of class interests, cultural levels, and degrees of political understanding. Further, the Party's own vanguard role is perceived as not only intensifying existing cleavages but independently generating new ones as well. The Party, in its concern to promote change, may seek to utilize these cleavages as levers to stimulate desired changes. In the face of

48

existing conflicts and the Party's own approach to change, the process of achieving integration is difficult and minimally requires, in the view of many Chinese writers, leadership skilled in reconciling conflicts of interest among its supporters; disciplined organization, permitting the development and assertion of a unified program embodying efforts at reconciling such conflicts; a set of common values, or agreed-upon criteria for selection of goals; consensual or consultative procedures, designed to yield flexible policy adjustments; and most important, policy that over the long run is genuinely congruent with the fundamental aspirations of the citizenry.

In practice, developing responsive policy on the basis of consultation and skillful political adjustment requires active citizen input. Only when Party leaders have a clear grasp of popular attitudes, and a sense of the sources and intensity of opposition and support, can policy be adjusted to deflect opposition and maximize support, and Party educational efforts be intelligently geared to address real citizen reservations. In this essentially "feedback" model of the mass line, full integration in Mao's sense of "unity of understanding, policy, planning, command and action"[8] requires policy that is consultatively developed and substantively responsive.

This stress on correct policy, that is, policy that is ideologically sound, realistic, and appropriately responsive to citizen needs is partly grounded in the educational requirements of the mass line. It is assumed that some support for correct policy will be naturally forthcoming from progressive elements in society but that persuasion will often be necessary to secure the acquiescence of the rest. Such efforts at consensus building will be straightforward if policy is sound but will be badly handicapped by poor policy. Mao makes the point succinctly in a comparison of the Great Leap Forward with preceding periods of Party history. During the Revolutionary War period and the period of the First Five-Year Plan, the General Line, Mao pointed out, had "abundant persuasive power," which made it possible for the Party to "unify the understanding of the cadres and the masses." In contrast, during the Great Leap Forward it "was not possible to have unified understanding and action."[9] Hua Kuo-feng has similarly praised the policy line of the eleventh Congress precisely for its putative capacity to elicit unified mass support.[10]

If correct policy facilitates unity or integration, participation is seen as the key to correct policy. As Mao has argued the case, "democracy" permits the Party to "collect opinions from all sides," and develop "communication between top and bottom." Without such communication, the Party, Mao suggests, will be prone to formulate decisions on the basis of "one-sided and incorrect materials" which in turn will make it impossible for the Party to "summarize experience correctly."[11] In this view, only when the Party gets a sense of popular response to particular initiatives can it properly appraise their workability and formulate in response the basis for an appropriate compromise. In Mao's words, "without democracy there can't be any correct centralization because people's ideas differ, and if their understanding lacks unity, then centralization cannot be established."[12] A corollary justification stresses the Party's fallibility, emphasizing that since the truth may at times be in the hands of a minority, it is essential to guarantee the democratic rights of minorities as a potential long-term corrective.

A *Red Flag* article in 1978 summarized part of this argument succinctly:

> The purpose of practicing democratic centralism and letting the masses speak out is to become acquainted with conditions at lower levels, to grasp the actual situation, to exchange views between higher and lower levels, and to commit fewer or no errors with regard to subjectivism, bureaucracy and other things, so that our party can have a centralized and unified leadership which is genuine and staunch instead of fake and weak. In stressing democracy we do not mean to discard centralization. The exact opposite is true. We want to create proper conditions so that we will achieve centralization. Our centralization embodies the centralized opinions of the masses. It never advocates "what I say counts." Therefore, our system differs from an autocratic dictatorship. Ours has scientific centralization—it centralizes the correct opinions of the masses.[13]

It is clear that the notion of correctness remains ambiguous since its two crucial criteria—public acceptability and ideological soundness—can be differentially stressed to justify particular policy compromises. The Party's current stress on the congruence between its policy and mass interests—as justification for new incentive policies, for example—suggests the polemical uses of this ambiguity.

Mass participation, it should be stressed, has a number of other functions, some of which also affect the process and level of societal integration. Participation can enhance an individual citizen's sense of efficacy, offer safety valves for pent-up dissatisfaction, check cadre abuses of power, or promote the internalization of Party norms, all of which advance the process of elite-mass integration.[14] What is being singled out for discussion here is the impact of institutionalized "airing of views" on the formulation of "responsive" state policy, which, I suggest, is the crucial mediating link between participation and integration.[15]

Mass Democracy and Citizen Participation

In the Party's view, a correct policy line requires a correct organizational line. The notion of an organizational line denotes not only the desired consultative style of leadership but also the appropriate provision of adequately institutionalized channels of communication between citizens and cadres. Among the formal input channels and instruments that have received specific legislative or constitutional sanction are work-unit elections, public meetings, cadre criticism sessions, letter offices at newspapers and government organs, opinion boxes, big-character posters, and so on. Jointly, these constitute the basis of "mass democracy."[16] The Party has recognized that its own occasionally "feudal autocratic" style of leadership and the lack of a "popular democratic tradition" in China have tended to inhibit the use of these channels, and therefore periodically encourages the use of these instruments to tap their potential fully.[17]

Yet citizen response to many of these channels appears to have been less than overwhelming, particularly in the past decade. One need not accept in toto the current assertions that the Gang of Four and Lin Piao imposed a "fascist dictatorship" after 1966 to regard as plausible many of the described failings of socialist democracy in China. The current effort to stimulate the revival of "democratic" instruments has focused on two kinds of systematic violations of citizen political rights in the past decade. The campaign to study the experience of Hsun-yi County has focused on cadre violations of peasant economic rights and rights of person. The campaign for socialist legality has provided evidence supporting the charges that many citizens who utilized their constitutionally sanctioned rights of criticism were penalized or suppressed by officials who used big-character posters, oral criticism, or letters to the government as evidence in making political charges against their critics.[18]

Even discounting some of the more extreme allegations since 1977, the general tenor of the criticism is at least partly confirmed by a recent interview-based study of citizen use of those democratic instruments.[19] The findings of that study, though of limited use because of the small number of respondents (37) and the unrepresentative nature of the respondent group, at least sustains impressionistically the thrust of official commentary. None of the respondents in the sample interviewed, for example, had ever written a *chien-chu hsin* (letter of complaint) to a newspaper or to an upper-level official. They were of course aware of the Party's nominal policy of support for *jen min lai hsin* (people's letters), but regarded them nonetheless as hollow and ineffective forms. Their attitudes toward big-character posters were similarly skeptical. Most had written such posters during the Cultural Revolution when urged to do so, but few had used this particular form of communication in the aftermath of the Cultural Revolution. The common opinion box provided in most units was similarly ignored as a means of communicating with the leadership. Finally, when invited to criticize their leadership for policy or style failings, most typically demurred on the grounds that it would prove either ineffective or counterproductive.

The explanations respondents offered for their diffidence confirm much of the official earlier critique. The major constraint on the use of these channels was fear of the economic and political consequences. To speak out at a meeting, to write a letter of complaint, to write a big-character poster was to run the risk of speaking or writing "incorrectly"— in Chinese terminology, *fan tsuo wu* (to make a mistake). Such mistakes of adopting a deviant ideological posture could carry penalties of varying severity, ranging from being asked to recant, to being required to undertake study, to being subjected to "struggle," or even ultimately detention and incarceration. Similarly, to criticize a cadre, even if invited to do so, was to risk retaliation in the long run, in lesser or greater degree. Cadres controlled access to promotion, bonuses, economic benefits, leaves of absence, workpoints, job assignments, welfare, benefits, education, military service, and so on. Most respondents were therefore of the view that *tuo i shih pu ju shao i shih* (better to be safe than sorry). Such forms of retaliation were not legitimate within the idealized conception of the mass line, but they appear to have been common and they bulked large in the calculations of respondents. For example, a typical complaint against a leader at a minimum might generate a subtly discriminatory response in terms of work assignments, holiday requests, and so on.

On the other hand, these potential penalties were not seen as overwhelming deterrents to participation. Almost all respondents conceded that the penalties were not ordinarily that severe and that one could often be vindicated in a challenge to policy or leadership. Moreover, if the financial or personal stake involved was great enough, a more assertive posture was likely. The respondents expressed admiration for the courage of ideological dissenters such as the authors of the 1974 "Li I-Che" poster on socialist democracy but said that there were few who were willing to run such risks.

These constraints applied most clearly to the use of formal written instruments of communication whose use carried the greatest risks. Similarly, the sense of constraint applied most forcibly to sensitive issues of state policy. In the rural areas, for example, production and requisition quotas were not subject to serious, open discussion. Not a single rural respondent in the group interviewed was even familiar with the term *tzu hsia erh shang* (bottom to top) planning, despite the fact that it was a central tenet of the mass line. Factory wages and rural excess grain levies were additional examples of issues that simply could not be raised openly or directly in this period. During periods of mass political move-ments, ritualistic support of publicly approved themes was perceived as the best strategy for coping with the pressures for expression. Slogans endorsing going against the tide were seen as slender sanction for the expression of critical or dissenting opinions and were never invoked by respondents in this sample.

Given the convergence of emigré testimony and documentary data, there seems little reason to challenge this overall picture, although it is important to note that there have always been exceptions to the patterns described above. At Tien-an-men Square in 1976, for example, a major popular challenge to the radical leadership helped ultimately to topple it, and since 1977, significant currents of dissent have surfaced in China on both the left and the right.

The Causes of Constrained Participation

On the face of it, this pattern of citizen response is at considerable odds with the optimistic feedback model sketched earlier. What accounts for the disparity between ideals and practice? Of course, many factors, both long and short term, are involved, including the declining commitment of the Party to mass-line norms, widespread deferential values among the mass public, as well as situational factors specific to the Cultural Revolution decade, such as the escalating level of political conflict. But the long-standing and critical factor would appear to be the conflicting requirements of the Party's leadership role and the ambivalence of its approach to integration.

The extent to which the Party chooses at a given time to emphasize unity or conflict varies with the policy context and its own changing purposes. The Party may, in implementing radical initiatives, seek deliberately to build policy on a narrow basis of support, in the expectation that success will vindicate the policy and allow a retrospective consensus to be forged. A good example would be the speed-up of collectivization in 1955, or the Learn from Tachai campaign of the 1970s. Alternatively, the Party may seek from the beginning to design policy to capture the broadest possible range of initial support, as in the case of the current Four Modernizations program. In the former instance, leadership anticipating the likely negative thrust of public sentiment responds by delegitimizing input, purposely constricting the flow of information.

The Party's general ambivalence to "mass" input stems from its vanguard role and is clearly illustrated by its conflicting instructions to basic-level cadres, who constitute the point of contact between citizen and state. On the one hand, they are enjoined to accommodate mass demands; on the other, they are proscribed from tailing after the masses.[20] Their role is described not as inert reflectors of popular opinion but as active shapers of opinion. Their role is to move attitudes in the direction of a principled consensus supporting the Party's perception and definition of the real long-term public interest. Thus, while local

Party leaders are consistently urged to "heed to masses," they are also cautioned against using the "interests of the masses" as a "pretext for refusing to carry out instructions from higher levels."[21] While they are urged to adapt central policy flexibly to local reality they are warned against modifying *correct* decisions of the Party.[22] One can easily understand a local leader's plaintive query: "In listening to the opinions of the masses it is first necessary to listen to the correct opinions. *Yet how can we tell whether an opinion is correct or not?*"[23]

The psychological and political pressures to ignore mass input are evident in a revealing self-criticism by a county Party secretary who reported his experience with the local program for fertilizer accumulation in 1972. Distressed at the local custom of letting the pigs roam loose, he ruled that the "masses should be required to build pigsties for accumulating manure." Other county leaders objected that this "was a problem that the past secretaries of the county had been unable to solve," but he countered that "*if even the building of pigsties cannot be accomplished, why talk about learning from Tachai and changing the world?*"[24] The circumstances and the ironic denouement are best captured in his own words:

> After a few mass meetings I went to Machuang brigade to carry out propaganda but the masses just muttered that pigs yield more pork when let loose. . . . Sensing ideological problems, I asked the cadres to proceed with the work . . . they built the pigsties in 3 days. Enthusiasm in the rest of the county, however, remained low, therefore . . . I went to Machuang a second time in the hope of summarizing the experience for popularization in the entire *hsien*. When I arrived there my heart sank. There was a pigsty in every family but there were no pigs in the pigsties. The pigs were running loose as usual in the daytime and they came back in the evening. The pigsties thus had become hostels for pigs.

In the face of the ambiguities and pressures of their role, Mao's 1962 remark that many cadres "don't understand democratic centralism" and "don't like it" becomes explicable,[25] as does one local official's admission that "while everyone knows in principle that the leading officials . . . should serve the people, things [are] often upside down."[26] In fact, to many local leaders this inversion of principle made administrative sense, a view reflected in the bureaucratic dictum that "work can be carried out just the same without heeding what the masses say" and that "normal democratic life was an obstacle to centralism."[27] To local officials, there was little wrong with the view that central priorities should take precedence over local priorities. It was a view built into the conventional administrative distinction between "hard tasks" (upper-level demands)

54

that had to be fulfilled, and "soft tasks" (constituency demands), that were less binding.[28]

The bureaucratic mindset, though a long-standing feature of local administration, appears to have become increasingly widespread in the 1970s as a result of ideological pressures that discouraged material incentives and made certain forms of self-interested participation less legitimate. But importantly, the same views continue to undercut even the very strong post-Mao administrative reform program.[29] Although the state is advocating the increased autonomy of the production team as an institutional basis for peasant rights,[30] and is strongly critical of cadres who "order around the lower units without knowing their specific problems,"[31] infringing on legitimate peasant interests, cadres have been notably resistant to the reforms. This resistance is rooted in the conviction that their own capacity to lead the peasants in the ambitious new programs of agricultural modernization will be imperiled by the changes. The *People's Daily*, in noting the "rather influential view" among cadres that the administrative reforms were "incompatible with the implementation of rural reconstruction,"[32] has stated that "while nothing can be accomplished without drive . . . revolutionary drive should not be confused . . . with coercion and commands."[33]

The Consequences of Constrained Participation

The continuing gap between mass-line ideals and the political practice just described would appear to have significant implications for the level of integration in Chinese society. Specifically, the disparity would appear to imply a high degree of citizen alienation, a dangerously suboptimal flow of information from the grass roots to the leadership, and in consequence, declining responsiveness and flexibility on the part of public authorities. Paradoxically, not all of these implications appear to have been fully held in practice. Interview material collected in a 1975 study of rural local administration,[34] though of impressionistic value, revealed a surprisingly positive appraisal of local leadership by most peasants. Many of the respondents tended to view pressure from above for innovation as legitimate. They regarded higher-level initiatives as frequently beneficial to local welfare, particularly when they could be modified by the older, experienced peasants. Further, they were willing to risk innovation under state pressure on grounds that the state would not "let them starve." Moreover, local leaders were generally characterized as "flexible and responsive," with "little reliance on commandist methods." Most brigade and commune cadres, respondents asserted, *"had learned"* (emphasis added) how to adapt central policies to local conditions. In the words of one respondent, the "Great Leap Forward style" of "blind and coercive leadership . . . is seldom seen today." Of course, most informants could cite individual instances of cadre arrogance and inflexibility, and personally knew cadres "who did not modestly accept supervision by the masses." Significantly, such forms of behavior were seen not only as illegitimate but as "atypical." One representative view of the leadership's success in eliciting participation was that "the masses do not fear retaliation in expressing opinions on production matters." Further, the impression of observers that local leaders had in the 1970s become relatively more responsive to mass input is supported by the 1977 interview data as well. The consensus articulated by respondents in 1977 was that the Cultural Revolution had had a positive democratizing effect on political relations in the villages.

The general lack of strong grievance among these rural respondents, whose most recent experience prior to departing China had been with the erratic and sometimes forcible local imposition of the Tachai model, attests to the importance of "small democracy" in alleviating citizen-cadre tensions.

It seems clear from both studies that even during periods of enforced political change and rigid policy, the Party has sought to preserve a number of limited forms of "production democracy."[35] Thus, during campaign periods, some significant possibilities remained for inputs on both a formal and an informal basis. This particularly applied to the meeting arena, where citizens apparently found oral communication less risky. Although discussion in such local public meetings was often monopolized by specialists, there was frequent opportunity for comment by ordinary citizens, and 30 out of 37 of the respondents interviewed in 1977 reported speaking out independently at least twice a year at mass meetings. Individuals had the right to air personal grievances and to address themselves to a limited range of remediable problems within the framework of existing policy. Thus, youths who had been sent down felt secure in invoking state policy to press for better housing and better treatment. They often used meeting forums and unit elections to work for these aims. Similarly, factory workers could appeal within state law for a fair share of economic supplements, housing, and other benefits. Peasants particularly addressed themselves vigorously to securing equitable distributions of workpoints, private plots, and so on.

Unit elections were viewed as offering opportunities for interest articulation and input. Important meetings to decide details of economic policy were often well attended and frequently lively and combative. Although the limits on debate were well understood and the scope of input tended to vary with degree of policy consensus at upper levels and the tightness of the current policy line, even within those limits there were many areas for communication. Where villages were united internally, they often exercised significant leverage as well.

Further, a variety of informal and quasi-legal modes of interest articulation, from grumbling to work slowdowns, enabled citizens to communicate their responses to local leaders. These forms of citizen input were not insignificant in providing useful feedback, minimizing cadre-citizen friction, and helping in the smooth adaptation of policy, despite the rigidities discussed earlier. In short, the stifling of demands appears less fragmenting and damaging in the rural context than one might expect.

Rigidity and Responsiveness in Policymaking

Yet, as the previous discussion indicated, the mass line implies more than simple "production democracy." It also implies a broader if indirect public capacity to at least partly shape state policy. The Maoist critique of "small democracy" during the Cultural Revolution specified as its key weakness its inability to sustain a challenge to fundamental policy, in this instance to the allegedly revisionist line of the 1960s.[36] The current leadership similarly has attributed the persistence of "inappropriate" "ultra left" policies through the 1970s to precisely the same lack of popular control over basic policy. Certainly the view of the current moderate leadership that there was an unacceptable degree of policy rigidity in the 1970s and a lack of sensitivity and responsiveness to mass material needs and interests, seems correct. The euphoria with which the purge of the Gang of Four was greeted, and the rapid pace of change since 1977 in all areas, powered by pent-up societal and bureaucratic demands, lends credibility to this view. More significantly, the decline in the degree of substantive policy responsiveness in the 1970s appears to have been genuinely fragmenting in its long-term impact on public attitudes toward the Party and state leadership.

In addressing the current problems of malaise and alienation, the leadership is once again stressing the importance of democratization as a means of renewing earlier levels of integration and consensus; but drawing on the lessons of the 1970s they have rejected those forms of direct democracy (such as the four freedoms) that were the institutional outgrowth of the Cultural Revolution. The rationale for this rejection stresses that the high levels of both politicization and polarization that accompanied the Cultural Revolution in fact decreased meaningful participation, and paved the way for the repression of the early and mid-1970s. As self-serving as this analysis may be, it seems clear that China in the 1970s, beset by factionalism, its leadership divided by ideological and personal conflicts, lacked the very organizational and political preconditions on which mass line democracy was based.

The current shifts can be seen in part as a return to the predicates of the mass line described earlier. The integrative role of the Party has been restored, along with its correlates, Party discipline, and rank-and-file democracy. The united front has been restored to its former importance as the symbol of consultative policymaking. Basic level units have been guaranteed the right to assert and defend their legitimate economic interests against overbearing administration. The new electoral and local government laws that went into effect in 1980 are intended to expand the scope of citizen influence and choice through strengthened representative channels. The right to criticize and control cadres has been augmented by the creation of a new legal framework offering greater protection to citizens in the exercise of their political rights.

Given the fate of Cultural Revolution reforms, which had the same nominal objectives, one may be skeptical of the efficacy of these efforts, and particularly of Chinese aspirations to develop *kao tu min chu* (enhanced democracy) by the year 2000 as the political concomitant of modernization.[37] Such skepticism, however, may be misplaced. If the current policy direction remains in force, it will in all likelihood presage a significant shift in the Party's vanguard role. As alternative development options vanish, the Party may be constrained from adopting radical initiatives and may find that a more permanent and institutionalized system of elite-mass communication is more suitable to the requirements of the current era. The cleavages likely to be generated by the current modernization program, though serious, may be more adequately dealt with by a stable set of policies, input channels, and legal guarantees.

This may not necessarily enhance the political efficacy of the average citizen, who may find power slipping into the hands of technocratic elites, and it may not be comforting to the Party, which is likely to feel a similar discomforting erosion of its corporate vanguard position. But to the extent that the informal rules governing mass-elite communication become more stable and routinized, and the channels of communication less constrained in the scope of demands they can carry, and more insulated from short-run political fluctuations, the result may be both better yield of information and more responsive policy. Such a system might well come closer to achieving the elusive blend of "small" and "large" democracy articulated in mass-line theory that has proved so difficult to achieve in practice since 1949.

NOTES

1. Integration perspectives are probably most useful in studying the period 1947–1957 during the main phase of institution-building in China. For a good application of such perspectives to problems of administrative integration, see Dorothy Solinger, *Regional Government and Political Integration in Southwest China, 1949–1954* (Berkeley: University of California Press, 1977). For a discriminating effort to tailor integration perspectives to China's revolutionary setting, see James Seymour, *China: The Politics of Revolutionary Reintegration* (New York: Thomas Y. Crowell, 1976).

2. The problems of analyzing the macrosocietal impact of participation on integration are best explored in Samuel P. Huntington and Joan M. Nelson, *No Easy Choice* (Cambridge, MA: Harvard University Press, 1976).

3. Claude Ake, *A Theory of Political Integration* (Homewood, IL: Rosey Press, 1976), pp. 74–75.

4. Huntington and Nelson, *No Easy Choice*, p. 4.

5. Ake, *A Theory of Political Integration*, pp. 8–11.

6. Mark E. Kann, "The Dialectic of Consent Theory," *The Journal of Politics* 40 (1978): 386–408.

7. There is a significant exegetical literature on the "mass line." One of the earliest and still sound summaries of the concept can be found in John W. Lewis, *Leadership in Communist China* (Ithaca, NY: Cornell University Press, 1963), Chapter 3.

8. Stuart Schram, ed., *Mao Tse-tung Unrehearsed* (Harmondsworth, England: Penguin Books, 1974), p. 164.

9. Ibid., pp. 177–178.

10. Hua Kuo-feng, "Unite and Strive to Build a Modern, Powerful Socialist Country" [Report on the Work of the Government, Delivered at the 5th N.P.C.] Text, BBC World Broadcast, Part III, Far East [FE/5758].

11. Schram, *Mao Tse-tung*, pp. 164–165.

12. Ibid., p. 163.

13. Ma Wen-Jui, "Restore and Carry Forward the Fine Tradition of Democratic Centralism," *Hung Ch'i* [Red Flag] no. 7, 1978 in *Foreign Broadcast Information Service*, 5 July 1978, p. E5.

14. For an excellent inventory of such functions, see Pierre M. Perolle, "Mao's Legacy: The Legitimacy of Political Opposition," paper delivered at the New England Political Science Association, Boston, April 1978.

15. For a similar and more fully developed exposition of this point, see Jerry F. Hough, *The Soviet Union and Social Science Theory* (Cambridge, MA: Harvard University Press, 1977), particularly Chapter 8.

16. See, for example, Mao Tse-tung, *Selected Works*, 5 vols. (Peking: Foreign Languages Press, 1977), 5:343–346. Also see *Peking Review* 44 (1978):16.

17. Ma Wen-Jui, "Restore and Carry Forward," pp. 6–7.

18. *Jen-min Jih-pao* [People's Daily], 9 October 1978.

19. Victor C. Falkenheim, "Political Participation in China," *Problems in Communism* 27 (3) (1978):18–32.

20. Lewis, *Leadership in Communist China*, pp. 85–86.

21. *People's Daily*, 7 September 1972.

22. Ibid., 23 January 1972.

23. Ibid., 20 February 1972; emphasis added.

24. Ibid.; emphasis added.

25. Schram, *Mao Tse-tung*, p. 160.

26. *People's Daily*, 25 October 1972.

27. Ibid., 20 February 1972.

28. Ibid., 25 October 1965.

29. For a good summary of the early phases of the campaigns to study Hsiang-hsiang, Hunan, and Hsun-yi, Honan, see Ch'en Ting-chung, "A Look at the Chinese Communists' Adjustments in the Rural Economy," *Chung-kung Yen-chiu* [Research on Chinese Communist Affairs] 12 (8) (15 August 1978):20–35.

30. Wan Li, "Conscientiously Implement the Party's Economic Policy in Rural Areas," *Red Flag*, no. 3 (March 1978):92–97.

31. *People's Daily*, 26 July 1978.

32. Ibid., 3 August 1978.

33. Ibid., 26 July 1978.

34. A set of open-ended questions focusing on subcounty administrative relationships was posed to 29 rural respondents in mid-1975 by the author and a research assistant, Mr. Yang Sai-cheung. The class breakdown of the respondents was: 9 poor peasant background, 3 lower-middle peasant background, 1 middle peasant background, 2 rich peasant background, 3 landlord background, 2 artisan background, 4 working background, 1 petty bourgeoise background, 1 overseas Chinese background, 2 office workers, 1 unknown. The transcripts are available from the author on request.

35. The following discussion draws on Falkenheim, "Political Participation in China."

36. Lowell Dittmer, "Mass Line and 'Mass Criticism' in China: An Analysis of the Fall of Liu Shao-Ch'i," *Asian Survey* 13 (1973):772–792.

37. *People's Daily*, 18 September 1978. For an interesting Hong Kong leftist commentary on this article, see Kao Man, "The Chinese Communists Advocate the Realization within the Century of Higher Democracy," *Tung Hsiang* [Momentum], 20 October 1978, p. 27.

4

The Mass Line and Leader-Mass Relations and Communication in Basic-Level Rural Communities

Marc Blecher

The Chinese Communist Party has developed probably the most sophisticated approach to leader-mass relations, both in theory and historical practice, of any major revolutionary party or group.[1] As a methodology of leadership,[2] the mass line, which lies at the heart of the Chinese Communist Party's strategy of leader-mass relations, embodies two major elements. First, the relationship between leaders and masses should be founded upon a basic equality of condition. Every comrade should "identify himself or herself with the masses wherever he or she goes, and instead of standing above them, should immerse himself or herself among them."[3] Second, leaders should strive to establish close, even intimate relations with the masses. The mass line directs leaders' attention not just to collecting the masses' simple opinions or preferences, but more importantly, to grasping their needs, hopes, problems, feelings, ideas, and existential situation, to all of which their opinions and preferences give but imperfect expression. In this sense, the mass line is a radical strategy of leader-mass communication. The emphasis is on understanding the masses' viewpoint as well as their views.

Of greater significance, the mass line posits a necessary relationship between equality and intimate communication between leaders and masses. On the one hand, intimate communication and in-depth understanding between leaders and masses depend on the existence of some basic equalities between the two groups. "The cadres of our Party and state are ordinary workers and not overlords sitting on the backs of the people. By taking part in collective productive labor, the cadres maintain extensive, constant, and close ties with the working people."[4] On the other hand, close contact with the masses can contribute to leader-mass equality. As Mao told Andre Malraux, "Equality . . . is natural to those who have not lost contact with the masses."[5] ·

The English language provides us with a single word, "communion," which combines these aspects of equality and intimacy. The first two definitions of communion offered by the *Oxford English Dictionary* are "sharing or holding in common with others" and "fellowship, in action or relations; mutual intercourse." (The use of the word to describe certain religious ceremonies, though perhaps the most common one in contemporary parlance, is a specific usage derived from the more general one.) The etymological link between "communion" and "commune," though obvious, alerts us to the simple fact that, in order to live up to its name, a commune must embody particular kinds of social relations both among members and between members and leaders informed by equality and mutual intimacy.

Viewed in all its richness, then, the mass line is far more than a set of principles about leader-mass *communication*, although it includes them. It addresses leader-mass *relations* in their broadest and fullest sense. It cannot be reduced to epigrammatic formulations like "from the masses, to the masses," or to Western concepts such as political participation, interest articulation, or political solicitation, though to be sure all these forms of citizen communication to leadership do have their place in the mass line. The mass line places the question of leader-mass communication squarely within the political, social, economic, organizational, administrative, and historical contexts that surround, condition, inform, constrain, promote, or even express the possibilities for open and intimate leader-mass communication, effective leadership, and heightened consciousness.

In this chapter I shall look at some of the ways in which these various features of local organization, political practice, and nationwide political movements and changes have intersected with the mass line's concern for fostering a communion of equality and intimacy between leaders and masses—in this case, cadres at the team, brigade, and commune levels[6] on the one hand and, to use the Chinese (official as well as vernacular) term, commune members (*she yuan*) on the other. The chapter has three parts. The first uses accounts by emigrés interviewed in Hong Kong in 1974–1975 to discuss the ways in which some of the basic features of political organization and activity in rural China affect leader-mass relations at the grassroots level. The picture that emerges is, on the whole, positive; informants tended to describe a relatively high degree of intimacy and equality between basic-level cadres and commune members; more important for our purposes, their accounts related this to a number of factors in rural organization and political activity. The second part looks at a stunning example of the decline of what I have called communion in leader-mass relations—in Hsun-yi County, which became a focus of press attention in mid-1978—with an eye toward identifying some of the causes of the problems there. Let me emphasize that neither of these parts offers explicitly, or is intended to offer implicitly, an argument about the actual level or degree of leader-mass communion that has been attained in rural China; answers to this question still lie well beyond the possibilities presented by the data available in contemporary studies of China. Nor do these parts of the paper attempt to offer causal arguments about the relationship between some set of independent variables on the one hand and the level of communion on the other. Here the goal is more modest: to use interview and press accounts to look at the qualitative ways in which some of the features of rural politics in China can function to promote or obstruct the development of intimate and egalitarian relationships between leaders and masses that are envisioned in the mass line. The third part of the paper returns to the interview materials to suggest some of the implications of leader-mass communion—when and where it may exist—for local politics and leader-mass communications at the grassroots level.

Local Organization

Production teams and brigades have been organized around the natural historical contours of the Chinese countryside—that is, they coincide with the traditional boundaries of communities that cohered and continue to cohere by virtue of preexisting spatial, kinship, historical, customary, or cultural ties. Relations between local leaders and commune members usually exist within the close affinities of such tightly knit communities. As one youth put it:

> The team head has grown up and lived with the people of the team all his life. . . . People in the village have lived together for generations. They understand not only your situation, but even as far back as your grandfather. . . . The team head may not understand everyone in the team equally well, but still he understands everyone very well. The only difference may be how much he knows about your great-grandfather.[7]

The organization of political and economic life around these natural communities-cum-production teams and brigades helps make for easy accessibility and frequent, intensive contact between local leaders and masses. Opportunities for communication between team cadres and commune members on a wide range of political and economic matters are provided by the team's regular meetings, political study sessions, militia drills, Youth League activities, and on-the-spot conferences.[8] More informal opportunities for intimate contact between cadres and members are also legion. One is the casual gatherings or "bull sessions" that take place in most teams after the evening meal.

> In the evenings, eight to ten people usually gathered under some trees in front of the team office. Yes, there were cadres there too—after all, they are just the same as the team

members. While sitting there, people talked about all sorts of things: production, complaints, grudges against the other lineage group, and so forth.[9]

At the bull sessions in our team, which were attended by 20 people including some cadres, people discussed things they had read about in the newspaper, such as China exploding an atomic bomb, or Chou En-lai or Mao hosting a foreign guest. . . . There were also small controversies over what to do with a certain piece of land, how much fertilizer to put down when, or how much grain this piece of land can produce.[10]

When the team cadres receive a production quota from the brigade, they go over to the peasant association office where there are often people sitting around shooting the bull in the evenings. The cadres just sit down to chat, and after a while, at the appropriate moment, they bring up the quotas.[11]

Sometimes, if the members had opinions about the performance of a cadre, they would bring it up in the evenings when people were sitting around shooting the bull.[12]

The myriad moments—along the road to market, on the way to the fields, while walking around the village—when commune members bump into their neighbor-leaders can also be used as opportunities for communicating views, feelings, ideas, and problems. The workers on one state farm were unhappy about the elimination of private plots. A cadre told me:

The masses raised opinions at livelihood meetings (*sheng-huo hui*) about how long it took them to go to the market to buy vegetables. They also complained to the cadres at other times when they happened to bump into them. For example, some of them bumped into me in town one day when I was buying vegetables. I was walking pretty quickly, and they asked me why. I replied, "You know how short time is. I have to get home and cook." They said, "Yes, look at how miserable things are since we have no more private plots. You ought to talk to the higher levels about this.[13]

In contrast to the findings of some political scientists that citizens in the "democratic" politics of the West often do not know who their leaders are or which leaders to contact about particular matters, or that the leaders are somewhat inaccessible to the citizens,[14] in rural China no one can fail to know who the local leaders are, and no one can have much difficulty finding them.

Leadership Recruitment

The pattern of recruitment of local leaders in rural China also reflects a concern with equality and intimacy between leaders and masses. Most basic is the fact that all leaders at the brigade and team levels, including Party secretaries, are local people. Team leaders are chosen directly by the team members with little interference by the higher levels, and brigade leaders are chosen through various processes which combine the preferences of the members expressed in voting with suggestions, nominations, or approval by the commune level.[15] Moreover, team and brigade cadres find themselves on the payrolls of their collective units, not the state.

Despite their local origins and their dependence on the village collective units for their incomes and their continued tenure in office, it is possible that local leaders may still be drawn from or may grow into a village socioeconomic elite. The available evidence suggests, however, that this is not the case. In my sample of 282 team, brigade, and even commune leaders who served 21 villages between 1958 and 1974, 17 percent were women, 36 percent had had two years or less of primary education, 57 percent were illiterate or semiliterate, and 56 percent were not Party members. Twenty-four percent were described as having "poor" economic situations, 37 percent "average," and 39 percent "good." Twenty-four percent were aged 25 or less, 23 percent between 26 and 35, 32 percent between 36 and 45, and 20 percent over 46 (including 12 percent between 55 and 66).

Moreover, in the wake of the Cultural Revolution's emphasis on increased representation and political power for young people, women, and people with lower levels of education, the data show a marked increase in the diversity of local leaders' backgrounds on each of these dimensions. The standard deviation of the ages of team cadres in my sample for 1958–1965 averaged 8.8 years, whereas between 1966 and 1974 it averaged 11.3 years, indicating a considerably greater spread in age. While women are still proportionately underrepresented in local leadership, the percentage of women rose from an annual average of 8.8 percent in the 1958–1965 period to 16.2 percent in 1966–1974.[16] The percentage of local leaders with no education rose from a low of 6 percent in 1968 to 19 percent in 1974. Those with upper-middle school education, of whom there were none before 1967, occupied 11 percent of the local leadership positions in 1974. Those formally classified as middle and upper-middle peasants increased their representation from an average of 5 percent in 1958–1968 to 8.5 percent in 1969–1974.

In short, while the pattern of leadership recruitment at the most basic level is complex, with considerably more equal representation (in proportional terms) on some lines of stratification than others, the data suggest that, at least for this sample, local leaders are not drawn from a local elite or a narrow set of social and economic groups. Finally, between the start of the Cultural Revolution and 1974, the distribution of various social classes and groups was growing more equal.

Establishing the intimate leader-mass relationship envisioned by the mass line, balancing the demands of the members with those of the higher levels, and maintaining the unity, activism, and support of the members while trying to provide frequently divisive incentives or pressures for greater sacrifices all require leaders to possess and master certain complex interpersonal skills. The ability to forge and maintain good relations with the members despite these tensions and cross-pressures is an important criterion used in selecting local leaders. At the production team level, this is particularly true for the selection of team heads—whose positions are the most ambiguous and demand the widest range of political and interpersonal skills—and for study advisers (*fu tao yuan*) who are specially concerned with the team's political life.

> The head of ——— team is a middle peasant. He is the only middle peasant cadre I can ever recall. He has headed the team ever since it was established, which is very rare. [The reason is] that he has good relations with the masses and is good at production.[17]

> The team head must have . . . a personality that can get along with the members.[18]

> In general, the cadres would nominate a man of the people (*ch'un chung ti yi chung jen*), someone of whom the masses have a good impression [to be poor and lower-middle peasant representative]. You'd be nominated only if a lot of people— not just one—had good things to say about you.[19]

> The most important criterion used in selecting me [to be team study adviser] was my ability to unite with the masses.[20]

> The criteria for selecting Mao Tse-tung thought study activists were concerned with the collective, taking the socialist road, *uniting well* [with the masses], leadership qualities, and ability to propagate Mao's thought. . . . If the nominee had good relations with the masses, no one would object [to selecting him or her].[21]

Interpersonal skills and a leadership style that fosters good relations with the members were mentioned prominently among criteria for recruitment of leaders at the brigade level as well, including, interestingly, Party leaders.

> The brigade Party secretary is selected by the Party, but obviously the Party elections follow those of the masses. For

example, once our Party secretary was not chosen by the masses to be director of the brigade revolutionary committee [i.e., brigade head], and so within the Party he was also not selected to be Party secretary. His shortcoming was a bad attitude—he had official airs and little leadership ability. The head of the brigade militia battalion was also unable to be reelected. Both these people were not welcomed by the masses.[22]

The brigade Party secretary should be the kind of person who can settle arguments and solve problems. The main thing [you look for in selecting someone] is leadership ability—i.e., the ability to resolve contradictions [among the masses].[23]

The head of our brigade was very capable [in production] but too dictatorial. He was not democratic. . . . We called him "emperor." Many people feared him. . . . He wanted to become brigade secretary, but people didn't let him, because of his strictness.[24]

Leadership at the team and brigade levels demands a complex set of agricultural, technical, and managerial skills as well as political and interpersonal ones. Expertise weighs heavily in the criteria for selecting local leaders in China, as I have argued elsewhere.[25] Yet there was a clear recognition among the members and leaders of the mass-line principle that local leaders, to be effective, must supplement their technical and managerial skills with the ability to forge and maintain good, close relations with the members—in Chinese terminology, to "unite with the masses."

Leader-Mass Equality

Like the members, team and brigade cadres rely for their incomes primarily on the value of their units' workpoints and the number of workpoints earned, which may not exceed the value of the highest number earned by a team member. Though cadres often receive supplements of workpoints, cash, or goods, informants also pointed out that these supplements are given in part to offset the cadres' lower level of private income, since their official duties do not permit them to devote as much time as ordinary team members to their private plots. And as we have seen, the local leaders in my sample came in approximately balanced numbers from poor, average, and good economic backgrounds.

The social distance between the members and local leaders is generally quite low. Informants stressed that holding a position of leadership is not itself a source of prestige or respect in the community—that is, political stratification is not a source of social stratification.[26] Team cadres are addressed in the same informal terms with which the commune members address each other—"Old Li" or nicknames. Their dress is indistinguishable from that of the members, and they do not decorate themselves with insignia or other symbols of their authority. As one youth put it: "The team cadres are just like the members; there's no difference."[27] All the members know the brigade secretary and brigade head to some degree, and many—particularly those from his or her home village—may know him or her as well as they know each other. In turn, brigade secretaries and heads generally know many, if not most, of the members by name. The members address them in terms varying from "secretary" at the most formal extreme to nicknames at the other—one brigade secretary in my sample was known to one and all as "old fruit skin."[28] Some members reported that they spoke quite freely (t'an te lai) with the brigade cadres, while others were more reserved. Nevertheless, most rusticated youth reported that relations between the members and brigade cadres are much more intimate and open than those between urban residents and basic-level cadres in cities.[29]

Commune members place a high value on social and economic equality with their local leaders. In sharp contrast to many other societies and cultures, a large gap between leaders and masses in rural China reduces the masses' respect for the leaders, rather than enhances it.[30]

> A commune cadre who came down to "squat on the spot" [tun tien] in our team had a very unpresentable expression. He wore cadre clothes and did not participate much in labor, so the peasants did not look up to him too much.[31]

> Aside from a very few, none of the Party members in our state farm . . . have special prestige among the members. The main reason is that they are separated from the masses. I know one Party member whom the masses respect and who has high prestige among the masses. . . . He maintains the same standard of living as the masses at large. He is always first in labor, doing the most arduous and dangerous work. Because he could share joys and sorrows with the masses, he gained our respect.[32]

Just as important, social and economic equality help promote the intimate communication and understanding between leaders and commune members that is a basic principle of the mass line. "Because the squad heads [state farm equivalent of team heads] were so close to the state farm employees (chih kung), it was easy for them to understand the situation of the masses."[33] That is, the workers felt more comfortable in raising their opinions freely with the local cadres, and the local cadres had a better understanding of the masses' problems and views even, as we shall see, in the absence of direct mass expression.[34]

70

Cadre Participation in Labor

The policy of participation by local leaders in productive labor on a regular basis—which has not been suspended despite all the recent policy shifts—is another expression of leader-mass equality. Despite their official duties, 54 percent of the local cadres in my sample (excluding those, like accountants, whose jobs require them to remain in their offices all day long) participated in labor more than three-fourths of the time, and another 29 percent participated between one-fourth and three-fourths of the time. Cadres' participation in productive labor helps promote a feeling of equality between local leaders and commune members.

> Q: You said that the vice-head of your team liked to have good relations with the peasants. What does this mean and how did he go about achieving it?
> A: He liked to participate in labor, and he did it well. So his prestige among the peasants was pretty high.
> Q: How does a cadre go about establishing good relations with the masses?
> A: *He has to be good in labor* and not take advantages.[35]

> The people in the brigade didn't like the vice-secretary. They said she didn't work enough.... She didn't have their respect.[36]

> The peasants had a lot of opinions about our team head, because he didn't go out to labor often.[37]

Cadre participation in productive labor also creates opportunities for informal contact and communication between leaders and members. It is particularly valuable in bringing brigade- and commune-level cadres, whose relations with the commune members are generally mediated through team cadres, into direct contact with the members.

> When a commune-level cadre came to our team to participate in labor, he recognized some of the team members, and they all recognized him. While working, he spoke with the members, and he could tell how they felt after speaking just a few sentences.... It's easy to talk while working; it doesn't interfere with work at all.[38]

> During rest breaks in the fields, most of the masses began to discuss the abolition of the old pension system. Since we cadres of the work district [a state farm unit equivalent in size to a brigade] were in the fields with them, we were in on these discussions.... During work, all five of us members of the work district revolutionary leading small group, each of whom was

working in a different squad [size equivalent to a production team], heard lots of discussion about the pension plan.[39]

During work, when lots of people are chatting, they raised opinions to the team cadres.[40]

The peasants don't always make a specific point of telling the team head what their view is. But they just talk while they are working in the fields. . . . They say whatever they feel like saying.[41]

Political Solicitation

The various ways in which team members communicate with their local leaders that have been discussed thus far all constitute forms of political participation, which is commonly defined as "activities by private citizens that are more or less directly aimed at influencing the selection of governmental personnel and/or the actions they take."[42] In their now classic study of political participation in the United States, Verba and Nie point to a significant problem for democratic politics posed by participation—namely, that it expresses the view of participants only. "Interest, intensity of opinion, resources, skill, and all the other characteristics that determine successful participation give greater voice to some citizens than to others."[43] Still more serious is their general finding that "the characteristics that determine successful participation" are not randomly distributed, but on the contrary are positively correlated with socioeconomic class.[44]

Verba and Nie contrast the "participation strategies" of citizen communication to leaders with what they call "polling strategies," in which leaders "go out and ask the citizenry about their preferences, being careful to speak to all citizens or a representative sampling of them."[45]

Beginning with the earliest days of the Kiangsi Soviet, the Chinese Communist Party has used and developed a systematic program of seeking out the masses and soliciting their views, feelings, problems, and ideas. The emphasis given in China to what I have called political solicitation is based on the recognition, garnered in years of revolutionary experience, that the masses do not or cannot always take the initiative to express themselves to their leaders fully, accurately, or equally. While the program of political solicitation as practiced in China is a "polling strategy" in Verba and Nie's sense, it also goes well beyond the common political poll. For though polling is usually restricted to ascertaining the citizens' preferences among a range of specific and, usually, narrowly drawn alternatives formulated by the poller, solicitation involves the leadership in a deeper and more complex exploration of the masses' existential situations, problems, hopes, ideas, and feelings as well as their preferences.

72

The use of cadre participation in productive labor for solicitation reflects the Chinese leadership's concern with gaining a grasp of the local situation in its totality—the commune members' problems and ideas as well as their mere preferences.

> During the busy season, many commune-level cadres went from team to team participating in labor and *learning about conditions*.[46]

> While the brigade head participated in our team's work, he talked with the commune members. He asked them about all sorts of things.[47]

> Before picking a slate of nominees for the team elections, the team cadres sometimes try to get a grasp of the members' opinions. While working, or at bull sessions in the evening, they asked people who they thought was capable, responsible, and so forth.[48]

While a simple poll would be a much less arduous and time-consuming mode of political solicitation, participation in labor exposes cadres to a range of information significantly deeper and broader than mere preferences, at the same time helping cadres gain the respect of the commune members and build the kind of egalitarian relationship with them that promotes open, forthright expression.

Where certain production teams have been unable to solve persistent problems, leaders from the brigade or the commune may go and squat on the spot (*tun tien*). This too is a form of political solicitation. In choosing to "squat on a spot," a local cadre implicitly rejects a cursory investigation in favor of an explicit attempt to gain a thorough understanding of the team's situation and problems in all their complex historical, social, economic, and political contexts as well as the concerns, ideas, motivations, and views of the members regarding them. For example, in one team, the wife of a brigade-level revolutionary committee member insisted that their son be given a higher workpoint rating than the members felt he deserved. The brigade head became concerned about the problem, in part because it involved a brigade cadre. In addition, the disagreement threatened the future of the then current Tachai workpoint system throughout the whole brigade, for the successful use of which this team had been singled out as a model. For these reasons, the brigade head decided to "squat" in this team.

> He asked the members of the team about her history and her expression. He spoke to some people in groups and others individually. He talked to people both in the fields and in their homes. During the investigation, he did not speak to those

people with whom he was friendly. He also sent people from the militia to investigate her own family. He carried out his investigation for a long time, and in the end collected lots of material proving that she was a bad person. . . . Meetings were then held for quite a few evenings to criticize her. Finally it was decided that her son would get 9.6 workpoints, not 9.8 or 9.9 as she had wanted. . . . This is a good example of how the brigade head held heart-to-heart talks, interviews, and small group meetings, and mobilized the militia and the team cadres to solve this problem.[49]

Another account of "squatting" captures both the depth of understanding sought by the cadre as well as his recognition that this would depend on his ability to establish egalitarian and intimate relations with the masses, through participation in productive labor and "heart-to-heart talks" (*t'an hsin*):

In 1969, the brigade secretary came to squat on the spot in our team, because our team had the worst production in the brigade and the members' ideology was very bad. He squatted for over a month, during which time he participated in labor with us each day. He chatted with us during rest periods in the fields and used this time to hold meetings for heart-to-heart talks. . . . Sometimes in the evenings he went to the team headquarters to see what was going on and find out about tomorrow's work. His main purpose in squatting in our team was to gain an understanding of the members' mood (*ch'ing hsu*) and ideology (*ssu hsiang*)—to gain an understanding of why our production was so bad and clarify people's ideology.[50]

Work teams too engage in systematic, in-depth political solicitation. Like "squatting on a spot," the very idea of a work team is an implicit rejection of superficial investigation or preference polling as bases for citizen communication to leaders to solve local problems. Work teams are charged with gaining a detailed understanding not only of the members' views, but also of the history, economic conditions, social relationships, and political situation in the production teams, that condition those views and give them meaning. This requires an extended period—sometimes several months—of systematic investigation. Because the work team depends for its success on the cooperation of the members, who are sometimes unwilling to divulge sensitive information to outsiders, it must concentrate on developing a good relationship with the members and gaining their trust at the same time as it is carrying out its investigation. Here, then, is still another link in practice between the leader-mass intimacy and equality that are the two core elements of the mass line.

An account by a member of a Socialist Education Movement work team illustrates some of the ways in which work teams tried to establish egalitarian leader-mass relations in their quest for an intimate, comprehensive understanding of the commune members through detailed, systematic investigation. After a preliminary check of the brigade files, the work team undertook in-depth interviews with every poor and lower-middle peasant and hired hand in the team—a process that took a full month and was known as "interviewing the poor and miserable" (fang p'in wen k'u). "We interviewed them at various times and places: their homes, the fields during breakfast, while they were cooking, before they went to sleep." During this phase, the members of the work team spent about half of their time participating in labor.

The second stage was called "sinking roots and linking up" (cha ken ch'uan lien) with the people who had been identified in the interviews as the "most reliable." "The purpose of finding these reliable people was to discover and uncover the problems in the team." To forge these links in the most effective way possible, the members of the work team moved into the homes of these people, took their meals with them, and worked with them in the fields—a practice known as the "three togethernesses" (san t'ung). "The purpose of moving in with them was to gain a better understanding of the conditions in the team." They continued to participate in labor, and while working they probed the commune members about the cadres. They also carried out more interviews in off-hours.

The third stage, known as "organizing the struggle," began with yet another complete round of interviews with everyone in the team (except former landlords and rich peasants). The interviews focused on the problems that had been identified in earlier stages. In addition, meetings of a newly constituted poor and lower-middle peasant association were held to familiarize people with the work team's findings and persuade and mobilize them to participate in struggle meetings. Considerable time was spent persuading those members who feared revenge by the local cadres to speak out.

After the struggle meetings came a fourth stage, known as "cleaning class ranks," in which the work team "checked and re-analyzed all the materials which had been gathered from brigade records, interview notes, investigations outside the village, and struggle meetings, on the basis of which final evaluations of the cadres were to be made."[51]

This account demonstrates that the work team sought out not only the commune members' views about the local cadres, but also a relatively complex understanding of the situation in the production team that conditioned, produced, or provided the context for those views. At the same time, it was constantly trying to cultivate good relationships with the members. Perhaps most interesting is the the work team's perception of a necessary and reciprocal link between these two endeavors. On the one hand, the systematic search for "reliable" people demonstrates how the investigative part of the work team's work served its goal of cultivating close relations with commune members. On the other hand, the team's repeated use of the "three togethernesses," including in particular regular participation in productive labor alongside the peasants, reflects its recognition that only by developing close, egalitarian relations with the commune members could it achieve its goal of gaining a relatively complete understanding of the situation in the team and the various members' problems with, feelings and opinions about, and evaluations of the local cadres.

Factors Working against the Development of Leader-Mass Communion: The Hsun-yi Case

In August 1978, some shocking revelations appeared in the Chinese media. Commune members in Hsun-yi County (Shensi) had been suffering physical and verbal abuse at the hands and mouths of county, commune, and brigade-level cadres. Whippings had occurred. Some commune members had been driven to suicide and insanity, others crippled, still others subjected to severe fines and deprived of food. It is hard to imagine a relationship between leaders and masses further from the communion of equality and intimacy called for in the mass line.

Just as the preceding sections of this chapter were not intended to generalize a rosy picture of leader-mass relations in rural China, the "Hsun-yi experience" is not raised to paint a generally gloomy picture. Instead, it will be analyzed for insights it can provide into the question of the features of local political organization and practice that mitigate against the fulfillment of the mass line's goal of developing a relationship of equality and intimacy between local cadres and commune members. This analysis is limited and conditioned by the scope and content of the official media reports, which provide the sole sources of available information on the particulars of the Hsun-yi case. The difficulty is compounded by the fact that details are relatively sketchy and the analysis of the causes of the problem rather superficial. This case was publicized in mid-1978, a time when penetrating and suitably complex critical analyses of China's experience in socialist transition up through the Cultural Revolution were not yet emerging with much clarity in public forums. Most serious ills—including those raised in the Hsun-yi case— were attributed to "interference and sabotage by the Gang of Four"[52] or, somewhat more benignly, to the fact that hapless cadres were "deeply influenced by the[ir] propaganda."[53] Precisely what this means or how it produced the problems that appeared in Hsun-yi are not fully spelled out in the Hsun-yi materials. But in light of subsequent elaborations of the analysis of the significance of the Gang of Four and the Cultural Revolution, which point to the problems of commandism and coerciveness resulting from the tendency to interpret nearly everything as an aspect of a two-line struggle, the following passage gains significance:

> The offending cadres['] . . . ways of coercing, upbraiding and fining the masses during the production effort were their response to the gang [of four's] slogans calling for "the use of forms that suit the philosophy of struggle," and "24-hour-a-day dictatorship over small production." They thus set themselves up as dictators over the people they were to serve.[54]

This passage suggests that Hsun-yi cadres acted as they did under the intense ideological or political pressures of "struggle." In other words, firm ideological positions and/or the pressures from higher-level leaders to conform to a given line are identified as having caused local leaders to abandon the "Chinese Communist Party's traditions and style of work,"[55] that is, the mass line.

The Hsun-yi cadres' behavior is also attributed to pressures on them to increase production in the absence of material incentives. The media reports call for full implementation of "the principle of 'from each according to his ability, to each according to his work,' " for "people [to] receive more for working more," and for the "unreasonable burdens on the peasants" to be reduced.[56] In this situation, in which commune members were not given sufficient incentives to work and were expected to undertake work that did not benefit them directly, local cadres succumbed to pressures to increase production by dealing with them in the most summary manner:

> Taking food from the masses and fining them were common practices. Those who failed to meet production quotas, such as the required number of pigs, eggs, and potato seeds; primary school pupils and other auxiliary labor forces who didn't take part in collective productive labor . . . were all subjected to fines and loss of food.[57]

Cadres were specifically accused of "attempt[ing] to force up production by . . . vicious practices."[58] Seen in this light, the renewed emphasis in recent policy changes on creating clear, direct material incentives acquires a powerful and poignant political significance.

The Hsun-yi cadre abuses were not linked to questions of rural organization. Organizational issues have been the focus of much recent criticism of rural policy before 1976, and of the reforms since then; specifically, brigade-level accounting has been attacked, production teams have been urged to subdivide into "work groups," and even individuals and households have been legitimated as production units under some of the new "responsibility systems" that are emerging.[59] In the context of the fundamental rethinking of the question of rural organization by the new Chinese leadership, then, it is surprising that the Hsun-yi events are not understood in organizational terms—for example, as results of the existence of overly large rural units. "Bureaucratism," which is in part a matter of organizational size, is mentioned, but only with respect to the failure of larger, higher-level units of administration— specifically, the county and the province—to take seriously reports they had been receiving in letters from commune members that problems in leader-mass relations existed at the basic levels.[60] But "bureaucratism" is not mentioned as a cause of the behavior of team, brigade, or even commune-level cadres.

Finally, it is significant that the Hsun-yi materials call for the solution of the problems there in part through many of the tried-and-true mass line methods discussed earlier. Investigation groups and work teams were to be sent down to the local levels, offending cadres were to be subjected to criticism and to make self-criticism with an eye toward reformng rather than punishing all but the worst cases, meetings of poor and lower-middle peasants were to be convened by "leading cadres of all prefectures and counties," three-level cadre meetings[61] were to be convened with the attendance of "representatives of the poor and lower-middle peasants to help the leadership rectify its work style," and the like. This was understood in general terms as a return to "the mass line" and the practice of "pay[ing] close attention to the opinion of the masses,"[62] which were reaffirmed as "the Party's fine tradition and work style."[63]

> The relations between our cadres and the masses have remained as close as fish to water. We must rely on powerful and meticulous ideological and political work to deepen this kind of relationship. . . . [64]

In a period when all aspects of Chinese politics were coming under critical scrutiny and many formerly sacred cows were beginning to be desecrated, and in particular at a moment when relations between local and regional party and state leaders on the one hand and the masses of peasants on the other were at their lowest ebb, it is highly significant that the mass-line principles governing those relations were reaffirmed, not criticized.

Yet even as the mass line was being reaffirmed, the Party leadership was beginning to come to grips with the realization that the mass line was not self-enforcing. Clearly, leadership could not be counted on to implement it on its own, out of good will or revolutionary fervor. At the same time, the post-Mao leadership, most of whom were victims of the Cultural Revolution, were wary of the Maoist corrective for bad leadership, namely, the direct action of the masses themselves. Thus they struck out in a new direction: the development of "socialist legality." Citizens were now to be protected from all sorts of leadership abuses by legal rights and codes backed by judicial power. Thus, the Hsun-yi materials speak repeatedly of "violations of state law" as well as of "Party discipline."[65] Offenders were understood to have committed political errors like "confusing the relations between the enemy and ourselves," but also to have "undermined the socialist legal system and encroached on the people's democratic rights."[66] They were to be "punished according to law" as well as "handed over to the masses for criticism and struggle."[67]

In mid-1978, the theme of "socialist legality" was only just beginning to be articulated, and at this writing (mid-1981) it was understood in practice in only the sketchiest and most formative way, especially in the rural areas. There has been some movement in the direction of improved and more formalized processes of election, with guarantees of candidate competition and secret ballots. But beyond this, precisely what institutional forms the new socialist legality in the countryside will take, what political effects they will have, and in what ways they will resonate to the principles of leader-mass relations embodied by the mass line remain to be seen.

Mass-Line Communion: Implications for Leader-Mass Relations and Communication

In the years since Mao's death, the mass line has been reformulated. Factors of mass spontaneity, mobilization, and direct political action have been deemphasized, while more egalitarian, intimate, cooperative, responsive relations between leaders and masses have been emphasized anew. In Hammond's terms, the sociological and epistemological moments of the mass-line dialectic have been played down, and the methodological played up.[68] There is a strong sense in China that during the Cultural Revolution years—and indeed, at important points throughout the entire period since 1958—leadership got badly out of touch with the masses, and that this must be put right very soon if China is to solve its myriad other political and economic problems. In doing so, it appears (at least at this writing) that the time-tested principles of the mass line, and even some of the specific political practices associated with them, are being reaffirmed, although partly in association with a new legalism with which they may or may not be fully consistent.

If this is the case, it will be useful to conclude with a brief discussion of the implications of the mass line's dual emphases on leader-mass intimacy and equality for local politics, and in particular for leader-mass communication at the grassroots level. Although Mao never spelled out the implications of the mass line in detail, some of the possibilities can be identified from those moments in basic-level political practice when some level of communion between leaders and masses has been achieved, even if only fleetingly.

One implication of leader-mass communion is that it can enable leaders to understand the unexpressed concerns and views of the masses. For example, the members of one commune in Kwangtung were unhappy with a 1958 administrative boundary that switched them from Tungkuan County, with which they had strong historical, ethnic, and economic ties, to Polo County.

> Q. Did the masses ever talk about or demand returning to Tungkuan's jurisdiction?
> A. Sometimes. But most peasants don't care to raise such things. . . . They would not go to the commune to demonstrate for their demands. But if you are a cadre, you can have frequent contacts with the masses and talk with them; in this way you can find out what they are thinking. This is what the Communist Party calls "words of the heart" (*hsin li hua*)—i.e., what they are thinking deep down inside but do not verbalize.[69]

As noted, in every political system some individuals and groups express their views and concerns more frequently, vocally, and effectively than others. In China as elsewhere, a "participation strategy" of leader-mass communication—in which leaders rely on the expressed views or articulated interests of the masses—always portrays an uneven and sometimes systematically biased picture of the masses' opinions.[70] To the extent that the leadership strategy of and methods informed by the mass line help put the leaders in contact with the masses' unexpressed views and thoughts, they may help ameliorate one major type of political inequality by compensating for the unevennesses and biases in the pattern of political expression.

Second, the mass line can help the leaders correctly interpret and, if necessary, reformulate the masses' expressed views and political actions. This in turn can help them guide their units to more effective solutions to local problems. For example, in one state farm a semiannual summary of the year's progress unexpectedly showed that only 60 percent of the planned work for the year had been completed in the first half of the year, compared with 75 percent in most other years. It emerged that the main reason for the drop was that the male workers in the second wage grade had been slacking off. While it might have been presumed that these men wanted their pay increased, investigations by, and small group discussion with, basic-level cadres revealed quite a different situation. The level-two men were not dissatisfied with their own absolute wage grade, but rather with the fact that a group of eight women had had their wage grades increased from level three to level two by cadres who were trying to dispose of a surplus in a payroll account. In the absence of an intimate understanding of the motivations and feelings that underlay the actions of the people involved, the solution to the problem might have been sought in raising the wage grades of the level-two men. This, as it happened, would have both angered the level-one men and embarrassed the level-two men, who "felt that they were not as good workers as the level-one men." Instead, the women's wage grades were restored to level three, which they were able to accept after some persuasion that their original raises had been improper in the first place.[71]

In another instance, cadres of the work district (i.e., the middle) level of the state farm were aware, from their daily contacts and shared situation with the state farm workers, of discontent about a new policy, adopted during the Cultural Revolution, of making deductions from the pay of people who did not work a certain minimum number of days each month. The cadres decided to air the issue within a broader framework by raising for mass discussion the question of the pros and cons of all the policy changes that had come out of the Cultural Revolution. Unexpectedly, in these discussions "the masses brought up very minor problems, such as an insufficiency of space for raising chickens and ducks." The cadres suspected that the workers were responding indirectly to the pay deductions by wanting to raise more animals. When at a later mass meeting the cadres raised the question of pay deductions directly, the members enthusiastically expressed their disapproval. The resulting clamor caused the policy of pay deductions to be rescinded. Having been obviated by the change in pay policy, the question of space for animal raising was dropped from the masses' list of concerns.[72] This anecdote richly illustrates how the cadres, by virtue of their close contact and equality of condition with the masses (the cadres also suffered under the deduction policy), were able to reinterpret the masses' expressed views and reformulate (or, in Mao's phrase, "concentrate") them in a way that the masses found even more appropriate to their problems and concerns than what they themselves had been suggesting.

Third, the mass line in leader-mass relations can help the leaders mobilize the political energies and participation of the masses. The following example, related by a brigade political study adviser, illustrates the link between communion in leader-mass relations and mass mobilization:

> One team-level political adviser in our brigade reported that the level of discussion and interest in his team's study meetings was not as good as in the other teams. So I decided to go down to this team. But first I and the other teams' advisers talked with him, to try to understand what the problem was. We taught him how to prepare for study meetings, and we paid special attention to him when we were preparing our lessons.

Then I went down to sit in on one of the study sessions in his team. After he finished presenting the lesson, I added a few words, and then I helped the members participate in the subsequent discussion by raising a few examples. . . . Not only that, but during the busy season I went to work with this team in the fields. I tried to work as hard, long, and fast as possible, to give them an example. After all, if you can't do it yourself, how can you teach others? Also, because I was working with them, I was able to find out who in the team was good and who wasn't. In this way I could help the team adviser learn how to use the method of praising the good and criticizing the bad [in study meetings]. This also helped him learn how to identify and cultivate activists. I also met with the militia, to try to encourage them to speak out at study meetings and to teach them how to do so. . . . I did help to raise the consciousness of the masses in this team. In fact, this was later turned back on me, when they criticized me [on an unrelated matter]![73]

In this case, the mobilization of the team members' political interest, self-awareness, and resulting action was the result not merely of simple-minded exhortation and propaganda, but rather of a careful, sustained effort by a local cadre who, inspired and guided by the mass line, sought to establish a communion of equality and intimacy between herself and the team's members.

Finally, the mass line is, as Edward Hammond has pointed out, an epistemology. It envisions a dialectical process of development in which the masses become increasingly capable of appropriating politics for themselves (through practical experience and heightened levels of consciousness), making the role of leadership increasingly circum-scribed and even unnecessary.[74] While this is, to the extent that it occurs at all, a long-term historical process, one can see some traces of it in the last account cited. The brigade study adviser's long and hard work to establish a relationship of equality and intimacy with the members of a backward team was successful in increasing their level of political activism and awareness. This in turn gave them the capacity to appropriate political affairs for themselves by criticizing her at a later time on a different issue.

NOTES

1. In her comparison of the French, Russian, and Chinese Revolutions, Theda Skocpol has written: "The Chinese Communists established more direct links to peasants than did radical elites in Russia or France. The Chinese Revolution, at least in its closing stages, thus has more of the aspect of an elite/mass movement than the other great historical social revolutions." Theda Skocpol, "France, Russia, China: A Structural Analysis of Social Revolutions," *Comparative Studies in Society and History* 18:201.

2. Edward Hammond, "Marxism and the Mass Line," *Modern China* 4 (1), esp. pp. 15–16.

3. Mao Tse-tung, "On Coalition Government," in *Selected Works of Mao Tse-tung*, vol. 3 (Peking: Foreign Languages Press, 1965), p. 315.

4. Mao Tse-tung, *On Khrushchev's Phoney Communism and Its Historical Lessons for the World* (Peking: Foreign Languages Press, 1964), pp. 68–69.

5. Andre Malraux, *Anti-Memoirs* (Harmondsworth, England: Penguin, 1970), p. 424.

6. A production team is a hamlet—or larger village neighborhood-sized unit—of about 150 to 200 people. A production brigade is composed of either a larger village or several small hamlets, averaging around 2,000 people. A People's Commune, consisting of around 12 brigades, averages about 23,000 people. These size estimates are from William L. Parish and Martin King Whyte, *Village and Family in Contemporary China* (Chicago: University of Chicago Press, 1978), pp. 35–36.

7. Informant BLM3/transcript p. 46. Transcripts of these interviews, conducted at the Universities Service Centre (Hong Kong) in 1974–1975, are on file in my office. Each informant is identified by a code name, e.g., BLM3.

8. For a fuller discussion of these modes of political participation, see Marc Blecher, *Leader-Mass Relations in Rural Chinese Communities: Local Politics in a Revolutionary Society* (Ph.D. dissertation, University of Chicago, 1978), Chapter 4.

9. BLM1/15.

10. TMG1/19–20.

11. PNM1/11.

12. XHM2/11.

13. LJM1/40.

14. See, for example, Dilys M. Hill, *Participating in Local Affairs* (Harmondsworth, England: Penguin Books, 1970), esp. pp. 99–100.

15. See Blecher, *Leader-Mass Relations*, pp. 78–82; also, John Burns, "The Election of Production Team Cadres in Rural China: 1958-74," *China Quarterly* 74 (1978): 272-296.

16. The sample was based on interviews conducted at the Universities Service Centre, Hong Kong. For details, see Blecher, *Leader-Mass Relations*, Appendix 2. Appearances to the contrary, there is no discrepancy between these figures and the overall average of 17 percent female cadres cited in the preceding paragraph. The 17 percent figure refers to the entire sample of cadres, in which each cadre who ever served is counted only once, regardless of length of tenure in office. The time-series data are based on a method of aggregation that counts all cadres who were serving in a given year, regardless of whether they had served in previous years or not; hence, in these over-time data, there is considerable double counting of cadres who served in several years. This is an unavoidable function of my use of the data to ascertain a profile of leadership in each year. The two figures, then, are not directly comparable, though they are consistent with each other.

17. BLM3/48.

18. ZCM1/25.

19. TGM1/17.

20. FGM1/8-9.

21. BAF1/8, my emphasis; also, see Burns, "Election." [Editor's note: The study of Mao Tse-tung thought has been deemphasized since the arrest of the Gang of Four.]

22. BLM1/11.

23. BLM3/34a.

24. BAF1/57.

25. Blecher, *Leader-Mass Relations*, Chapter 3.

26. Ibid., pp. 45-46.

27. BLM1/15.

28. LJM1.

29. BLM3/46; XHM1/41.

30. I recall a conversation with a Chicago taxi driver, a Black Muslim, as we drove past the palatial residential and business headquarters of the Black Muslims. In reply to my inquiry about whether he resented the group's leadership's opulent digs in light of the fact that he had to drive a cab all day, he replied: "Hell, no! When I see that, it makes me feel proud!"

31. BLM1/7. Squatting on the spot, or *tun tien*, is a practice of sending higher level cadres to live and work in a production team for an extended period in order to become acquainted with problems in the village.

32. LJM1/53, 54.

33. LJM1/27.

34. LJM1/passim.

35. KCM1/17; my emphasis.

36. BAF1/49.

37. HYM1/8.

38. BLM3/8.

39. LJM1/27–28.

40. XHM2/11.

41. BLM3/46.

42. Sidney Verba and Norman Nie, *Participation in America: Political Democracy and Social Equality* (New York: Harper & Row, 1972), p. 2.

43. Ibid., p. 268.

44. Ibid., passim.

45. Ibid., p. 268.

46. BLM3/8; my emphasis.

47. BAF1/44.

48. XHM2/9.

49. BAF1/35.

50. XHM2/35–36.

51. GYM1/passim.

52. For just one example, see *Jen-min Jih-pao* [People's Daily], 3 August 1978.

53. New China News Agency (NCNA) broadcast, 2 August 1978, in *Joint Publications Research Service Daily Report* (hereafter, *Daily Report*), 4 August 1978.

54. Ibid.

55. Ibid.

56. Shensi Provincial broadcast, 6 August 1978, in *Daily Report*, 10 August 1978.

57. NCNA broadcast, 2 August 1978, in *Daily Report*, 8 August 1978.

58. NCNA broadcast, 2 August 1978, in *Daily Report*, 4 August 1978.

59. For a thorough discussion of the emerging responsibility systems, see Tang Tsou, Marc Blecher, and Mitch Meisner, "Policy Change at the National Summit and Institutional Transformation at the Local Level: The Case of Tachai and Hsiyang County in

the Post-Mao Era," in Tang Tsou, ed., *Select Papers from the Center for Far Eastern Studies* no. 4 (Chicago: Center for Far Eastern Studies, University of Chicago, 1981), pp. 328–338.

60. NCNA broadcast, 2 August 1978, in *Daily Report*, 8 August 1978.

61. It is unclear in the report which three levels of leadership this refers to.

62. *People's Daily*, 3 August 1978.

63. Ibid.; the phrase is repeated in many of the contemporary reports, including NCNA broadcast, 2 August 1978, in *Daily Report*, 8 August 1978.

64. *People's Daily*, 3 August 1978.

65. Ibid.; also NCNA broadcast, 2 August 1978, in *Daily Report*, 8 August 1978.

66. *People's Daily*, 3 August 1978.

67. Ibid.

68. Hammond, "Marxism and the Mass Line."

69. BLM3/7–8.

70. Blecher, *Leader-Mass Relations*, Chapters 4 and 6.

71. LJM1/38–39.

72. LJM1/33 ff.

73. BAF1/36–37.

74. Hammond, "Marxism and the Mass Line," pp. 16–17.

III. Coordination and Interest Articulation

A major means of communication by which the Party informs the Chinese citizens of important decisions and enlists their support is the Central Committee Documents. By issuing directives, soliciting opinions, and providing guidance on sensitive political issues, the Central Documents play a critical role in shaping the views of Party cadres, and through them, the views of the people about the Party's policy agenda.

Kenneth Lieberthal presents data on two such documents, one on the death of Lin Piao and the other on the campaign to criticize Lin Piao and Confucius, to answer questions about the dissemination of the Central Documents: Who actually receives the original texts? Under what circumstances and by what means are the contents transmitted to wider audiences? What roles do the mass media play in further explaining the issues raised in the documents? And what is the potential for distortion in the transmission process? These questions bear directly on the processes by which the Party leadership in China informs its key cadres of societal goals and coordinates the means to achieve these goals.

Beyond the dissemination of information on policy matters, national coordination requires concrete action programs at the local level that in turn necessitate intergroup cooperation among different units. The agricultural mechanization program that Steven Butler has analyzed illustrates how such coordination is achieved in China.

For agricultural mechanization, the various units in a county—the communes, the production brigades, and the production teams—must take actions that not only pool their resources in an aggregate sense, but rather have sequential and reciprocal implications to one another. Difficulties arise when the goals of the various units are not mutually consistent. While higher-level units are more concerned with fulfilling campaign objectives, lower-level units—the production teams—are more interested in raising their own income.

The goal divergences that Butler has discussed need not be viewed only as a communication problem. They also indicate a strength of the present Chinese system in that they reflect a high degree of local autonomy among the peasants.

The task of coordination today is how to reconcile central planning with local autonomy. The Chinese system contains sufficient communication channels for the contending units to meet, and to discuss and resolve their different goal perceptions. The examples cited by Butler from the early 1970s, however, indicate that central policy has a tendency to overtake local concerns. The new Party leadership is cognizant of the problem and seeks remedial measures.

An important structural mechanism by which the Party can bypass bureaucrats to reach the villages directly for upward information is the work team, known as *kung tso tui*. The work team concept reflects Mao's philosophy of leadership: "No investigation, no right to speak." That is, only when the leaders are intimately acquainted with the situation at the local level can they formulate correct policy.

John Burns presents a detailed analysis in Chapter 7 of how the work team carries out its tasks under varying circumstances: for example, to rectify corruption among local cadres, restore unity to a divided production brigade, promote a production campaign, or correct deviant practices among the peasants. In the process, the work team can receive, transmit, and act on the demands of the peasants, thus functioning as a channel for grassroots interest articulation.

Burns discusses the limitations of the work team as a communication channel. The decision to dispatch work teams, for instance, lies in the hands of the Party elite, although sometimes work teams are initiated in response to local dissatisfaction. The effectiveness of the work teams as a mechanism for interest articulation, Burns shows, depends largely on whether the peasants' interest coincides with the policy being implemented by the work teams.

5

Communication from the Party Center: The Transmission Process for Central Committee Documents

Kenneth G. Lieberthal

The central authorities in China use a range of vehicles for communicating their views and decisions to lower levels. Written intra-bureaucratic communications are undoubtedly the tool most often employed, although this documentary system is buttressed by other channels of communication. The public media are some of these, as are various limited circulation publications.[1] Meetings bringing together central leaders and responsible people from various locales have been used both as part of the process of reaching decisions and as a means for communicating the substance of these decisions to the pertinent lower-level officials.[2] All of these vehicles operate in concert, moreover, to coordinate the perception of major events and policy decisions among cadres throughout the political system in China. Unfortunately, however, not all are equally susceptible to outside observation and analysis,[3] and therefore we must remain content with investigations that illuminate key parts of this system while being aware that other important dimensions escape our notice.

In this chapter I seek to expand our knowledge of communication between Peking and the lower levels of the political system by analyzing the means by which perhaps the most important bureaucratic document stream in China—the so-called *Chung-fa* (Central Committee Document)—is transmitted, including the use of the national news media in the process.

Central Committee Documents (CDs) play a critical role in shaping cadres' views about the Party Center's current policy agenda and decisions, for this document stream is the bureaucratic vehicle for written communications from the Central Committee to other organs of the Party. In reality, Central Documents are issued in most instances by the Politburo in the name of the Central Committee, and during the 1970s, they came forth in a rather steady stream of between twenty-five and sixty in the average year.[4] This is a flexible instrument of

Reprinted by permission of The University of Michigan Center for Chinese Studies from *Central Documents and Politburo Politics in China*, pp. 51–73, by Kenneth Lieberthal, copyrighted 1978.

communication for the Politburo in that it has been used to serve a wide range of functions—to issue commands, solicit opinions, commend people and experiences, provide guidance on sensitive political issues, and circulate materials for reference.[5] Thus, the Party leadership can use Central Documents to communicate with its intended audience in the broadest sense of the word and is not confined to making this channel convey only decisions and instructions.

Transmission of CDs

The following questions guide our analysis of the *ch'uan-ta* (transmission) of Central Documents: Who receives the original texts of CDs? Under what circumstances and by what means are the contents of these documents transmitted to wider audiences? What roles, if any, do the public media play in further explaining the leadership's thinking on issues raised in CDs? And what is the potential for distortion during this transmission process? All these questions bear directly on our understanding of the degree to which Central Committee Documents inform and coordinate the views of key individuals in China about both societal goals and the means to achieve these goals.

The available evidence suggests that considerable variation attends the process of transmitting Central Documents, depending in part on the content of the particular document concerned. Still, certain common elements evidently apply to the transmission of virtually all CDs, regardless of the process by which they are drafted, how widely they are disseminated, their level of classification, their function in the system, and so forth. The following outline specifies these common dimensions of the process and indicates some of the types of variations that may be encountered as different documents flow through the system.

Many (perhaps most) Central Documents have a two-tiered transmission process: the first involves circulation of the document and is almost invariably intrabureaucratic; the second involves a wider dissemination of the contents of the document—sometimes beyond the confines of the bureaucracy, and often without the document itself being made available.

Every CD specifies the units to which the document should be sent, typically in its first paragraph. These units define the first tier of the transmission process. On almost all such documents available in the West, the units (called *chu-sung chi-kuan* in the vocabulary used concerning official documents in China) are both military and civilian[6] and encompass the Central down through the provincial (and sometimes *hsien*) levels. Typical is the list of such organs for CD(72)4[7] on the Lin Piao affair: "To the Party committees of each province, municipality (directly under the Central Government), and autonomous region; the Party committees of each military region, provincial military district, and field army; the Party committees of each general department of the Military Affairs Commission and each service branch; the leading groups and Party core groups of each department, ministry, and commission of the Central Committee and the State Council."[8] During the Cultural Revolution, CDs tended to be circulated more extensively, as this document stream was used to fulfill a wider range of communication functions. This wider dissemination is reflected, for instance, in the list of *chu-sung chi-kuan* for the CD on the "Suspension of the Big Exchange of Revolutionary Experience All Over the Country" issued by the Central Committee on 19 March 1967: "To Party committees at all levels, Party committees of all military regions and districts, revolutionary committees of all provinces and municipalities, and all revolutionary mass organizations."[9] Note that this list not only includes organs down to the basic level but also encompasses non-Party as well as Party recipients.

In addition to the *chu-sung chi-kuan* detailed at the beginning of the CD, typically the last paragraph of the Central Document stipulates the groups to which the second tier of dissemination should be directed. To use the two CDs just cited, for example, the final paragraph of CD(72)4 calls for transmission to be "divided into two steps: the first is to transmit it among the cadres, and the second, to the masses." The CD of 19 March 1967 concluded with the instruction: "This circular may be posted in cities, the countryside and armed forces units."[10]

The First Tier

Central Documents are sent out simultaneously to all organs on the *chu-sung chi-kuan* list. When the Party General Office receives the CD at, for instance, the provincial level, the head of the General Office of the provincial Party committee sends the CD to the first secretary of the provincial Party committee, who in turn decides upon the process of further discussion and dissemination of the CD. If the document covers a relatively routine and functionally specialized subject, the first secretary may decide simply to consult with the Party secretary responsible for that area of work and, having decided on the best means of implementing the document, to send it down through channels from there. If the CD is of broader scope and greater importance, the first secretary will probably convene a meeting of the Standing Committee of the Party to discuss how to transmit and implement the document. Almost certainly, the Party General Office would, under orders from the first secretary, have made enough copies of the document for each of the members of the Standing Committee to use for reference. The Standing Committee would most likely stipulate the forms to be used in the further dissemination process, perhaps under some guidance from Peking, and write its own covering document expressing its opinions on the implementation of the CD in the area under its jurisdiction.

The Standing Committee can then convene a meeting of the entire Party committee, of key cadres from the department under the Party committee or from several levels down the hierarchy, or of any other groups appropriate for purposes of transmitting the contents of the document. Alternatively, it can eschew a meeting process entirely and rely instead strictly on written communications passed along the appropriate bureaucratic channels. Thus, the actual process of transmission of a document varies according to the needs of the moment, and the entire process typically is geared to achieving the most effective implementation of the demands of the CD without violating the instructions of the Center and the possibilities afforded by local conditions.

When the Standing Committee receives a document that its members feel warrants dissemination via a meeting format, then *ch'uan-ta hui-i* (transmission meetings) in relevant units are convened.[11] At these, the responsible person (usually the first secretary of the unit) announces that "CD(year)(number)" has just been received, then either reads or summarizes the text of the document to the meeting. The rules on taking notes vary and are specified at the beginning of the meeting. At the end of the secretary's recitation, he or she may proceed to call attention to some particular points that are regarded as the central elements in the document or provide some other explanatory information. The secretary then calls for questions, which at this point are usually limited to requests that some part of what was said be repeated because the person could not hear or understand it all. This type of request occurs quite frequently and is always honored.[12]

Sometimes the people attending this *ch'uan-ta* meeting break up into small groups to review the document item by item and gain a clearer and more detailed understanding of both the contents of the CD and the way the material should be handled. In these small groups the participants can raise detailed questions about the material—questions that will be referred to higher levels if necessary. The range of questioning, however, will be dictated in part by whether the CD is labeled an "order," a "directive," a "circular," or some other rubric from among the roughly eighteen such titles available to the issuing authorities. Each rubric in itself conveys some sense of how the directive should be handled by lower-level organs.[13]

Thus, the first tier transmission of the CD typically involves key personnel and consists of a relatively full rendition of the contents of the document, efforts to unify thinking on the issues concerned, and concrete preparations for wider dissemination. The first tier transmission of CD(72)4 illustrates this dimension of the *ch'uan-ta* process. This Central Document circulated the "second batch" of materials on the "Lin Piao/Ch'en Po'ta anti-Party clique." The "second batch" included prominently the famous "571" document, Lin Piao's purported plan (drafted by Lin Li-kuo and his colleagues) for an armed coup d'etat against Mao Tse-tung.[14]

The Lin Piao affair presented the Central leadership with one of its greatest challenges since 1949. Mao had personally anointed Lin his heir apparent, and the traumatic Cultural Revolution had been widely seen as issuing from the political alliance of the Party Chairman and his head of the armed forces. Thus, Lin's dramatic demise in a plane crash while reportedly fleeing to the Soviet Union after an assassination attempt against Mao Tse-tung sent shock waves throughout the Party and the country. The task of explaining this event to Party officials throughout the bureaucracy as well as to the masses posed a major problem, and CD(72)4 conveyed one of the key sets of documents concerning this affair. Clearly, this was a CD that had to be handled with more than the usual amount of care given to the process of transmission, for the issues involved were potentially explosive and cynicism toward the explanations given was likely to be widespread.[15] Not surprisingly, then, this document spread through a somewhat more elaborate transmission process than was typical, but the basic outlines remained the same as those just sketched.

The *chu-sung chi-kuan* listed for CD(72)4, as previously noted, included the Party committees of both the provinces and the military regions. Since in Yunnan the seats of both of these are in Kunming, the leadership at this level decided to transmit the CD via a joint meeting of cadres of both the Yunnan Provincial Party Committee and the Party Committee of the Kunming Military Region. Our information about the *ch'uan-ta* process for this document comes almost exclusively from the available text of the summation speech given at this joint meeting by Wang Pi-ch'eng, who at that time concurrently served as commander of the Kunming Military Region, second secretary of the Yunnan Party Committee, and first vice-chairman of the Yunnan Provincial Revolutionary Committee.[16] The *ch'uan-ta* meeting itself assumed a format resembling that of a work conference, with an initial plenary session, followed by a number of days of small group discussions of the issues concerned, and capped by a final plenary session and summary report. The entire meeting lasted ten days and involved 1,851 participants, of whom 841 were from the military system and 1,010 were from the civilian sector.

CD(72)4 was issued by the Central authorities on 13 January, and the Yunnan transmission meeting convened from 28 January to 6 February. Thus, it took almost a month before this document was presented by the provincial leadership to the provincial level cadres specified in the *chu-sung chi-kuan* list. Such a delay in transmission is not very much out of the ordinary, except that in this case the document was of such high priority that one would have anticipated more rapid dissemination. The pause seems to be accounted for by the fact that the

Central leadership took the precaution of first disseminating the document in key points to test the reaction it would cause—the kinds of questions raised and how best to deal with them. Indeed, this key point transmission went all the way down to the grassroots level before the document was more widely distributed among the Party cadres throughout the country[18]—an indication of the extraordinary concern Peking displayed over the possible reactions to the revelations contained in the material. Having analyzed the response this document engendered at the key points, the leadership felt confident enough to disseminate it more widely within the Party—certainly with appropriate directions to the leading personnel at each level on what questions they should anticipate and how they should handle them. The CD itself also provided some guidance on what should be stressed in the study of the accompanying reference materials.

The provincial-level transmission meeting in Yunnan began with an address by Chou Hsing, a vice-chairman of the Yunnan Revolutionary Committee and political commissar of the Kunming Military Region.[19] Chou first read verbatim the text of CD(72)4 and the appended materials to the audience assembled and then criticized the contents of the "571" documents, thereby indicating the way this extraordinarily sensitive revelation of a coup plan should be handled. The meeting then broke up into separate study groups, and over the following eight days the participants attended both these groups and one or more plenary sessions. In the small groups, these participants criticized line by line the materials provided on Lin Piao's plans and studied what these materials revealed about Lin's real character, motives, and politics.[20] They were also provided with appropriate materials from Lin's public utterances in recent years so as to highlight the contrast between what he said in public and what he actually felt as revealed in the reference materials circulated with the CD (thus proving what a double-dealer Lin actually was).[21] People were encouraged to express their views during the study groups, and a number of them took advantage of this opportunity to indicate that they had misgivings either about the materials circulated by CD(72)4 or about presenting these materials to a wider audience later on.[22] The plenary session(s) presumably summed up the discussions on each point, specified the key problem areas, and provided some guidance to put the small group discussions back on a smooth track. During this small-group study period, the various participants also developed concrete plans for disseminating the document to wider audiences—including eventually the general public—as had been called for in the second tier dissemination instructions in the CD. These plans stipulated a process, in the following order, of: transmitting the document to key test points in order to gain experience; having the cadres study the document well so that they could deal with all problems that might arise; cultivating "backbone" personnel to help lead the

94

discussion of the document; and developing a clear plan as to how to direct each phase of the masses' study of the document. Only when all these preparations had been made would the masses be told the contents of CD(72)4.[23]

Wang Pi-ch'eng summed up the work of this meeting at a plenary session on the final day of the convocation. His speech, which was classified *chueh-mi* (absolutely secret), reviewed the progress of the transmission meeting, recounted some of the problems that had been encountered, laid out in no uncertain terms the correct attitude to take toward the range of issues that had been raised both by the Central Document itself and by the discussions over the preceding days, provided a pep talk to those who still held doubts about what the public response to CD(72)4 would be, and laid out in broad brush the plans for further dissemination of the document. This last item in Wang's speech shifts our attention to the second tier of dissemination of a CD and the problems involved in making the contents of a CD known to a wider audience.

The Second Tier

The second tier dissemination of a CD varies extremely widely in the techniques used and the time period involved. In part, it involves further transmission of the document within the bureaucracies—to lower-ranking cadres, general Party members, and non-Party civil servants. For some documents, such as CD(72)4, there is further dissemination to the general public. What is actually circulated at these levels is typically not the original document but rather a copy of it made by one of the *chu-sung chi-kuan*,[24] which sometimes excludes the CD covering letter[25] and conveys only the reference materials originally attached as appendices. The different techniques employed make it worth tracing this second-tier dissemination separately in its intra- and extrabureaucratic dimensions.

A CD is usually sent simultaneously to all bureaucratic units involved in the second tier transmission. Sometimes, communicating the contents of the CD can take the form of convening a multilevel cadre meeting for relevant personnel from the second-tier units, who will then return to their individual units to report on what they have been told. At other times, a copy of the CD itself is sent to the second-tier units, along with a covering document from the *chu-sung chi-kuan* that indicates any opinions that organ has on the issues concerned. A third method entails sending out cadres from the *chu-sung chi-kuan* to the second-tier units to instruct them on the contents of the CD and how to handle it. For instance, as part of the process of transmitting CD(74)21 on the need to "grasp revolution and promote production" in the campaign to criticize Lin Piao and Confucius, the Kiangsi Provincial Party Committee convened a meeting of leading members of the provincial departments. The committee then dispatched these leading cadres to the rural and industrial and mining areas to help units in these places implement the CD.[26]

A telephone conference is another frequently used vehicle for transmitting the contents of a document from one level to the leadership cadres of the next lower level. This type of conference is probably of particular value in large provinces and in the rural areas. On 8 July 1974, for instance, Szechwan's Provincial Party Committee convened a telephone conference to transmit the contents of CD(74)21. This conference linked together the leading Party cadres of all regional, municipal, autonomous *chou* and county committees, and provincial departments. Li Ta-chang, secretary of the provincial Party committee, spoke at the conference and transmitted the basic contents of CD(74)21.[27] Other provinces using telephone conferences to transmit this directive included Yunnan,[28] Kiangsu,[29] Honan,[30] and Heilung-kiang.[31] In sum, the forms used for dissemination can vary widely. Not infrequently, moreover, only the summary of a CD, not the CD itself, is circulated in the second-tier units.

When *ch'uan-ta* meetings have been ordered as part of the process of intrabureaucratic second-tier dissemination of a CD, the format of these meetings seems to follow closely that used in their counterparts in the first tier organs. One non-Party informant described a part of this process thus:

> Following the [second tier] *ch'uan-ta* meeting, the participants usually break up into their usual study groups. The person leading each study group has been briefed in advance on the contents of the document and has been given advice on how to handle the discussion of it. Often, he begins the study groups by again reading the document or its summary to the participants. The document itself, however, is not circulated for their perusal, as every effort is made to keep the number of original copies down to a minimum and exercise tight control over their dissemination. The study group leader entertains requests for yet another reading of portions that remain unclear, and then he leads discussion of the contents of the document. This discussion of contents can be very detailed or rather pro forma, depending on how directly relevant the document is to the particular unit concerned. Indeed, for some CDs that are considered not very important for the receiving unit, the leadership can disregard the *ch'uan-ta hui-i* and utilize only the study group format for introducing and discussing the document. For others more directly pertinent, the *ch'uan-ta* process may include serious discussion of the means to implement the Central decision.[32]

Any person under a political cloud is excluded even from the transmission of the document to the non-Party people in the unit. This exclusion automatically applies to the five bad elements,[33] and it is usually also applied to anyone who is currently under suspicion even if that person is not yet aware of being in political difficulty. Other types of exclusion can also come into play. For instance, it is not very rare for a document to be transmitted only to those non-Party cadres above a particular civil service rank or to those who specialize in the areas with which the CD is concerned. Thus, if a cadre knows that a CD has been transmitted in his or her unit and has not been invited to participate, it behooves him or her to find out what the subject of the document is. If it concerns a general political issue (such as the purge of Lin Piao), the cadre might take exclusion from the *ch'uan-ta* process as a fairly firm indication that he or she is under investigation for some offense.

The sphere for second-tier transmission of a CD is, as mentioned earlier, determined by the leadership in the pertinent first-tier organ in conformity with instructions from the Center and the contents of the document. Clearly political issues evidently receive wider dissemination, as there is no functional demarcation inherent in the subject matter that excludes a particular portion of the people. Naturally, some of the "political" CDs may concern issues so sensitive that they remain tightly held within the Party bureaucracy. The more functionally oriented CDs are evidently more likely to be transmitted only to those whose jobs make it desirable for them to be briefed on the contents.

Wang Pi-ch'eng's summary speech again provides an underpinning for some of these generalizations, which were derived primarily from interviewing. Wang, for instance, stresses the need to have the cadres and discussion leaders fully understand the CD before it is more broadly communicated.[34] He also notes that further transmission will bring the CD to the attention of everyone in China *except* the five bad elements.[35] Thus, the transmission of Central Documents in the PRC proceeds level by level (i.e., from the top down) and from the inside to the outside (i.e., from the Party core to non-Party bureaucrats and then to the public), with the leaders stipulating a cutoff at any point they deem appropriate. The political outcasts of society are evidently always felt to be beyond the pale in the *ch'uan-ta* process.

Techniques for Dissemination

Once one goes beyond the strictly intrabureaucratic sphere and looks at how the substance of a CD is transmitted to the masses, the variety of techniques encountered becomes extraordinarily rich. The common people may be brought into the *ch'uan-ta* process via listening to appropriate speeches on radio or television, reading editorials and feature articles in the newspapers, attending a special rally or a meeting of the mass organization to which they belong, or learning the contents of a document through a meeting of their regular study group.[36] A person may also become aware of a document through being invited to participate in an endeavor that grows out of a Central Document, as was the case for people who participated in the National Agricultural Science and Technology Conference of February–March 1963. The twelve hundred scientists who attended had clearly been drawn into work mandated by the Tenth Plenum of the Eighth Central Committee the previous September.[37] The one common feature among dissemination techniques is that only rarely are the contents of an entire CD communicated verbatim to the public. Again let us turn to a case study— this time a detailed review of the transmission process for CD(74)21—to highlight some important aspects of the process of transmitting the contents of a CD to the public.

As noted earlier, CD(74)21 was issued on 1 July 1974, at a time when the campaign to criticize Lin Piao and Confucius had peaked and caused widespread disruption, which in turn was paralyzing sections of the economy. While affirming the correctness of the campaign and the value of this experience, therefore, the CD focused particularly on the need to "grasp revolution and promote production," leaving no doubt that it was the latter part of this well-known slogan that should be the touchstone of policy in the current period. In somewhat more detail, the contents of this CD's ten articles are as follows:[38] *Article 1* praises the current situation and asserts that industrial and agricultural production will continue to improve as the campaign to criticize Lin Piao and Confucius is continued and deepened; *Article 2* calls for "serious attention" to be devoted to shortfalls in coal and steel production and in rail transport, with the major offending locales stipulated in the text; *Article 3* attributes a part of these problems to deviations in carrying out the Criticizing Lin Piao and Confucius movement, asserting that these have allowed "a small handful of class enemies to take the opportunity to bring up the surges, engage in destruction and disrupt order"; *Article 4* focuses on Mao's evaluation that "the great majority of cadres are good" and calls for policies to allow cadres who have made mistakes to rectify them and to be again on good terms with the masses; *Article 5* articulates a series of measures for dealing with the problem of cadres who have ceased coming to the office because they are under fire; *Article 6* condemns "economism" and stipulates that questions about wages that have arisen are to be put off until the latter stage of the campaign; *Article 7* stresses that "going against the tide" must be carried out based on a class analysis and condemns those who engage in mountain strong-holdism and factionalism; *Article 8* calls for the leadership to suppress people who disturb social order and commit economic crimes; *Article 9* calls on all Party and Youth League members to help propagate the experiences of those who successfully integrate the Criticizing Lin Piao and Confucius movement with promoting production; and *Article 10* directs the Party committees at various levels to review the situation and effectively mesh the campaign against Lin and Confucius with fulfillment of the various economic plans of the state.

Overall, then, this document touches on a wide range of dimensions of the problem of increasing production, instilling discipline, and maintaining public order while continuing to carry out the campaign to criticize Lin Piao and Confucius. It calls for continuing attention to the campaign but makes clear, as happened in the Cultural Revolution and previous political movements, that the campaign's goals had in fact changed—in this case, that the campaign must now serve the cause of increasing production. This multifaceted document was one of the most important CDs issued during 1974. It bore the rubric *t'ung-chih* (circular), thus indicating (not surprisingly, given the tremendous variations in local conditions around the country) that the Central authorities expected local leaders to act in accordance with the spirit (*ching-shen*) rather than the letter of this document.[39] The first-tier dissemination of this document was stipulated down to the provincial level[40] with second-tier dissemination required to the counties[41] and then to the general public. In some provinces, second-tier dissemination commenced as early as 5 July while in other provinces there is no visible evidence of this level of dissemination until as late as early August. Fourteen of the nineteen provinces on which such data are available, however, commenced second-tier dissemination by 15 July.[42]

Not surprisingly, there is no geographical pattern that explains the sequence of second-tier dissemination for CD(74)21. Distant Yunnan commenced this process within five days of the issuance of the CD, while nearby Shantung did not show evidence of engaging in this work until almost four weeks later. The overall rapidity of dissemination is noteworthy, however, and seems to have resulted from two factors. First, the document was considered top priority and therefore received urgent treatment. Second, the document was sufficiently broad in scope, with specific references to economic conditions in various units and a wide range of concrete policy prescriptions, that the drafting process for it must have involved quite a few provincial and subprovincial-level bodies. The lower levels were therefore probably well aware of the general thrust and contents of the document in advance of its formal adoption and issuance,[43] and this familiarity may in turn have facilitated the process of dissemination.

The level-by-level and inside-to-outside approach to second-tier dissemination of the contents of CD(74)21 emerges clearly from the local media reports of July–August 1974, as illustrated by the following examples from individual provinces. The Yunnan Provincial Party Committee convened a telephone conference for Party cadres on 5 July. Four days later, the provincial and Kunming municipal Trade Union Federation, Women's Federation, and Youth League sponsored a "pledge rally" attended by workers, poor and lower-middle peasants, and the staff and workers of the finance and trade from in the city to convey the contents of CD(74)21.[44] Szechwan Province began its second-tier dissemination process with the 8 July intrabureaucratic telephone conference mentioned earlier that linked up the leading Party cadres at the provincial level with those in the prefectural, municipal, autonomous *chou*, and *hsien* Party committees. Seven days later, the provincial Party committee convened a ten-day provincial conference on grasping revolution and promoting production in industry and communications attended by some 1,700 cadres and regular employees from that functional system. The purpose of this conference was to transmit and discuss how to implement the contents of CD(74)21.[45] On 18 July, the Szechwan provincial and Ch'engtu municipal federations of trade unions held a joint "oath-taking rally" attended by 13,700 workers from the industry, communications, finance, and trade fronts at which the leaders transmitted the contents of CD(74)21 to this large audience.[46] Finally, on 22 July, the *Szechwan Daily* published an editorial that transmitted the basic contents of CD(74)21. Indeed, this editorial quoted extensively from several articles of the CD, albeit without mentioning that they were direct quotations.[47] In Kiangsu, likewise, the second-tier dissemination began with a telephone conference convened on 8 July by the provincial Party committee, which transmitted CD(74)21 to responsible cadres at the provincial, prefectural, municipal, and county levels in the Party, government, and mass organizations.[48] Two days later, the municipal Party committee in Nanking convened a rally of 50,000 representatives of the cadres and masses at Wutaishan Stadium to transmit the message of the CD. A rash of other meetings was held in the municipality on the same day to exchange experiences relevant to grasping revolution and promoting production, to take oaths to carry out the spirit of CD(74)21, and to commend model units who exemplified the virtues called for in the Central Document.[49] On 15 August Kiangsu Radio carried an editorial from the province's *Hsinhua Daily* entitled "Uphold the Great Principle of Grasping Revolution and Promoting Production." This editorial also conveyed the contents of CD(74)21.[50] In each of these instances, then, second-tier dissemination went from provincial-level to lower-level to the general public and, on the whole, from Party cadres to non-Party cadres to ordinary citizens.

Among the plethora of groups that met to hear the contents of CD(74)21, one type that appears repeatedly in different provinces is meetings of the functional systems for which the Central Document is particularly pertinent. Kweichow, for instance, convened a special conference on finance and trade for 10–22 August;[51] Shantung held a telephone conference on grasping revolution and promoting production in the province's coal industry on 16 August;[52] Kiangsi also convened a provincewide conference on the coal industry[53] as well as a related meeting on the metallurgical industry,[54] while Kirin convened an eight-day conference of personnel from the industrial and communications system.[55] Hupei held a conference of Party secretaries responsible for industry,[56] and Szechwan convened the afore-mentioned conference of people from the industry and communications system.[57] Another frequently seen meeting was that convened by the trade union organizations, which in mid-1974 were just recently reconstructed after having been virtually destroyed during the Cultural Revolution. A significant component of CD(74)21 focused on matters of primary concern to workers—factory discipline, production quotas, and wages. Thus, it is wholly appropriate that the newly reorganized trade unions should have been called on to play a major role in communicating the contents of this CD to the workers in various enterprises. Ch'uan-ta meetings and rallies either sponsored or cosponsored by the trade union organizations were reported in Kiangsu,[58] Kweichow,[59] Szechwan,[60] and Yunnan[61] provinces. A common dimension of the second-tier dissemination process, then, is to convene meetings of functionally defined groups of people who are directly concerned with the message of the Central Document.

Other devices that were mentioned in the media (excluding the articles and editorials in the papers themselves) for communicating CD(74)21 to the public included oath-taking rallies,[62] regional broadcast rallies,[63] pledge rallies,[64] mobilization rallies,[65] and symposia to exchange experience,[66] in addition to the various specialized meetings and conferences already mentioned.

Selective Transmission

The media reports on these events seem to indicate that the leadership conveyed only parts of CD(74)21 to the public via these forums. Naturally, these seeming omissions may in fact reflect selective reporting of the events rather than the events themselves. Similarly, somewhat fuller versions of the document may have been transmitted via the study group network than were conveyed in the more ostentatious public gatherings (although one knowledgeable informant doubted that this would be the case). It is striking, in this connection, to find that local editorials written to convey the contents of the CD exhibited similar selectivity,[67] suggesting that this derived from a conscious policy of limiting the public dissemination of sections of the document. It appears from the media materials available that provincial political leaders conveyed only a part of the contents of the document to many people in the second tier of dissemination in their provinces. Indeed, in several instances there is evidence that provincial (in both senses of the word) considerations skewed the very transmission process in various locales as well as the ways in which this was done. This circumstance may well have reflected a conscious strategy of taking political advantage of the complexity of the ten articles in CD(74)21 and the flexibility generally allowed by the use of a *t'ung-chih* rubric.

Some local leaders simply conveyed a significantly different thrust on key issues from that contained in the CD—all in the name of transmitting the contents of the CD. For example, Article 8 of CD(74)21 states that "we must sufficiently (*ch'ung-fen*) mobilize the masses, make the dictatorial organs function properly, and resolutely attack those enemies who undermine the criticism of Lin Piao and Confucius, undermine the industrial and agricultural production, and undermine the communications and transportation." In short, the thrust of this article (and of the entire document) is to crack down on disruption so as to reestablish order, stop struggle, and increase production. The official summary of the 8 July Szechwan telephone conference that linked the provincial Party committee up with the leading cadres of the provincial departments and of the prefectural, *hsien*, municipal, and autonomous *chou* Party committees in order to transmit CD(74)21, by contrast, argued that "we must trust and rely on the masses and *give them free rein* . . . ,"[68] which goes directly against the spirit of the Central Document, although it plays off the CD's acknowledgment that one should continue to mobilize the masses "sufficiently." Indeed, this entire Szechwan telephone conference as reported in the media took on a distinctly different aura from that of the CD it was convened to transmit. For example, CD(74)21 begins with a brief review of the situation to date, which notes that "the campaign to criticize Lin Piao and Confucius *has already been* carried out in the cities and villages throughout the country and is developing deeply, universally, and persistently. The masses of people *have been* mobilized."[69] The remainder of the document, as noted previously, downplays the Criticizing Lin Piao and Confucius campaign and in fact completely restructures the goals of the campaign toward order, discipline, and production. The Szechwan telephone conference, by contrast, stressed that "the most fundamental thing is to grasp the line. *At present*, this means carrying out criticism of Lin and Confucius deeply, universally, and protractedly."[70] The original Chinese Central Document was clear in its use of the past tense on the mobilization phase of the anti–Lin Piao campaign—and the conference was equally clear[71] in shifting it to the present tense and making it the key focus of current policy. The conference summary argues further that the Szechwan leadership should "embrace still more firmly the idea of fighting a protracted war and strengthen spontaneity. . . . We must resolutely support the masses' proletarian revolutionary spirit and welcome their criticism and supervision. We should plunge among the masses, sum up experiences in mass struggle [which presumes—contrary to the message of the CD—that "struggle" should continue], concentrate them, and persist in them."[72] Thus, although this broadcast on the telephone conference also includes substantial terminology that is found verbatim in the CD, the policies stipulated by the conference, if accurately reported on Szechwan Radio and translated in *FBIS/PRC*, considerably shifted the balance between the tasks of revolution and of production from that dictated in CD(74)21.

Chekiang Province's dissemination of CD(74)21 provides an even more striking example of an attempt to refocus the thrust of this important Central Document. CD(74)21 had been issued on 1 July, and the provincial leadership clearly had the document in hand within a day or two, as indicated by the fact that second-tier dissemination had begun in Yunnan as early as 5 July.[73] Nevertheless, on 5 July a meeting was convened in the name of the Chekiang Provincial Party Committee and presided over by Weng Sen-ho, who has subsequently been denounced as one of the key followers of the Gang of Four. This mass meeting, attended by many high-ranking officials, was convened in the name of pushing forward the campaign to criticize Lin and Confucius and devoted most of its attention to the major themes of that campaign— criticizing those who want to "restrain oneself and restore the rights," denouncing those who would seek to become the head of state, and so forth. The meeting concluded that "it is necessary to continuously criticize the rightist trend which advocates retrogression and restoration, and negates the Great Proletarian Cultural Revolution and socialist new things."[74]

This same meeting called on cadres (almost as an afterthought, if the broadcasted review of the meeting accurately reflects the proceedings) to grasp production and map out effective measures for increasing production. It then closely paraphrased CD(74)21 in stating that the cadres "must fully mobilize the masses to resolutely strike at class enemies who are trying to sabotage the movement to criticize Lin Piao and Confucius."[75] This admonition differs in two crucial respects, however, from the actual decision expressed in Article 8 of CD(74)21. First, Article 8 clearly states that both the mobilized masses *and the dictatorial organs of the state* should be brought into play to suppress the class enemies, while the Chekiang meeting entrusted this task solely to the "mobilized masses." Second, Article 8 calls for suppression of those who oppose the Criticizing Lin Piao and Confucius campaign and of those who disrupt either industrial and agricultural production or communications and transportation. Weng Sen-ho's meeting omitted the latter two dimensions of this important stricture. By transmitting only a part of the text of Article 8, then, this meeting seriously distorted the meaning of the document the provincial leadership had just been told to disseminate.

Weng Sen-ho's meeting used another device that was also employed by other provincial leaders in transmitting this document—to wit, the meeting called on its participants to "further implement the *series of* important directives of Chairman Mao and the Central Committee. . . ."[76] Earlier CDs evidently had been more to the liking of the radicals, and CD(74)21 did not explicitly negate earlier Central Documents. Rather, it turned around the thrust of the Criticizing Lin Piao and Confucius movement simply by specifying the key current problems and tasks in a way that differed from earlier analyses. By meshing CD(74)21 with the earlier CDs on the campaign against Lin Piao and Confucius, therefore, provincial leaders could dilute somewhat the parts of CD(74)21 that they found objectionable.[77] The fact that during 1974 the provincial leaders were receiving a new CD virtually every ten days must have made this an attractive ploy to use in the transmission process.[78]

Thus, Weng Sen-ho and his colleagues in the Chekiang provincial leadership distorted CD(74)21 in the process of transmitting it. Specifically, they focused on the campaign instead of on increasing production and upholding discipline. They quoted from one of the major articles of the CD, but omitted a key passage on the use of "dictatorial organs" and left out two of the three objects of exercising dictatorship. Finally, they "packaged" CD(74)21 by meshing it with a whole series of CDs on the Criticizing Lin Piao and Confucius campaign, thus mitigating some of the force of this individual document. Not surprisingly, Weng Sen-ho came under fire as a member of the radical faction soon after the October 1976 purge of the Gang of Four.

A meeting of the key military, Party, and government leaders in Hunan Province that was convened toward the middle of July[79] used many of the same tactics to distort the thrust of CD(74)21 in the province. This meeting, for instance, convened "with a view to implementing *the series* [emphasis added] of important instructions of Chairman Mao and the Party Center on criticizing Lin and Confucius and on various other work." The meeting then focused almost all its attention on overcoming the obstacles that had been encountered in fully carrying out the Criticizing Lin Piao and Confucius campaign in the province, giving barely a nod to the production issues brought up in CD(74)21. Since CD(74)21 was clearly on the agenda, though, the provincial leadership could not wholly ignore consideration of the task of increasing production. Rather, it called for an all-out effort to "propagate and implement on a grand scale the instructions of the Center on grasping revolution and promoting production." To implement this, it directed that "while devoting their main efforts to leading the campaign, the CCP committees must also strengthen their leadership over production"—a distribution of effort sharply at variance with the thrust of CD(74)21. This meeting thus managed to keep its focus on mobilization, struggle, and battles to prevent a reversal of verdicts on the Cultural Revolution and the socialist newborn things while also formally transmitting and studying CD(74)21.

Another critical dimension of the transmission process for Central

Documents is highlighted by some additional distortions of CD(74)21 in this Hunan meeting. In the name of uniting the cadres of the Party committees, the meeting called operationally for "unfolding within the CCP committees struggle between the correct and incorrect lines and struggle between correct and incorrect ideas." While quoting from Article 4 of CD(74)21 to the effect that "the great majority of cadres are good. . . . In compliance with the principle 'learn past mistakes to avoid future ones and cure the sickness to save the patient,' we must take a correct attitude to erring comrades," it inserted between these quoted sentences a sentiment not found in CD(74)21—namely, that "the masses must exercise revolutionary supervision over leadership cadres and vigorously support their work."

Where did these discordant ideas originate? The answer, in this case, is clear: from the *People's Daily* editorial published on the same day that CD(74)21 was distributed! This 1 July editorial[80] did not launch a frontal attack on its Central Document counterpart. Rather, it partly complemented the message in the CD (that the Party committees must assume firm leadership over the anti–Lin Piao campaign); partly ignored it (by, for instance, mentioning "grasp revolution, promote production" only in the final line, and even then merely as a slogan without specific content); and partly undermined it (by calling for *struggle* as the means to attain unity in the Party committees and stressing the mobilization of the masses and their supervision over the leadership). In mid-1974, provincial leaders around the country and their subordinates thus received two highly authoritative communications from Peking with identical dates. Both were very important (a wide-ranging Central Document articulating a new policy line on a current political movement and the annual 1 July editorial in honor of the founding of the Party), and yet the spirit of each differed enough to allow lower-level leaders to modify the message of either by adjusting the mix between them in the dissemination process. Some provincial cadres, such as those that convened the mid-July transmission meeting in Hunan Province, clearly took advantage of the latitude afforded by this situation.

Role of *People's Daily* Editorials

Did *People's Daily* editorials traditionally have an adversary relationship with internal Central Committee communications? Clearly not. Before the Cultural Revolution, indeed, major Central Documents as a matter of course generated one or more *People's Daily* editorials that amplified the points in either a part or the entirety of the document. Some of these editorials were published weeks or months after the dissemination of the Central Document so as to provide guidance on problems that had arisen in the process of implementation. Since *People's Daily* editorials are required subjects for study in most of the study groups in

China, they were used by the Central leadership as an efficient means to amplify policies communicated in CDs to lower-level cadres and the public. This is not meant to imply that all, or even a majority, of pre-1966 *People's Daily* editorials communicated the contents of Central Documents. It also should not be construed as indicating that all CDs generated their own *People's Daily* editorials. Rather, it simply indicates that an important and wide-ranging CD would very likely serve as the source for one or more *People's Daily* editorials during the weeks and perhaps months following its dissemination by the Central authorities.

A brief look at the use of *People's Daily* editorials to communicate the contents of the series of major Central Documents on the Socialist Education campaign during 1963–1965 illustrates the basic points about this editorial practice. Four important CDs initiated and then molded the contours of this campaign: the "Former Ten Points," the "Later Ten Points," the "Revised Later Ten Points," and the "Twenty-Three Points."[81] Mao Tse-tung authored the first and last of these, while Teng Hsiao-p'ing and Liu Shao-ch'i are said to have been responsible for the other two. The campaign was, moreover, a subject of intense debate in China during this period.[82] The dates of discussion of the contents of these documents in *People's Daily* editorials (without explicit mention of a CD itself) are listed in Table 5-1.

Several points stand out from this list. First, these documents were too long and complicated for any single editorial to deal with in their entirety. Each editorial, therefore, focused on only one or two major points in the document. Second, the *People's Daily* published a series of editorials on one particular point in a CD before moving on to a different point. This practice would suggest either that these complex programs were implemented in phases and that the editorials reflected this approach, or that the editorials really focused simply on a particular issue that had become a problem in the process of implementation. Third, the editorials concerned a political movement in the rural areas, and the hiatus in their appearance during the fall harvest and spring sowing periods suggests that they were intended as guides to immediate action in the countryside. Political campaigns directly affecting the rural areas in China since 1949 have almost without exception been suspended during the spring sowing and fall harvest. Fourth, the decline in editorials on the last two documents in the series is both obvious and somewhat misleading. There was considerable overlap among these Central Documents, as each modified rather than wholly replaced the previous one. The diminution in editorial coverage of the documents is at least partly explained by the fact that much of the material in the later CDs had already been covered in earlier ones. Further, the research on *People's Daily* editorials with respect to these documents only went up to the end of June 1965 and thus may have missed subsequent editorials published on the "Twenty-Three Points." Fifth, these editorials covered about

Table 5-1
Editorials Discussing
Socialist Education Campaign CDs

Document and Article Number Reflected	People's Daily Editorial Date
"Former Ten Points"	
6	29 May 1963
9	2 June 1963
9	4 July 1963
9	17 July 1963
9	21 July 1963
9	29 July 1963
9	17 August 1963
"Later Ten Points"	
1	29 November 1963
1	7 December 1963
Introduction	1 January 1964
1	19 March 1964
1	24 March 1964
1	26 March 1964
7	28 August 1964
7	30 August 1964
"Revised Later Ten Points"	
1	17 November 1964
"Twenty-Three Points"	
20	17 February 1965
4, 7	28 April 1965

equally (if one allows for repetition in documents) both CDs that reflected Mao's views and those that posited the other side of the argument. This dimension of the system was sufficiently institutionalized before the Cultural Revolution that in cases of dispute where each side managed to have its views adopted in CDs over time, the People's Daily helped convey the contents of the CDs almost regardless of the internecine fighting behind the scenes. Finally, the list shows clearly that People's Daily editorials were used to convey only parts of these major Central Documents, while other sections were ignored in this medium.

Before the Cultural Revolution, People's Daily editorials played an important role in communicating the contents of many Central Documents and amplifying the decisions contained in them.[83] These editorials directly addressed problem areas and seemed to have been impervious to the politics behind the documents themselves. I have found no examples in pre-1966 editorials of any attempt by the People's

Daily editors to undermine the thrust of a major CD recently promulgated by the Party leadership. These editorials in their totality did, however, frequently convey the contents of only portions of a major CD rather than the entire contents of the document.[84]

Often, it should be noted, the *People's Daily* editorial quoted extensively from the Central Document that had sparked it, without directly mentioning that it was revealing the contents of a recently issued CD. A major segment of the 25 July 1963 editorials, for example, quoted verbatim the language found in the introduction to the "Former Ten Points," running on for several paragraphs. The same is true for excerpts from Article 9 of the "Former Ten Points" as conveyed in the editorial of 2 June 1963. At other times, the editorials dealt directly with the issues raised in one of the articles in the CD but did not use any of the specific language of the document itself. The 28 April 1965 editorial reflecting the contents of Articles 4 and 7 of the "Twenty-Three Points" typified this approach, referred to in China as conveying the spirit (*ching-shen*) of a document.

The role of the *People's Daily* in transmitting and explaining major CDs, moreover, was not limited to editorials. Short commentaries (*tuan-p'ing*), and signed and unsigned feature articles were also often employed. As an example, an article by Chang P'ing-hua in the 2 November 1964 *People's Daily* (p. 5) focused on issues raised in Article 1 of the "Revised Later Ten Points," at one point even quoting from that article without naming it. The *People's Daily* also published both New China News Agency reports on statistics relevant to the problem raised in a CD and various articles on model experiences throughout the country that were relevant to a CD. Sometimes, indeed, these have been "model" reports that were circulated as appendices to the CD itself. Through providing this range of material, the *People's Daily* often played a significant role in communicating and amplifying the contents of Central Documents for a larger audience.

After the Cultural Revolution, by contrast, the *People's Daily* generally played a greatly diminished role in communicating and amplifying CDs for the populace, and in 1974, factional political considerations clearly began to affect what coverage the paper did give to this area. For the years 1970–1973, no editorials reflected the contents of any of the available CDs at all,[85] with the minor and insignificant exception of some very general references to "swindlers like Liu Shao-ch'i," "splittists," and so forth, evocative of the Lin Piao affair during the period when the series of CDs on that affair was being issued.

Mainland China sources have revealed that the radicals gained control over the *People's Daily* shortly after the Tenth Party Congress, which convened in August 1973.[86] Almost immediately, the pattern changed somewhat. CDs on the campaign to criticize Lin Piao and Confucius were issued on 18 and 22 January[87] and probably subsequently during the course of the spring as well. Then on 2 and 20 February and 15 March, *People's Daily* editorials appeared on this campaign, each conveying the radicals' perspective (as did the equivalent CDs). When CD(74)21 came out on 1 July and refocused the campaign away from the issues dear to the radicals, however, the *People's Daily* editorial of that date turned a deaf ear to its CD counterpart, as analyzed previously. During 1974, the radicals managed to use *People's Daily* editorials to convey their own policy preferences in the first part of the year. Prior to July, this meant that the editorials played their pre–Cultural Revolution role vis-à-vis CDs, insofar as the CDs themselves also reflected the radicals' preferences. At mid-year, however, the contents of the Central Documents changed, and editorial support for them immediately ceased. Only once from mid-1974 to the end of 1975 did a *People's Daily* editorial seem to reflect the contents of a CD—when the 11 March 1975 editorial evidently evoked some of the spirit of the CD on railway transportation.

Other dimensions of *People's Daily* guidance in carrying out the policies contained in Central Documents also seem to have deteriorated after the Cultural Revolution, presumably reflecting an attempt by Yao Wen-yuan and his colleagues to mitigate the force of policy directives with which they disagreed. An intensive review of *People's Daily* coverage during the months following the issuance of CD(74)21, for example, finds few articles that come squarely to grips with the issues raised in the CD and provide concrete guidance on how to handle the problems encountered. A former PRC cadre who examined these articles termed them *k'uang-tung-ti* (vacuous) and comparison of them with the equivalent *People's Daily* coverage before the Cultural Revolution simply highlights the vast change that seems to have occurred during this period.

Treatment of CDs in the provincial media seems to have varied somewhat according to the political ties of the provincial leadership, as illustrated by the preceding analysis of the transmission of CD(74)21. Clearly, though, the media in many provinces continued to present the kind of amplification and guidance that the *People's Daily* and they had together provided before the Cultural Revolution. For instance, the provincial newspapers of the following provinces carried editorials that actually reflected CD(74)21: Inner Mongolian Autonomous Region, Fukien, Shantung, Kiangsu, Hunan, Szechwan, Heilungkiang, Sinkiang, and Yunnan.[88] Virtually all these editorials quoted directly, and often extensively, from the text of CD(74)21, albeit without indicating that they were direct quotations. In other ways already analyzed, however, some editorials twisted the letter and/or the spirit of the original document, and supporting feature articles, reports, and model experiences conveyed in the provincial papers of these months did likewise.

Conclusion

In sum, the process of transmitting the contents of Central Documents is complex and flexible. It begins with a diffusion of the document itself to a selected group of units for study and implementation. It then may lead to an increasingly widely ramifying set of efforts to communicate the contents of the document to wider circles of people. This transmission process is one that proceeds roughly step by step from the highest to the lowest levels of the system and also tends to move from the "inside" to the "outside"—that is, from Party cadres to other civil servants to the public. The dissemination of a particular document is cut off at the point stipulated by the authorities who issue it.

Generally, the original CD circulates only to the limited groups of units on the *chu-sung chi-kuan* list. Further transmission, which can utilize a rather bewildering variety of vehicles, frequently carries increasingly truncated versions of the document downward. This process of continual summarization and condensation during transmission increases the likelihood that periods of political conflict will produce efforts to distort the thrust of a document, by omission if nothing else. It also means that since many of these documents are broad in scope and cover a substantial range of issues in their various articles, the people in one locale might be briefed on the substance of some articles while those in another are being given information from a quite different set of articles. Thus, people at the basic levels in different provinces might well receive very different pictures of the same document. Another possible method of distortion, as noted, relies on transmitting the contents of several CDs to lower levels and the public at once.

The only systematic change in the transmission process clearly evident from this research is in the role that the *People's Daily* plays in it. Before the Cultural Revolution, it gave guidance from the Center on the issues raised in major CDs; after the Cultural Revolution, however, this virtually ceased to be the case (I have not carried out research to determine whether the *People's Daily* has reverted to its previous role since the arrest of the Gang of Four—most importantly, of Yao Wenyuan—in October 1976). Although political factionalism clearly affected the relationship between the *People's Daily* and Central Documents during the year or so after the Gang of Four gained control over the *People's Daily* in late 1973, this does not seem to have been the case for any year before the Cultural Revolution. The findings of this research effort support and lend substance to the widely held belief that the moderates basically controlled the executive organs of the Party during the early and mid-1970s, while the radicals had to rely on their leverage over the *People's Daily* and several other media outlets to blunt the thrust of the decisions taken by their adversaries within the councils of the Party. In a real sense, then, the political strife of the 1970s caused a deterioration in the process by which the Central leadership transmitted the contents of its decisions and provided guidance on their implementation.

In all probability, the integrity of the transmission process for Central Documents has been substantially restored during 1977–1978. The Hua Kuo-feng administration's constant emphasis on discipline and on fidelity to administrative rules and regulations, combined with the severe purge of the *People's Daily* staff, suggests that the Party Center is now again in most instances able to communicate accurately its concerns and decisions to important cadres throughout the political system. It bears highlighting in this connection that most officials in China learn the contents of Central Documents only indirectly (through the second-tier dissemination process), if at all, and therefore during the period of factional strife before Mao's death, many responsible leaders at the lower levels received incorrect information about the desires of the Central Party leadership even through in-house channels. Insofar as the integrity of this intrabureaucratic system of communications has been restored, therefore, the Central Party leaders have decidedly enhanced their ability to coordinate the perception of major events and policy decisions by cadres throughout the system.

NOTES

1. These limited circulation publications include, for example, the *Ts'an-k'ao tzu-liao* (published regularly in approximately eight million copies and distributed to a wide range of cadres throughout China) and other, less well-known publications, such as the "internal journal" published by *Jen-min Jih-pao* [People's Daily]. On the latter, see: New China News Agency, 15 June 1978—*Foreign Broadcast Information Service, People's Republic of China* (*FBIS/PRC*).

2. On the role of meetings in the policy process, see Kenneth Lieberthal, *Research Guide to Central Party and Government Meetings in China, 1949-1975* (White Plains, NY: International Arts and Sciences Press, 1976), pp. 3-23.

3. We, for instance, know almost nothing about the limited circulation publications.

4. Specifically, the average number of CDs issued per month (calculated from the CDs available outside China) during the 1970s has been:

Year	Average No. of CDs per Month
1970	6.6
1971	6.8
1972	2.9
1973	4.1
1974	2.7
1975	n.a.
1976	1.9
1977	4.1

   Source: Lieberthal, *Central Documents*, p. 17. The figure for 1977 is updated based on the information in CD(77)37 given in *FBIS/PRC*, 30 August 1978, E-1-31.

5. Lieberthal, *Central Documents*, pp. 6-20, passim.

6. The well-known "Some Problems Currently Arising in the Course of the Rural Socialist Education Movement" (usually referred to as the "Twenty-Three Points") is one of the extremely few pre–Cultural Revolution Central Documents for which we have listed the *chu-sung chi-kuan*, and the list for this major document excludes the military. Is the inclusion of the Party groups in the military on the CD routing, then, primarily a phenomenon generated by the Cultural Revolution? The text of the Twenty-Three Points is available in R. Baum and F. Teiwes, *Ssu-ch'ing: The Socialist Education Movement of 1962-1966*, China Research Monographs no. 2 (Berkeley: University of California Press, 1968), pp. 118-126.

7. Central Committee Documents are numbered seriatim beginning with the number 1 at the start of each calendar year. They are usually identified by stating the year of issue in parentheses, followed by the serial number of the particular document in question. Thus, CD(72)4 indicates that this is the fourth Central Document issued in 1972.

8. Ying-mao Kau, *The Lin Piao Affair* (White Plains, NY: International Arts and Sciences Press, 1975), p. 78. This Central Document circulated a collection of reference materials on Lin Piao's crimes that had been uncovered during the investigation of the

former defense minister after his death in September 1971. For a similar list on another CD, see the text of CD(74)21 in *Issues and Studies* 11(1):101–102.

9. Text in *CCP Documents of the Great Proletarian Cultural Revolution, 1966–1967* (Kowloon: Union Research Institute, 1968), pp. 377–378 (hereafter cited as *CR Documents*).

10. See texts cited in notes 8 and 9.

11. See Michel Oksenberg, "Methods of Communication within the Bureaucracy," *China Quarterly* 57 (January–March 1974):12–15 for additional information on "transmission meetings."

12. One informant commented that in his unit such requests were often made rather rudely after the Cultural Revolution. A person would say, for instance, "Your *p'u-t'ung-hua* is so bad that I could not understand what you said. Please reread the document."

13. For a fuller discussion of rubrics and their implications, see Lieberthal, *Central Documents*, pp. 10–15.

14. Partial text in Kau, *Lin Piao*, pp. 78–95. This CD was issued on 13 January 1972.

15. Oksenberg reports in "Methods of Communication," p. 13, that such cynicism was in fact a serious problem.

16. The text of Wang's speech is given in *Chinese Law and Government* 7(3):7–32.

17. Ibid., p. 7.

18. Ibid., p. 16.

19. Actually, Chou had been the political commissar for the Kunming Military Region (MR) at the outset of the Cultural Revolution and was identified as a "responsible person" of the MR in 1972. I am assuming that he retained his position as political commissar.

20. *Chinese Law and Government* 7(3):8.

21. Ibid., p. 10.

22. For a summary of these opinions, see ibid., pp. 15–17.

23. Ibid., pp. 20, 26–27.

24. The available copy of the "Twenty-Three Points," for instance, was printed by the Fukien Provincial Party Committee; see Baum and Teiwes, *Ssu-ch'ing*, p. 118.

25. When a Central Document is used as a vehicle for circulating materials for reference, technically the CD itself is simply the covering letter from the Central Committee that stipulates the *chu-sung chi-kuan*, gives instructions on how to handle the attached reference materials, and specifies any further dissemination of the material that should be carried out. The reference materials themselves are considered appendices rather than intergral parts of the Central Document. For further explication of this issue, see Lieberthal, *Central Documents*, pp. 9–10.

26. Kiangsi Radio, 18 July 1974—*FBIS/PRC*, 23 July 1974, G-4. This CD was issued on 1 July 1974.

27. Szechwan Radio, 14 July 1974—*FBIS/PRC*, 15 July 1974, J-1-2.

28. Yunnan Radio, 6 July 1974—*FBIS/PRC*, 8 July 1974, J-4-5.

29. Kiangsu Radio, 9 July 1974—*FBIS/PRC*, 11 July 1974, G-1-3.

30. Honan Radio, 12 July 1974—*FBIS/PRC*, 17 July 1974, H-1.

31. Heilungkiang Radio, 14 July 1974—*FBIS/PRC*, 18 July 1974, L-1-3.

32. If the reference materials being circulated with the CD include pictures or graphics of some sort, as was the case with CD(72)24 on the Lin Piao affair (text in Kau, *Lin Piao*, pp. 96–105), then these visual materials are circulated among the participants in the study group but the text is not, according to this informant. The same informant commented that a senior cadre in his study group would occasionally simply reach over and take a document off the table to peruse during discussion. Lower-ranking cadres would not dare to take such liberties.

33. Landlords, rich peasants, counterrevolutionaries, rightists, and bad elements, all of whom have been treated as permanent pariahs in the People's Republic of China. In early 1978, a large number of people branded as "rightists" in the Anti-Rightist campaign of 1957 were rehabilitated, and thus at the time of this writing, it is not clear whether "rightists" are still considered a permanently ostracized group. See Hong Kong AFP, 18 May 1978—*FBIS/PRC*, 19 May 1978, E-3.

34. *Chinese Government and Law* 7(3):26–27.

35. Ibid., p. 15.

36. Oksenberg covers variations of this in his "Methods of Communication," pp. 12–14.

37. The National Conference convened from 8 February to 31 March 1963. Documentation on this conference and on the preceding Tenth Plenum is provided in Lieberthal, *Research Guide*, pp. 198–199 and 191–193, respectively.

38. Texts in *Issues and Studies* 11(1):101–104; *Chung-kung yen-chiu* [Chinese Studies] 8(12):6/20–6/21.

39. Lieberthal, *Central Documents*, pp. 10, 13.

40. More precisely, to Party committees at various provinces, (directly administered) municipalities, and autonomous regions, Party committees at various military regions, provincial military districts and field armies; Military Affairs Commission; Party committees at various general headquarters of armed services, various arms and branches; and the leadership groups and core groups of the departments of the Central Committee and of the ministries and commissions of the State Council.

41. Actually, to both the counties and the regiment level in the People's Liberation Army.

42. These dates should be understood, of course, to indicate the *latest* time by which second tier dissemination began in each province. For the provinces where

information on second-tier dissemination of CD(74)21 appeared in the media, the
dates for the earliest evidence of this dissemination are shown in Table 5-2.

Table 5-2
Second-Tier Dissemination of CD(74)21

Province	Date of Earliest Second-Tier Dissemination Mentioned	Date of Provincial Radio Broadcast	*FBIS/PRC* (date & pages)
Yunnan	5 July	6 July	8 July, J-4-5
Chekiang	5 July	8 July	10 July, G-1-4
Kirin	6 July	7 July	8 July, L-2-4
Szechwan	8 July	14 July	15 July, J-1-2
Kiangsu	8 July (approx)	9 July	11 July, G-1-3
Shanghai	8 July	10 July	11 July, G-4-6
IMAR	9 July	10 July	11 July, K-1-3
Kweichow	10 July	10 July	15 July, J-2-3
Kwangtung	10 July	12 July*	15 July, H-4-5
Anhwei	10 July	10 July	17 July, G-1-3
Honan	11 July (approx)	12 July	17 July, H-1-2
Heilungkiang	12 July	14 July	18 July, L-1-4
Hunan	14 July (approx)	15 July	16 July, H-1-4
Tsinghai	15 July	15 July	19 July, M-1-2
Kiangsi	18 July (approx)	18 July	23 July, G-4
Hupei	18 July (approx)	18 July	23 July, H-7-8
Shensi	27 July	29 July	30 July, M-1-3
Shantung	28 July	28 July	31 July, G-6-7
Sinkiang	4 August	4 August	7 August, N-3-6

*Canton City broadcast.

43. This is strongly suggested by the fact that broadcasts from a few provinces in June 1974—that is, during the month *before* CD(74)21 was issued—clearly and concretely anticipated the contents of this document. See, for example, Canton Radio, 21 July 1974—*FBIS/PRC*, 26 June 1974, H-4-5.

44. Yunnan Radio, 6 July 1974—*FBIS/PRC*, 8 July 1974, J-4-5; ibid., 10 July 1974—*FBIS/PRC*, 11 July 1974, J-1.

45. Szechwan Service, 28 July 1974—*FBIS/PRC*, 29 July 1974, J-1-2. This conference convened from 15-25 July in Chungking and attracted participants from all over the province.

46. Szechwan Radio, 19 July 1974—*FBIS/PRC*, 29 July 1974, 22 July 1974, J-1-2.

47. *FBIS/PRC*, 23 July 1974, J-1-3.

48. Kiangsu Radio, 9 July 1974—*FBIS/PRC*, 11 July 1974, G-1-3.

49. Kiangsu Radio, 24 July 1974—*FBIS/PRC*, 25 July 1974, G-10-11.

50. Kiangsu Radio, 15 July 1974—*FBIS/PRC*, 18 July 1974, G-5-7. The broadcast does not give the date of the editorial, but usual practice is to broadcast an editorial within one day of its publication in the paper.

51. Kweichow Radio, 22 August 1974—*FBIS/PRC*, 27 August 1974, J-1-2.

52. Shantung Radio, 18 August 1974—*FBIS/PRC*, 21 August 1974, G-7-9.

53. Kiangsi Radio, 20 August 1974—*FBIS/PRC*, 23 August 1974, G-1-2.

54. Ibid., G-3-4.

55. Kirin Radio, 28 July 1974—*FBIS/PRC*, 30 July 1974, L-5-8. The conference convened from 15-22 July.

56. Hupei Radio, 18 July 1974—*FBIS/PRC*, 23 July 1974, H-7-8.

57. Szechwan Radio, 28 July 1974—*FBIS/PRC*, 29 July 1974, J-1-2.

58. Kiangsu Radio, 24 July 1974—*FBIS/PRC*, 25 July 1974, G-10-11.

59. Kweichow Radio, 23 July 1974—*FBIS/PRC*, 25 July 1974, J-1.

60. Szechwan Radio, 19 July 1974—*FBIS/PRC*, 22 July 1974, J-1-2.

61. Yunnan Radio, 9 July 1974—*FBIS/PRC*, 11 July 1974, J-1.

62. Szechwan Radio, 19 July 1974—*FBIS/PRC*, 22 July 1974, J-1-2.

63. IMAR Radio, 10 July 1974—*FBIS/PRC*, 11 July 1974, J-1; Chekiang Radio, 11 July 1974—*FBIS/PRC*, 16 July 1974, G-1-4; Anhwei Radio, 15 July 1974—*FBIS/PRC*, 17 July 1974, G-1-3.

64. Yunnan Radio, 9 July 1974—*FBIS/PRC*, 11 July 1974, J-1.

65. Canton Radio, 12 July 1974—*FBIS/PRC*, 15 July 1974, H-4-5.

66. Hupei Radio, 26 July 1974—*FBIS/PRC*, 29 July 1974, H-1-2.

67. See, for example, the editorials in *Inner Mongolia Daily*, 10 July 1974—*FBIS/PRC*, 12 July 1974, K-4-5; *Fukien Daily*, 11 July 1974—*FBIS/PRC*, 12 July 1974, G-5; *Tachung Daily* (Shantung)—*FBIS/PRC*, 19 July 1974, G-7-9; and *Szechwan Daily*, 22 July 1974—*FBIS/PRC*, 23 July 1974, J-1-3.

68. Szechwan Radio, 14 July 1974—*FBIS/PRC*, 15 July 1974, J-2. Emphasis added.

69. Article I. Emphasis added.

70. Szechwan Radio, 14 July 1977—*FBIS/PRC*, 15 July 1977, J-1. Emphasis added.

71. If the *FBIS/PRC* translation is accurate.

72. Szechwan Radio, 14 July 1977—*FBIS/PRC*, 15 July 1977, J-1.

116

73. Yunnan Radio, 6 July 1974—*FBIS/PRC*, 8 July 1974, J-4-5.

74. Chekiang Radio, 8 July 1974—*FBIS/PRC*, 10 July 1974, G-1.

75. Ibid., G-2.

76. Chekiang Radio, 8 July 1974—*FBIS/PRC*, 10 July 1974, G-1.

77. Ten years earlier, Liu Shao-ch'i purportedly used a similar tactic to blur the differences between Mao's "Ten Points" and Liu's "Revised Later Ten Points" by lumping them together and referring to them as the "Double Ten Points"; see Stuart Schram, ed., *Authority, Participation and Cultural Change in China* (Cambridge: University Press, 1973), p. 79.

78. For another instance of the use of this ploy in the transmission of CD(74)21, see for example, Shanghai Radio, 10 July 1974—*FBIS/PRC*, 11 July 1974, G-4-6.

79. Hunan Radio, 14 July 1974—*FBIS/PRC*, 16 July 1974, H-1-4.

80. Text of translation in *Survey of People's Republic of China Press*, nos. 5648–5652, 8–12 July 1974, pp. 217–219.

81. These, of course, are simplifications of the titles of these documents. The documents themselves were issued, respectively, on 20 May 1963; September 1963; 10 September 1964; and 18 January 1965. Texts are available in Baum and Teiwes, *Ssu-ch'ing*, pp. 58–94 and 102–106. I am indebted to Richard Baum for providing me with the original Chinese copies of several of these texts.

82. On the differences among these and the political disputes over them, see Baum and Teiwes, *Ssu-ch'ing*, pp. 11–48; and Richard Baum, *Prelude to Revolution* (New York: Columbia University Press, 1975), passim.

83. That this was by no means merely a reflection of the *People's Daily* treatment of the Socialist Education campaign CDs is proven by similar research conducted on other major documents of the pre-1966 period. Table 5-3 gives two examples in the same form used in Table 5-1 for the SEC documents.

84. A somewhat analogous situation seems to have been the case with respect to *People's Daily* coverage of secret central meetings and policy debates occurring behind the scenes. Sometimes, as in the debate over "bourgeois right" taking place in late 1958–early 1959, the *People's Daily* carried articles that evoked the points in contention rather fully. See, for example, the articles discussing "bourgeois right" of the following dates: 3, 6, 12, 24, and 26 December 1958; and 3, 9, 20, 24, and 27 January 1959. For information on the politics of this discussion at the Party Center during this period, see Lieberthal, *Research Guide*, pp. 128–129. At other times, major debates have taken place in-house that have found no echo in the *People's Daily* of the period. One of the most dramatic instances of this occurred during the month-long meeting of 7,000 cadres during January–February 1962, which focused on a series of critical issues including an evaluation of the Great Leap Forward, the sensitive issue of rehabilitation of people purged during this time, and how to reestablish a spirit of democratic centralism within the administrative apparatus. The only article in the *People's Daily* that bore a direct relationship to the issues being discussed at this massive conclave was a major piece on united front work by Li Wei-han that was reprinted in five parts in *Peking Review* 8–12 (1962). On the 7,000-cadre meeting, see

117

Table 5-3
Editorials Discussing Two Major Pre-1966 CDs

Documents and Article Number Reflected	People's Daily Editorial Date
"Regulations on the Work of Rural People's Communes" (draft)*	
26	25 November 1960
2	21 December 1960
20	29 December 1960
27	12 January 1961
15, 25	20 January 1961
10	23 January 1961
4	27 January 1961
1, 2, 10, 16, 20, 27	2 April 1961
33, 55, 57	6 May 1961
6, 27, 36–39	21 June 1961
"Seventy Articles on Industry"†	
42	22 July 1961
2	8 August 1961
34, 35	6 September 1961
37–47	17 December 1961
9	24 December 1961
1	12 January 1962

*Issued in May 1961. Chinese text available in the Asia Library at the University of Michigan. This text was itself a revision of an earlier twelve-article version.

†For summary of text, see *CR Documents*, pp. 689–694. Date of issue is uncertain.

Lieberthal, *Research Guide*, pp. 179–181. I have not conducted the research necessary to make more rigorous generalizations about the relationship of the public media to private policy discussions at the highest levels.

85. These are listed in Lieberthal, *Central Documents*, pp. 195–197.

86. *Peking Review*, 44 (28 October 1977):19.

87. For the Chinese texts, see *Chung-kung nien-pao* (1974), Section 7, pp. 17–19.

88. Texts are in, respectively, the following *FBIS/PRC*: 11 July 1974, K-4-5; 12 July 1974, G-5; 19 July 1974, G-7-9; 18 July 1974, G-5-7; 16 July 1974, H-4-5; 22 July 1974, J-1-3. This clearly need not exhaust the list of provincial editorials reflecting this CD. Others may have been published but not broadcast or were broadcast but not translated in *FBIS/PRC*. Also, the search in *FBIS/PRC* for these carried only through the end of August 1974, and it is possible that more editorials appeared in September and later. This list is, therefore, illustrative rather than definitive.

6

Goal Structure and Coordination in China's Rural Local Administration

Steven B. Butler

"Low effectiveness is a general characteristic of organizations. Since goals, as symbolic units, are ideals which are more attractive than the reality which the organization attains, the organization can almost always be reported to be a failure."[1] Such appears to be the case for most of China's local administrative units, even when compared with the realized success, as opposed to ideals, reported in advanced units such as Hsiyang County. Measured against the ambitious goals promulgated by China's central leadership, local administrators have much yet to achieve. But the gap between goals and achievement may not tell us much about the quality of local leadership. One reason is that the structure of goals that purportedly guide administrative decisions contains serious internal contradictions. In this chapter I shall argue that because of these internal contradictions, the communication of goals, featured so prominently in China's mass communication system, cannot hope to achieve the intended coordination and integration. Conversely, the selective promulgation of specific goals inhibits coordination, since attainment of one goal may prevent attainment of others.

As a means of studying the communication system in counties, I have selected the goal of agricultural mechanization as a focus of analysis. China's leaders have felt this goal of sufficient importance to institute a prominent national campaign around it. The program of agricultural mechanization provides a convenient starting point to look at problems of coordination in local administration since, in the process of mechanization, all of the four lowest levels—from county to production team—play an important role. In addition, several functional systems that cut vertically through these levels provide important inputs to the process.

Coordination is both a process and an outcome (goals indicate only outcomes). In complex organizations, outcome may be defined as a situation in which subcomponents of an organization achieve at least minimally acceptable results on indicators intrinsic to their own function while contributing to the overall achievements of the organization. For example, a machinery repair factory may contribute heroically to helping production teams and brigades reduce costs, but if in the process it goes bankrupt and closes down, coordination will not have been achieved. A more pedestrian example would be the repair shop that does not adjust its capacity to fit the agricultural seasons. Machines tend to break down when they are used most, which also is the time when they are most needed. Coordination will not have been achieved from the point of view of production teams and brigades should the repair shop fail to adjust its schedule.

In this example, the need for coordination as a process arises because each unit depends on the other unit to perform its function adequately. If interdependence is the root cause of the need to coordinate, a discussion of interdependence will be helpful, since some kinds of interdependence are more difficult to coordinate than others.

Following James D. Thompson's typology, interdependence can be distinguished as pooled, sequential, or reciprocal.[2] *Pooled interdependence* describes a situation in which units of local administration make a general contribution to the performance of the whole, yet their individual performance may have no direct relationship to the performance of other units. In this sense, all production teams make a general contribution to the performance of counties by selling surplus grain, and failure to do so damages the performance of the county. At the same time, the failure of one team to perform well does not normally affect the ability of other teams to produce. (There will of course be individual exceptions, such as when teams jointly own tractors or use the same limited water resources.) *Sequential interdependence* describes a situation in which the output of one unit becomes input for the next. The output of a local fertilizer factory becomes the input for a production team, and if the factory does not reach its planned output, teams will suffer. *Reciprocal interdependence* means that the outputs of each of two units become inputs for the other. An example is the relationship between production teams or brigades and commune machinery repair shops. The output of the maintenance shop, a working machine, is an input for the team, while a by-product of team operation is a machine needing maintenance, which becomes an input for the repair shop. By these definitions, all units that have reciprocal interdependence also have their sequential and pooled aspects.

As should be apparent, the difficulties of coordination and consequent need for communication increase as organizations encounter more and more sequential and reciprocal interdependence. The drive for agricultural mechanization has precisely this effect on local administration. Units located at different administrative levels and in different functional systems perform specialized tasks that must be coordinated to further overall goals. I shall first examine these goals in the context of local administration, then see what kinds of coordination for goal achievement are handled by which communication channels.

Goals in Local Administration

The official goal of China's Communist Party is broadly conceived as total transformation of the society to achieve communism. Since this goal is, however, clearly too abstract to be of much help to local administrators, Party leaders have tried, through a difficult political process, to arrive at a set of subgoals that can be an effective guide to action. The achievement of basic agricultural mechanization by 1980 was one such goal. But even this target fails to give very concrete directions. Basic mechanization means that 70 percent of production tasks will be performed by machines, but 70 percent is to be the average of counties in China, so that some counties will be 100 percent mechanized, while others will fall considerably below 70 percent. If the Chinese have clear standards by which to measure the percentage of mechanization, they are not available in the West. One recent traveler to China, observing fields being plowed by oxen, was told that the unit had achieved 100 percent mechanization. Local cadres explained that they used their tractors to transport materials.[3] Because of the prominent national campaign to encourage mechanization, we can expect that local administrators will try to increase use of machines; but simple knowledge of this goal will not be likely to serve as a predictor of administrative action, since this aim is embedded in a more complex structure of subgoals.

The complexity of this structure causes two related problems for local administrators—subgoals can be inconsistent; and administrators at different administrative levels and in different functional systems rank the priority of subgoals differently. Before discussing manifestations of these problems, we might note the intimate relationships between administrative goals and assessment of administrative performance. Within counties, an elaborate system of cadre and mass meetings, work teams, and propaganda devices is used to popularize a set of goals. But frequently, higher levels have few means to detect whether lower-level units commit resources to achieve maximum possible fulfillment of these goals. This results both from imperfections in the monitoring capacity of the communications system and also from great complexity in the chain of cause and effect relationships that may nonetheless result in easily measured outcomes, such as increases in grain yields. Consequently, higher-level administrators may use simplified indicators of performance, such as grain yields. This causes lower-level cadres to strive for adequate performance on indicators actually used by higher levels, and with such performance assured, substitute their own goal structure for that popularized by higher levels.[4] In this fashion, the system of evaluating administrative performance plays an important role in determining behavior over and above promulgated goals.

The divergence of perceptions of goals follows from two different principles of dividing administrative tasks. The first reflects the hierarchical division of authority where higher levels of administration perceive goals differently from lower levels. The second derives from the functional division of tasks across levels, for example, work in finance and trade as opposed to work in culture and education.

Vertical Goal Divergence

To take a simple example of goal divergence reflecting hierarchical divisions, higher-level administrators frequently view the success of their mechanization program in terms of gross and per unit yields of grain or other crops. Production team cadres and team members place much greater emphasis on the amount of distributable income, and, in particular, the value of a standard day's labor. According to official Party lore, these goals are not inconsistent. Increased yields should result in greater benefit to the state, the collective, and the individual. The Party recognizes that personal income from collective sources must rise if commune members are to continue feeling enthusiastic about collective labor. This notion appears frequently in the *People's Daily* when reporters note that the activism of peasants is dampened by stagnating personal income and, conversely, is aroused by higher income.[5]

Nonetheless, these two goals are contradictory, in some cases because of structural factors and in most cases because of the preferences of administrators. The contradiction is structural when units experience an increase in gross and per-unit yields of grain accompanied by a drop in net income. The reason for this is that some units have reached a point of diminishing returns, where the marginal productivity of further investment in agriculture approaches zero. Frequent reports in the Chinese press of teams that attain high productivity but low income (*kao-ch'an ch'iung-tui*) or teams that increase output but not income (*tseng-ch'an pu tseng'shou*) confirm this condition.[6] Previously, Chinese authorities attributed this phenomenon to mismanagement. They stressed that by reduction of overhead expenses and careful planning, income could continue to rise with yields. Li Hsiennien, however, in his speech to the National Conference on Farmland Capital Construction, has finally admitted that poor management cannot take all the blame. In some cases, he reported, the principal cause of the failure of income to increase lay in the relatively high prices of agricultural inputs (machines, fertilizer, etc.) and the relatively low prices for agricultural produce.[7]

A former cadre from a county Agricultural Bureau in mountainous Kwangtung expressed this same problem in describing agricultural trends in his county in the 1970s. The following quotation is from a summary transcript of an interview with him:

During this period the distributable income tended to fall. Although output may have gone up, it was not enough to compensate for the increase in population and the cost of the extra inputs: capital construction, fertilizer, triple cropping, insecticides. In one unit the distribution fell from 0.60 yuan per labor day in 1970, to 0.55 in 1971, and to 0.50 in 1972. Many of the peasants do not feel that it is economical to use insecticides to combat insects. Although it will kill insects and save some of the crop, it is expensive and the benefits do not outweigh the cost. However, they are required to purchase and apply fertilizer and pesticides. If they do not, the county will accuse them of disrupting production, which is a very serious charge.[8]

A conditioning factor here reflects the role of machines in increasing yields. One of the few ways to raise yields dramatically is to increase the number of crops planted each year. In south China, this was accomplished without the aid of machines, since in the warm climate, growing seasons are long and bottleneck labor shortages not as severe. One emigré from near Canton remarked to me, "Even in busy season we are not all that busy."[9] In the Yangtze region, however, production teams must squeeze two crops of rice into a 210- to 220-day growing season. Without the aid of machines to speed up the harvest of the first crop and plowing and transplanting of the second, the yield of the second crop could be damaged severely, even to the extent that the total annual yield might fall below what they could achieve with a single crop.[10] In the absence of such pressing seasonal labor shortages, however, the introduction of machines has the immediate effect of displacing labor. If local administrators can find an alternate productive use for this labor, the unit may happily find its income increasing. If not, income may decline.

Factors leading to a declining marginal productivity of agricultural investment are largely beyond the control of local administrators. Rural cadres, however, play an important role in determining whether production teams will actually make the decision to invest in grain production and how they will use any displaced labor. This role is crucial because, based on scattered data on Kwangtung Province from emigrés interviewed in Hong Kong, the only teams able to maintain both increasing grain output and increasing income were those that had a lucrative sideline.[11] These units used the income from sidelines to pay for investments in grain production, where they lost money. Recent articles in the Chinese press confirm the crucial role of sideline production and brigade and commune enterprises, and state very clearly that units relying only on grain production cannot raise the investment funds necessary to support expanded yields.[12] Only by setting up lucrative enterprises at the local level and raising money can units afford to purchase cement, steel, and other inputs necessary for capital construction that will improve irrigation and drainage, or level fields. Even if agricultural investments would pay off, it appears that the marginal return on sideline investment is higher. Rural cadres must adopt administrative measures to encourage production teams to opt for less profitable alternatives so that they can meet rising grain-production targets.

The Party handles such conflicts of goal structures by promoting notions such as *i-liang-wei-kang, ch'uan-mien-fa-chan* (take grain as the key link and promote all-round development) and criticizing the abandonment of agriculture for sidelines. But it is up to local administrators—from the county down—to decide where to draw the line. Rather than passing the buck by telling team cadres simply to make the most effective use of their resources possible, higher-level cadres develop indicators by which they try to judge whether teams have in fact allocated their resources effectively. These indicators include team fulfillment of quotas, gross and per-unit yields, use of tractors for agricultural rather than transportation work, percentage of laborers in nonagricultural work, sideline enterprises based on a fixed ratio of land and labor, limitations of the percentage of team income from nonagricultural sources, or level of distributed income.

A case from interviews will illustrate both the potential internal inconsistency among these measures and the inconsistency with income-maximizing goals of teams.[13] In 1970, a production team in Kwangtung promoted an activist and capable rusticated youth to the position of team head. The team head introduced new sideline production and new planting techniques that resulted in increased income, as well as more investment in grain production. Grain output rose. To keep team members happy and encourage their enthusiasm for production, the team head used higher team income to increase members' personal income. The value of a day's labor rose to 1.5 yuan, significantly higher than the surrounding teams. In addition, since higher levels placed limitations on the amount of grain the team could distribute, our team head concealed actual grain yields and distributed the extra amount to team members. Even so, grain sales to the state continued to rise. The team head came under severe pressure from the commune to reduce the level of distribution more in line with surrounding teams, where, at a commune meeting of team heads, he was accused of being a "stubborn power holder." He nonetheless stuck to his guns and refused to lower the distribution. He explained, in an interview, that the commune tolerated his refusal because he was young and new at the job, and also since grain output had in fact increased dramatically. After several years of attempting to deal with contradictory demands on his performance he resolved the dilemma by resigning. Several years later, he fled to Hong Kong.

Before discussing goal divergence among functional systems, we might note that the attempt to regulate team activities by the promulgation of operating standards and monitoring compliance involves the simplest kind of coordination, since it is a response to pooled interdependence among teams. The high costs of achieving coordination here reflect not great organizational complexity but rather difficulties in assuring compliance caused mainly by divergent goal structures.

Horizontal Goal Divergence

The divergence of goals among administrators performing different functional tasks is reminiscent of the red versus expert dichotomy. Bankers may have little quarrel with Supply and Marketing Cooperative cadres, or with factory managers, but they frequently rank their priorities differently from the central line of administrative leadership. This central line refers to the hierarchy of administrative units, from the production team to Peking, whose jurisdiction is defined territorially.[14] The divergence, however, is not so much a conflict between ideologues and professionals (as implied in the red-expert dichotomy) as between territorial and functional administrators, or perhaps, generalists and specialists. Functional specialists define goals and evaluate performance in relatively narrow terms intrinsic to the function performed, using criteria such as profit, growth, sales, and so on. Territorial administrators display more concern with the contribution that functional specialists make to the achievement of broader goals. For example, banks and credit cooperatives can loan money with less risk and be assured of faster repayment on loans to nonagricultural enterprises while territorial administrators may place more emphasis on agricultural development. Factories lose money on the repair of agricultural machinery, yet unless they provide this service cheaply, generalists cannot realize the projected benefits of mechanization.

Local cadres, it appears, often report to higher-level administrators using the more narrow indicators of functional specialists. For example, local bureaus in charge of farmland capital construction may report glowing success by citing figures for the number of labor days used and number of cubic meters of stone moved, indicators that have no necessary direct relationship to the final goal of raising productivity. In August 1978, Chi Teng-k'uei criticized such reports, and pointed out that more appropriate indicators would be the amount of land irrigated or increases in yields.[15] It is not that territorial administrators will be opposed to having construction departments move many tons of earth or to having banks insist that loans be repaid, but rather they will want functional administrators to evaluate their work in terms of its contribution to larger concerns. The consequences of unresolved divergence between narrow operational targets and larger goals are waste and misallocation of resources, which can easily occur even when everything is operating smoothly from the point of view of each functional system. For example, due to the relative profitability of investment in subsidiary production, if banks used profitability as the sole criterion for loan approval, virtually no agricultural loans would be issued. What appears wasteful and less profitable from the bank's point of view may be the top priority of territorial administrators.[16]

While the regulation of team activities is primarily a response to pooled interdependence, the activities of functional specialists frequently involve the more complex forms of sequential and reciprocal interdependence. Sequential interdependence occurs, for example, when units rely on the Materials Bureau, the Commercial Bureau, or the Supply and Marketing Cooperative for the delivery of goods. Machinery and repair shops are reciprocally interdependent with users of the machines that they service. One informant described the organization of a large-scale construction project that pooled a variety of resources including labor from production teams, technicians from county bureaus and commune departments, and materials and finance from a variety of sources. Project leaders wrangled with production teams over labor supply, borrowed large amounts of money from the credit cooperative and the bank, upsetting loan plans, and drew a disproportionate amount of construction materials, forcing other departments to adjust their plans.[17]

Goal Pursuit and Outcomes

Contradictions among various goals cited are more than abstract potentials. Frequently, local administrators are under great pressure for high achievement on one indicator of goal attainment. Performance on single indicators can frequently be improved, even dramatically, but usually not without expense. Sometimes the expense shows up when county administrators sacrifice production team goal priorities to their own, and in doing so violate Party policy on administrative procedure. At times, administrators manage to reach their own goals and satisfy production teams, but only by violating other policies, such as state trading regulations. Much like the Soviet factory director who must cut corners to fulfill the plan (a phenomenon not unknown in Chinese factories), rural administrators must frequently choose the lesser of evils, or fudge reports in order to please their superiors.

In 1970, Kwangtung Province raised a slogan that the average per-*mou* yield of grain should surpass 1,000 *chin*. In one county, in response, the county first secretary, who was a military man, did not understand agriculture and promoted a distance of 3" by 4" [for transplanting rice seedlings]. He felt that the more you planted, the more would be harvested. He selected two communes where all teams were required to use this transplanting distance. . . . The actual yield per *mou* did not drop, but it was necessary to use 80% more seeds. In addition, the crops were relatively unhealthy and were easily affected by blights and insects, requiring greater expenditures on insecticides. Thus, it was not economical to plant so closely.[18]

Here the ambitious undertaking resulted in gains to none and loss to the production teams.

In other actions, the same county gained by increasing grain yields, but the standard of living of peasants suffered.

Again in 1970, with the provincial call to surpass 1,000 *chin* per *mou*, the county secretary ordered an expansion in the acreage of grain. He ordered that land already planted in peanuts, already sprouting, must be plowed under and changed to paddy land. Fruit groves were also cut back. The county sent out work teams to go to all of the production teams and order them to do it, since they knew that there would be some resistance to this move. They would stay in the production team until they had already changed the fields. The teams must implement this kind of order. The grain output for the county did increase for the year, but the output of economic crops dropped sharply. There developed shortages in food products, such as peanut oil.[19]

After this, the county gave up on its big pushes to improve yields.

While such ill-advised policies are probably the exception rather than the rule, the example cited is not isolated. In another county closer to Canton, the county issued a directive requiring teams to cut back on their sideline activities in order to increase grain output. In one team where most income came from raising fish and other sidelines, income dropped dramatically. (The informant, who was an accountant, reported from memory that the drop was from 1.80 yuan to .80 yuan per day.)[20]

Moreover, a series of disclosures in 1978 has shown that even China's national models, their well-publicized Tachai-type counties, have had to cut corners to achieve highly visible results. The *People's Daily* has published many such disclosures in response to the campaign to study the experience of Hsiang Hsiang County in Hunan. While the campaign attacks a range of administrative malfeasance that results in "unreasonable" burdens on the peasants, one theme criticizes overly ambitious capital construction projects that do not result in immediate increases in distributable income, and the appropriation of team labor without adequate compensation.[21] In August 1977, Tung-p'ing County in Shantung received national attention for its ambitious response to the 1975 National Conference to Study Tachai.[22] It developed long-range, large-scale projects to improve its water control system. Even in 1977, its cadres emphasized opposition to polices that treated teams equally and arbitrarily transferred labor (*i-p'ing erh-tiao*). But in July 1978, Tung-p'ing's Party secretary admitted that they had achieved their success at the expense of certain Party policies. They didn't pay enough attention to the principles of mutual advantage and imposed too large a burden on commune members. In the first year of their project, commune members throughout the county greeted the project with great enthusiasm, but as the burdens continued with no quick results, enthusiasm declined in the second and third years.[23] In Tai-an County, county cadres did not listen to the opinions of the masses, tied up too much labor on a large project, some of which was not properly compensated for, and caused income to fall in places.[24]

Other advanced counties have violated different policies to gain their results. At the national conference on agricultural field construction, held from July to August 1978, participants asked the Party secretary from Wu-hsi County in Suchou how they managed to assemble so much construction material for their projects. The secretary responded that one-third came from the state distribution, one-third came from local processing factories, and one-third came from cooperative arrangements. At this remark, the provincial secretary guffawed and pointed out that so-called cooperative arrangements referred to improper material exchanges with outside units. Wu-hsi had been trading agricultural sideline products for factory goods from other areas.[25] Circulation of materials outside of state plans has come under recent attack in a *People's Daily* editorial,[26] which argued that plans are not met because of the practice. (It neglects the possibility that at times plans cannot be met *without* such deals.)

Hunan's model county An-hsiang experienced a fall in grain output in 1975, yet failed to report it properly to the province. In order to sell enough grain to the province to cover the gap, they made extra ad hoc procurements from lower units. The extra procurements had the effect of dampening the peasants' enthusiasm and lowering production outputs even further in 1976 and 1977 (according to the *People's Daily* analysis). Finally, the province discovered the discrepancy and the Party secretary, newly appointed in 1975, made a tearful self-criticism and vowed to reform. Now the county has been transformed into a model of how to correct past errors.[27]

The whole problem of negative consequences resulting from the pursuit of single goal indicators has received the clearest treatment in a series of articles about whether it is possible to accomplish "great things" while observing Party policy. Chi Teng-k'uei pinpointed the dilemma for local administrators by noting that many of them are afraid of three things: (1) that they will have to appropriate labor equally among teams and not repay them properly; (2) that if they start a project they will not have enough money or materials; (3) that there will be mistakes and others will criticize them.[28] The *People's Daily* concluded that great things *are* possible within the scope of Party policy, but they are clearly on the defensive and repeat that many cadres hold "incorrect," opposing opinions on the issue.[29]

I suggest that in these cases, when China's leaders exhort officials to observe policy, they have in mind something very similar to our notion of coordination, namely, that individual units be able to achieve at least minimally acceptable results on indicators basic to their own operation. For example, production teams must be able to increase income from the benefits of projects to which they contribute labor. Party policy when used in this way, refers to the detailed regulations that govern the operation of its rural institutions, principally, the Sixty Articles on Agriculture. The Sixty Articles give each level of administration a measure of autonomy with regard to the allocation of its resources. At the lowest levels, in particular, this was clearly designed to give them an incentive to use resources effectively and not squander them. Higher-level officials are much more inclined to engage in uneconomic undertakings since their personal incomes are not affected by the success or failure of projects. To prevent such uneconomic decisions, higher-level administrators are supposed to elicit support for large-scale projects by persuasion. Units voluntarily commit resources in proportion to the benefit they will receive from the project, and receive pay for labor where they receive no benefit. Production teams or other units will allow themselves to fall below these minimum acceptable standards of achievement if they have control over their own commitments. In other words, Party policy, in order to achieve coordination, calls for administrators to observe procedural rules by which team leaders are permitted to calculate the benefit they will receive from a project and refuse to send labor. This theme in the Chinese press addresses a recurrent administrative problem: Pressures for dynamic leadership cause administrators to ignore rules designed to preserve basic institutional integrity.

The student of organization theory may notice here a curious reversal of a well-known organizational disease found in the West: goal displacement. Robert Merton pointed out that because of the pressures of bureaucratic life and the need for stability and security, bureaucrats frequently become attached to administrative means—procedures and rules—in such a way as to prevent the organization from attaining overall goals.[30] The organization becomes more committed to maintaining itself

129

and its habitual way of operating than to attaining the ends for which it was originally set up. This phenomenon is the root cause of red tape and the origin of the common pejorative connotations of bureaucratism (also present in Chinese, *kuan-liao chu-i*). But if this analysis is correct, Chinese local administration seems prone to precisely the opposite bureaucratic dysfunction. Pursuit of dramatic, highly visible goals upsets procedural norms and may lead to organizational breakdown. To understand why, we need to look more closely at actual problems of coordination found in local administration. The inconsistency in goals that we perceive does not deter administrators from taking action. They must find ways to achieve in spite of multiple and inconsistent pressures placed on them. Thus, we now return to the nationally promulgated goal of mechanizing agriculture.

Coordination and Goal Attainment

To achieve coordination in the mechanization program, local administrators must assemble resources from a variety of functional systems and levels of administration. I shall review here briefly five areas of resource control and allocation and provide generalizations concerning the dominant mode of communication involved in decision making for each resource. Due to space limitations, it will not be possible to present detailed descriptions of the decision-making process for each case.[31] Five areas clearly of central concern are finance, technology, repair and use of machines, distribution of materials, and construction and management of infrastructural supports (e.g., water or electricity supply). My aim is to see which resources require coordination among different administrative levels, especially involving production team cooperation, and which resources involve coordination among functional systems.

Mobilizing finance involves coordination of both vertical and horizontal organs. Questions of loans from credit cooperatives and banks involve either decisions following routine procedures where demands for loans do not exceed planned loan targets for a particular category, or negotiations among cadres from administrative units (i.e., those with territorial jurisdictions) and cadres from the financial system. Such negotiations are necessary, since to lend money in excess of planned targets it is necessary to reduce targets in other categories or draw money from nontargeted funds to which everyone, in principle, has an equal claim. Frequently, funds for agricultural mechanization involve the latter kind of decision, because tractors and other industrial goods can be expensive. Where routine procedures can be followed, the interdependence between administrative units and financial institutions is sequential, and is handled primarily by planning. These plans are the province of higher administrative units. (Probably higher than the county for setting general targets, but evidence on this point is murky.) When loans exceed targets, interdependence becomes reciprocal among administrative units and the financial institution, requiring coordination by mutual adjustment. Cadres resolve these coordination problems by meeting and negotiating among themselves. The following quotation from an interview with a commune cadre illustrates the kind of problems involved and the means of dealing with them:

> At one point the commune Construction Headquarters wanted to purchase a hydroelectric generator that cost 10,000 yuan. The commune credit cooperative, however, reported that it could only lend 2,000 yuan, so the Headquarters appealed to the commune revolutionary committee to help solve their problem. The commune then ordered the credit cooperative to lend them 5,000 yuan, but this was still not enough. The commune Headquarters then went to the county Construction Headquarters for help. The county then sent someone down to "mobilize" (tung-yuan) the commune credit cooperative into lending the money. The credit cooperative complained that it would tie up too much of their funds, but they eventually came up with 8,000 yuan, which was still not enough. Finally, they had to go to the county credit cooperative (which is part of the bank), for the other 2,000 yuan.[32]

Investment funds from the budgets of administrative units, from the production team to the county, are not amassed, generally, by the upward transfer of funds. If teams or brigades pool funds to purchase machines, they generally establish something akin to ownership rights in the property. Decisions of this nature are, again, made by cadres in meetings, but their decisions are more constricted if they use production team funds, since the reaction of team members to large investments may be negative. If team members are actually consulted on individual decisions (I have no direct evidence on this point, although it seems likely from what is known about how teams operate), then the issue would naturally arise during the regular team meetings held to discuss production and political questions.

Downward transfers of funds for capital construction from counties to communes, and from communes to brigades and teams, are common practice. Use of such funds is contingent on approval by the higher level on a project-by-project basis, and the higher-level cadres will meet among themselves to review and decide on a proposed project.

Dissemination of technology involves primarily the downward flow of information on how to apply fertilizer and pesticides, how to use machines, techniques involved in improved seed varieties, how and when to weed. (I shall not examine the infrequent upward flows occasioned by local innovations.) The transfer of information usually takes place at meetings of team agricultural specialists (vice heads, heads, or team agricultural technicians) at the commune or the county. Usually county and commune Agricultural Bureau and Department cadres encourage teams to adopt new techniques based on demonstrated effectiveness. The degree of implied or explicit sanction involved in pressuring to adopt new techniques varies by administrative unit. In its most explicit form, in some places, county officials at county-level meetings inform team cadres that, should they refuse to use the technique and experience crop failure, the county will not send relief grain (only counties can make this decision). In a milder form, commune and county officials will pressure teams to try the technique experimentally before wholesale adoption. In other cases, higher officials simply supply information but make no effort to pressure teams to make use of it. Thus, while dissemination of technology takes place at cadre meetings, the actual adoption of new methods depends on team compliance. Since the nature of interdependence here is pooled, the method of coordination among teams involves standardization of techniques, such as setting transplanting distances between rice seedlings, or fixing when to flood and drain fields.

All three levels of the commune may own agricultural machines, but there is scattered evidence that as the number of tractors and larger machines increases, more and more of them are owned at lower levels, especially the brigade.[33] This makes sense since putting them at a lower level of ownership facilitates effective use in farming.[34] In Kwantung, some teams own their own hand tractors. Throughout the 1970s, the Chinese press has continued to address the problems involved in repair of machinery, focusing on three areas. First, machines are poorly made and break down frequently. Second, users of machines do not maintain them properly, causing waste. Third, repair costs are too high and repair services are poorly coordinated with users' needs. The first problem is largely beyond the control of local administrators. The nationally publicized solution to it, however, is to impose strict industrial standards, quality control, and also to make factories bear the costs of selling substandard machines. The second problem, training tractor drivers, presents few problems of coordination. The brigades must delegate peasants for training (and pay for it), and the communes or counties must organize classes, but once the labor force is trained, little coordination is required. As for repair services, many counties have set policies that require commune repair shops to operate at a loss, and communes make up the difference from general revenues. The county's ability to enforce such a directive over a long period clearly indicates the relative responsiveness of communes to higher-level control. This is another form of standardized rule enforcement.

More complex coordination of repair services and allocation of machinery occurs during the agricultural busy season. In the press, one reads of commune repair technicians who set up roving repair teams to work on machines in the field. Others, where repair shops also handle manufacturing jobs, cut back on that work to handle increased flows of broken machinery. These changes in work organization clearly result from the decisions of administrative cadres on the level that owns the shops. Where joint ownership of machines or joint use of machines owned by single units occurs, the units schedule their plowing or harvesting, which handles their sequential interdependence. Where fewer units are involved in sharing, however, schedules may be unnecessary, since the costs of constant communication for mutual adjustment of operations are relatively low. Nonetheless, in both cases cadres make decisions in meetings. In some places, communes have attempted to maximize the use of machines owned by lower units by centralizing plans for use during busy seasons. While such a high level of organization may be effective for communes that own few machines, where machines are more common, such a method of coordination would appear to involve extremely high costs in administration and also to be likely to decrease use while trying to fit the vagaries of local agricultural needs into a unified plan. Nonetheless, for cases where machine use is widespread, but isolated machines in short supply, such a system might increase use. Coordination for the use of agricultural machines involves meetings of cadres to draw up schedules and adjust plans.

The supply of materials is generally handled by functional systems, the Materials Bureau, the Commercial Bureau, and the Supply and Marketing Cooperative, but administrative units make decisions on the allocation of short-supply goods. Thus, the Supply and Marketing Cooperatives handle the transportation of fertilizer to the commune or brigade branch, but each administrative level decides how much fertilizer the unit beneath it will receive. (Frequently, counties or communes impose rules on lower units for allocating fertilizer, such as amount per unit of arable land.) The supply of fertilizer, pesticides, and seeds presents a relatively easy distribution problem, since even though they are in short supply, these goods are easily divisible. Allocation takes place by plan, based on decisions of cadres in meetings.

The distribution of nondivisible goods (e.g., tractors) or goods used in nondivisible quantities (e.g., it is futile to start building a canal with less than 20 tons of cement) is more complex. Generally, plans for the distribution of such goods extend down to the county level, and below that level are decided on a case-by-case basis. This has the effect of giving counties great discretion in selecting the priority of construction projects (and the temptation to disregard constraints imposed by other types of resources). The distribution of construction materials is the object of great politicking and shady commercial transactions, as when cadres trade goods through the back door, sometimes involving illegal grain or oil transactions.[35] The prescribed method for using such nondivisible goods is to follow long-range plans drawn up by the county to integrate individual construction plans of subordinate units. Units can, in effect, set plans for future investment, labor allocation, and income. When lower-level units need such materials, they submit requisitions to county authorities. Based on these requisitions, county cadres decide among themselves in meetings how to allocate materials. One informant described the process in his county:

> The county Materials Bureau will take the materials requisition form from each commune and submit it to the county Party committee office for approval. The county Party committee office usually respects the opinion of the Materials Bureau and approves its decision. Sometimes the commune will not have enough money for the purchase, and the county will consider whether to lend the money. . . . The county Party committee office will not conduct a careful investigation [to see if the commune really needs the material]. In the process of approval, sometimes personal relationships [between county and commune cadres] will affect the decision, but only for materials that are not expensive, such as motors.[36]

The construction of infrastructural supports to agriculture involves the most complex form of planning, since it requires many of the resources already considered—finance, technology, machines, and materials—as well as another resource—labor. (Labor could also be considered a disguised financial procurement from the teams when not paid for.) To handle all the interdependencies frequently encountered in construction, counties and communes set up ad hoc project task forces composed of experts drawn from various levels of administration and functional systems. These task forces cannot operate without the support of normal administrative units, and they are frequently invested with great power to draw labor from production teams, borrow large amounts of money (if they earn income; if not, they receive grants), and consume great quantities of materials. Planning for these projects is especially difficult because of the interplay between resource availability and opportunity cost. I suspect that county planners want to make the maximum feasible use of topographical opportunities that might call for very large projects beyond the capabilities of other resources under their control. After all, why not go for the big reservoir first, instead of the series of smaller projects where each has a relatively small payoff? County and commune officials can simplify planning problems by committing financial and material resources (and winking at expediters who purchase materials through the back door). But in principle, every team that commits labor to these projects must be convinced on the basis of equal benefit or fee for service. Fee for service is very expensive; equal benefit is difficult to calculate and establish. Construction projects may need constant amounts of labor, but agricultural labor needs fluctuate. Not only this, even if the proportional contribution of team labor matches its benefit from the project, excess labor extractions can have the effect of increasing the number of workpoints awarded in any one year and reducing the value of a day's labor. Frequently, because such projects do not pay off immediately or the return on investments of labor is not high, they are planned by cadres in meetings and labor is requisitioned without consulting teams. Most informants described such requisitions as *chih-shih* (directives) or *ming-ling* (orders). In many wealthy, highly commercialized Pearl River delta counties, peasants receive a substantial wage for participation in these projects, and production teams benefit from the portion that they must return to pay for their workpoints. Reports in the press, however, seem to indicate that in poorer regions, administrators caught in a bind between pressure to complete projects rapidly and inadequate resources choose to take the easiest route out—let production teams shoulder the burden.

Methods of Communication

How does the county means of coordination relate to its overall communication system? The system of decision making already described does not centrally involve China's most famous means of communication—study groups, work teams, mass meetings, *tun tien*,[37] or radio networks—for several reasons. First, many of the messages carried by these channels do not always have any clear operational content. They may serve purposes such as raising spirit and enthusiasm, or collective vigilance against enemies, but, if received, have only indirect effects on unit behavior. Even should a message imply action by the individual, it is not clear that exposure to mass media directly affects behavior. Parish and Whyte found that variable exposure to such communication did not generally correlate with social change in the direction encouraged by Party policy. Other variables served as better predictors of such changes.[38]

Second, when aimed at unit behavior, these means of communication aim to improve single unit performance. The target is to solve problems of pooled interdependence, and the intent, broadly conceived, is to promote standardization, namely, to encourage the unit to adhere to promulgated norms that may be more or less specific. For example, cadres may be sent to *tun tien* in units that deviate from norms encouraging limitations on private production, or sideline production, or, more frequently, have problems such as corruption or ineffectual leadership. The common practice of sending down higher-level cadres in

135

work teams is primarily targeted at leadership problems, as during the Four Clean-ups movement,[39] although sometimes higher levels dispatch teams to add punch to a new policy initiative, such as family planning.

In addition to the effect on the local unit, however, the *People's Daily* frequently points out that going down on work teams or to *tun tien* has beneficial effects on participating cadres. By working at the basic levels, they will come to understand the output of the bureaucracies that they head, and this greater understanding may enable them to serve as better administrators. Such experience promotes problem identification and may suggest solutions. In view of the complex problems of coordination in higher levels alone and consequent busy schedules of reports and meetings, it is easy to see why without such practices higher-level cadres might overlook detailed problems at the local level. Although it is difficult to assess the importance of this method of communication, it clearly provides an input that facilitates coordinating policy with local level considerations. Such investigations did not appear in the discussion of specific problems of coordination since their input to the process usually occurs at an earlier stage, where broad policies are considered. For example, a county official working in a production brigade discovered a successful interplanting technique that was later popularized around his county.[40] But the fact that many county cadres are now under criticism for "failing to consider the views of the masses" and initiating projects that place "unreasonable" burdens on the peasants would indicate that most decisions to initiate large projects do not incorporate these grassroots views. Upward flows of information from work teams that affect policy play the greatest role in fine tuning the system of rules that govern the internal operation of the teams, that is, adjusting standardized norms with which higher levels expect teams to comply. Such norms may include workpoint systems (*p'ing-kung* versus *pao-kung*),[41] or, as in the example cited, planting techniques. But the system of local investigations and *tun tien* appears to have relatively little input for decisions concerning the complex interdependencies encountered in the mechanization process, as outlined earlier.

Communication and Coordination: Conclusions

In conclusion, I shall draw together diverse points about goals, interdependence, communication, and coordination. Communication can be thought of as an administrative cost, incurred in the search for coordination, which tends to increase when organizations experience more complex forms of interdependence, and also when interdependent units have divergent goal perceptions, since compliance becomes a problem. In China's case, as mechanization proceeds, local administrative systems encounter more and more complex forms of reciprocal and sequential interdependence among different subunits, some of which have divergent perceptions about their goals. Consequently, the cost of coordination increases rapidly, often outstripping the capacity of the local administrative system.

But, as can be seen from the discussion of the different resources involved in the mechanization process, the capacity of the administration is more adequate for some areas than others. Counties have a tendency to centralize control over resources at higher administrative levels and use their greater authority to allocate them. Where resources could not be centralized because constituent units need continuous access to the resource (e.g., tractors or finance), cadres at a lower level met to formulate plans, and to make compromises and adjustments in their own activities. In spite of the possible divergences of goal perceptions between administrative units and functional specialists, both seemed ready to compromise and agree on concrete plans. Apparently, higher administrators within functional systems have given their subordinates sufficient leeway to adjust to the demands of cadres from administrative units, and, when faced with limited capacity on the part of functional specialists, administrative units will lower their sights. These adjustments may involve rancorous negotiations and political maneuvering, but once a decision is reached, unforeseen negative consequences are relatively unimportant and the issue is, more or less, settled. (There are areas of greater contention between administrative units and functional systems, but they are not so important as far as the specific goal of agricultural mechanization is concerned.)

But for some kinds of tasks, especially large-scale projects, the prospect of allowing all units involved to hammer out workable compromises in negotiation is simply not feasible. If, as outlined in the Sixty Articles on Agriculture, counties (with an average of 2,500 teams) and communes (with an average of 100 teams) negotiated with individual teams on the basis of equal exchange and voluntarism for commitments of labor, the costs in administration would be enormous. Consequently, many higher-level cadres simply requisition team labor in standardized quotas without regard for differential impact on the teams' economy, thus, in effect, exerting centralized control over labor as well as finance and materials.

Although recent *People's Daily* articles have criticized them, in the short run such practices may be an effective means for higher-level administrators to achieve some measurable success on high-priority goals. Over time, however, costs may outweigh benefits if high requisitions of labor have a negative impact on team performance. The situation described here reveals one of the few cases where teams have a reciprocal interdependence with higher authorities. The administrative costs are especially high because of the great number of units with differing situations on which higher levels depend, as well as because of the fragile incentive structure and differing goal perceptions of team members. For this reason cadres complain they cannot accomplish "big

137

things" without violating the team's autonomy. In other words, coordination cannot be achieved by using available methods of communication.

China's leaders have not simply given up, but the current strategy advocates longer-run development designed *not* to make the team more pliable, highly integrated, and thus subject to efforts to overcome problems of complex interdependence. China's leaders have chosen instead to make team cooperation increasingly irrelevant to the performance of complex tasks by developing greater resources available to higher levels of administration that do not depend on team cooperation. The current strategy stresses rapid growth of profitable small-scale enterprises at these levels. Income from these enterprises is to be used to support permanent labor brigades for construction. Brigades and communes will also purchase machinery, in effect subsidizing the modernization of Chinese agriculture for teams that cannot afford it themselves.

While this strategy will reduce the more complex forms of reciprocal and sequential interdependence involving teams, and thus reduce administrative costs, these developments will not eliminate the pooled aspect of team interdependence. All teams continue to make valuable contributions that serve the overall goals of higher administrators. As James D. Thompson points out, organizations tend to handle pooled interdependence by standardization.[42] The degree to which higher administrators might standardize team management in China has always been limited by the intensive nature of agriculture. From local blights to complicated lineage conflicts, too many unpredictable things happen in production teams to infringe too far on their decision-making autonomy. Nonetheless, higher levels have already introduced an impressive array of rules with which they expect teams to comply. The supposed periodic swings between emphasis on team autonomy and emphasis on team responsiveness to higher-level demands do not reflect a dichotomy between rules and no rules, but rather an effort to determine whether teams must comply with certain controversial rules in a context where they already must comply with a large body of accepted ones.

While China's leaders will undoubtedly keep most of these standardized rules in effect, there are indications that they are reevaluating the effectiveness of certain controversial ones and are considering an entirely different strategy. Rather than relying primarily on "administrative management," there is talk now of shifting toward "economic management."[43] Economic management would involve the manipulation of prices in such a way that teams would be offered an economic inducement to comply with planners' preferences. When higher levels cause teams to lose because of ill-advised administrative controls, teams might be given rights to sue for redress of damages. In other words, a controlled market may replace bureaucratic controls.

How such a system would operate in practice is not entirely clear, but consideration of these alternatives reveals clearly that China's leaders have recognized that the communication and coordination capacity of their own administrative system is limited. As modernization proceeds and interdependencies among large numbers of administrative subunits grow more complex, these limitations are likely to be felt with increasing severity, making market manipulation strategies more and more appealing.[44]

NOTES

I thank Andrew J. Nathan and Tang Tsou for helpful comments on an earlier draft of this chapter, and gratefully acknowledge support during preparation from the University of Chicago's research project "Political Leadership and Social Change in China at the Local Level from 1850 to the Present," which is funded by a grant from the National Endowment for the Humanities.

1. Amitai Etzioni, *Modern Organizations* (Englewood Cliffs, NJ: Prentice-Hall, 1964), p. 16.

2. James Thompson, *Organizations in Action* (New York: McGraw-Hill, 1967), pp. 54–55.

3. Personal communication.

4. See informants no. 10 and no. 12. Some of the data for this chapter are drawn from a series of interviews conducted in Hong Kong in 1977 with emigrés from China. References to these interviews include a number for each informant, a letter for each interview session, and page numbers of the session transcript.

5. See, for example, *Jen-min Jih-pao* [People's Daily], 10 July 1978.

6. For example, *People's Daily*, 10 July 1978.

7. *People's Daily*, 16 August 1978.

8. Interview 18Cp1.

9. Interview 3Cp4.

10. See discussion by Shigeru Ishikawa, "The Question of China's Agricultural Mechanization," *Ni-chu keizai kyokai kaiho* [Bulletin of the Japan-China Association on Economy and Trade] 58 (April 1978).

11. See Steven Bailey Butler, "Conflict and Decision Making in China's Rural Administration, 1969–76" (Ph.D. dissertation, Columbia University, 1980).

12. *People's Daily*, 23 July 1978.

13. Informant no. 10.

14. Chinese administrators may not accept the application of the term *hsing-cheng tan-wei* (administrative unit) to the production team or brigade, preferring to refer to them as *sheng-ch'an tan-wei* (production units). I have given the term a more precise definition than might be warranted by its common usage. For a more detailed description of these administrative terms, see Butler, "Conflict and Decision Making."

15. *People's Daily*, 18 August 1978.

16. This, of course, reflects the overall imbalance of the price structure, for which local administrators are not responsible. This imbalance appears difficult to eliminate, making it impossible to use profit as a criterion for deciding on economic priorities.

17. See 17H and 17L.

18. Interview 18Bp1.

19. Interview 18Bp4.

20. Interview 3Ap6.

21. *People's Daily*, 5 July 1978.

22. *People's Daily*, 10 August 1977.

23. *People's Daily*, 26 July 1978.

24. *People's Daily*, 30 July 1978.

25. *People's Daily*, 26 July 1978.

26. *People's Daily*, 8 July 1978.

27. *People's Daily*, 17 July 1978.

28. *People's Daily*, 18 August 1978.

29. *People's Daily*, 6 July 1978.

30. For a summary of this concept, see Etzioni, *Modern Organizations*, p. 12.

31. For a more detailed discussion, see Butler, "Conflict and Decision Making."

32. Interview 17Jp7.

33. See Steven Butler, *Agricultural Mechanization in China: The Administrative Impact* (New York: Occasional Papers of the East Asian Institute, Columbia University, 1978), p. 25.

34. For a discussion of this point in a broader context, see Benedict Stavis, *The Politics of Agricultural Mechanization in China* (Ithaca, NY: Cornell University Press, 1978).

35. See Steven Butler, "China's Host of Buying Agents Patch Up Oversights of Planning," *The Asian Wall Street Journal* (Hong Kong), 25 July 1978.

36. Interview 16Hp18.

37. *Tun tien* literally means "squatting on a point." It is a leadership method by which higher-level cadres stay at a basic-level unit for a period of time in order to discover and solve problems.

38. William L. Parish and Martin King Whyte, *Village and Family in Contemporary China* (Chicago: University of Chicago Press, 1978).

39. During the Four Clean-ups movement, which took place around 1964, teams of higher-level cadres entered production teams in order to root out a variety of management and leadership problems.

141

40. New China News Agency, 13 February 1977, in *Survey of the People's Republic of China Press*, 6284, 22 February 1977.

41. *P'ing-kung* is a system of awarding workpoints based on a time rate, while *pao-kung* is a system that awards workpoints according to tasks completed.

42. Thompson, *Organizations in Action*, p. 56.

43. These alternatives have been discussed in various articles in *Ching-chi Yen-chiu* [Economic Research] beginning in September 1978. Also see Hu Chiao-mu's three-part article "Observe Economic Laws, Speed Up the Four Modernizations," *Peking Review*, 10 November 1978, pp. 7–12; 17 November 1978, pp. 15–23; 24 November 1978, pp. 13–21.

44. This conclusion concurs with James Thompson's hypothesis that in the face of "intensive interdependence" among large numbers of organizations, the hierarchically structured, classical Weberian bureaucracy becomes increasingly unwieldy as a means of exercising control. The hypothesized response is that organizations will be erected whose sole responsibility is to manipulate environments to induce desired organizational response. He offers the Federal Reserve Board as an example of such an organization in the United States. See James Thompson, "Social Interdependence, the Policy, and Public Administration," *Administration and Society* 6 (May 1974):3–20.

7

Peasant Interest Articulation and Work Teams in Rural China: 1962–1974

John P. Burns

The study of communication and control in complex organizations has received considerable attention in Western organization theory.[1] As one study of bureaucratic behavior points out, "the methods used by the organization to collect, select, and transmit information are critically important determinants of its behavior."[2]

Superiors in large complex organizations are dependent on the upward transmission of information from subordinates within a hierarchy of authority. In the process of transmission, however, messages are often distorted, as Downs has pointed out.[3] To limit distortion, superiors in complex organizations employ a variety of means, one of which Downs has called the "by-pass"—that is, higher levels bypassing middlemen and going directly to lower levels in the search for reliable information. This function is performed by *kung-tso tui* (work teams) in rural China.[4]

Although work teams do function to collect information and obtain compliance—the functions of a by-pass, according to Downs—in rural China, they also serve as channels for demand making by lower levels, either passing peasant demands up the hierarchy, or making changes on the spot in response to interests articulated by peasants.

In the study of Chinese politics, the focus has been on the work team as a means of policy implementation and mass mobilization, especially during Land Reform, and the Four Clean-ups campaign.[5] This study differs from previous work in looking at work teams in terms of Chinese peasant interest articulation.[6] The point here is not how work teams implement policy and mobilize the peasantry, but rather how they receive, transmit, and act on the demands of peasants. In this chapter, then, I shall consider work teams sent to brigades and production teams as structures for the articulation of peasant interests in rural China.

Work teams receive peasant demands and often either act on them to make changes on the spot, or report them back to higher levels. Work teams are most receptive to peasant demands when the policy being carried out by the work team coincides with peasants' perceived interests. Although such a coincidence of interest has characterized both campaign and noncampaign periods in rural China, peasants have more often used work teams as a channel for interest articulation during noncampaign periods. If a work team is carrying out a campaign, especially a nationwide campaign, it will tend to be composed of outsiders, thus using the *san-t'ung* (Three Togethers) procedures, which, as we shall see, facilitate the articulation of peasant interests.[7] Second, the setting, whether campaign or noncampaign, affects peasant willingness to speak out and the incidence of peasant-initiated demand making. Both tend to increase in the noncampaign situation. Finally, other variables, such as the internal cohesion of the work teams and the status of the place being investigated (is it a "key point" or a "model"?) will tend to influence the ease with which peasants make demands of higher levels through work teams.[8]

This chapter, consisting of a series of case studies, is restricted in several ways. First, it considers only the period 1962–1974, a period chosen because of its relative institutional stability in the countryside. The narrow time frame is also necessary because the study relies heavily on emigré reports, and informants' memories of events before the early 1960s are less reliable than for more recent periods. Second, the chapter analyzes work teams dispatched to production teams and brigades. Although work teams were sent to every level of the administrative and Party hierarchy by higher levels (e.g., by the national levels to the county), I am concerned here only with those that came to the village levels. It is these work teams that come in direct contact with peasants and serve as a structure for peasant interest articulation.

Work teams may be defined as groups of two or more cadres organized at one level of the government or Party to go down temporarily to lower levels in order to investigate and report on conditions there, supervise the implementation of policy, and solve problems as they arise on the spot. In this sense, work teams are to be distinguished from *tiao-ch'a tui* (investigation teams), which are sent to lower levels to report back to their organizing unit on conditions there, but which do not have the power to make on-the-spot changes.[9]

Although undoubtedly investigation teams report peasant demands to higher levels, the content of these reports is in general not publicly available.[10] Where, however, investigation teams or cadres sent down to local levels have made changes on the spot (that is, have behaved like work teams), they have been included in this study.

Chinese Policy toward Work Teams

There are both theoretical and practical reasons for the existence of work teams in China. Mao's theory of leadership requires that leaders conduct investigations before they make policy: "No investigation, no right to speak."[11] Moreover, some part of these investigations is to be made personally by cadres.

Everyone with responsibility for given leadership . . . must personally undertake investigation into the specific social and economic conditions and not merely rely on reading reports. For investigation and reading reports are two entirely different things.[12]

Mao's effort to "combine leading with learning,"[13] and thus minimize bureaucratism among officials, has been summarized in the theory of the mass line, of which the work team is a manifestation.[14] Not only is one of its primary functions investigative, but the work team is specifically designed to put leaders directly into local situations.

Work teams also fill a practical need in rural China where leaders of local work units—the commune, brigade, and production team—are almost all local people. The team and brigade leaders live in these units with their families, and although they receive extra workpoints, their income is tied to production team income. Commune cadres often have been recruited from brigades in the commune, and almost all of them are from the same county. Work teams sent to these units from the county and above, then, form a valuable checking and control function.[15] Where work unit leaders are assigned from outside and paid out of state funds, as occurs in the rural Soviet Union, work teams are less frequently required to perform these functions.[16]

Although the sending of work teams "has been recognized as the proper means of organization in every movement since Liberation in 1949," as Liu Shao-ch'i explained during the Cultural Revolution, work team policy has not been free of controversy.[17] In fact, Liu's own experience in a Land Reform work team led him to be critical of work team methods in P'ing-shang.[18] Work teams continued to be controversial, as Lowell Dittmer has pointed out. In 1956, although Mao approved of the dispatch of work teams to the countryside, it was only with reservations: "Work teams must be sent, but it must be stated very clearly that they are being sent to help local party organizations, not to replace them."[19] Mao was aware of the tension that has often existed between local-level cadres and work teams, and thus gave less than an enthusiastic endorsement of their use.

From 1962 to 1974, work teams were sent to local levels for the Socialist Education campaign (1962–1966); the Four Clean-ups campaign (1964–1966); the Cultural Revolution (1966–1969); the Cleaning Up Class Ranks campaign (1969–1970); the Campaign to Rectify and Rebuild the Party (1970); the Criticizing Lin Piao and Confucius campaign (1973–1975); and the Campaign to Study Tachai (1969–1974).[20] On two occasions, however, first, the method used by work teams, and second, the existence of work teams themselves, came under attack.

There was intense conflict over the goals of the Socialist Education campaign, which was reflected in the struggle over work team methods. In the end, Mao came to see them as obstructionists:

> In short, we must rely on the masses, not the work teams. The work team either does not understand the situation or is ignorant. Some of them have become bureaucratic and obstruct the movement. Some of the persons on the work teams are not dependable.[21]

Work teams again became an issue for their role in the Cultural Revolution when they were sent out to schools and factories in urban areas by provincial authorities in defiance of directives from Peking.[22] By 1970, however, work teams had once again become legitimate, and they remained so throughout the rest of the period.[23]

What effect elite attacks on work teams had for peasant interest articulation is difficult to determine, either because the data are not available, or the work teams were sent to urban areas, thus lying beyond the scope of this chapter. More important than the work team's legitimacy for peasant interest articulation, however, seems to have been whether it was carrying out a policy that coincided with peasants' perceived interests. Nonetheless, it is likely that attacks on work teams while they were in the field would diminish the work teams' authority in the eyes of the peasants. Peasants might be less willing to talk to them, and the work teams themselves might be inhibited either from taking action on the spot or from reporting peasant demands up to higher levels.

From the Chinese leadership's point of view, work teams are sent to lower levels not only to investigate and report back local conditions and to discover and solve problems in the course of implementing policy, but also to "come to share the thoughts and feelings" of commune members. In this sense, it was completely legitimate for them to report back the real attitudes of peasants and to make policy and personnel changes in the interests of peasants.[24] Peasant interest articulation via work teams was, then, legitimate for most of the period from 1962–1974.

The following four case studies demonstrate that work teams have been receptive to peasant demand making when the policy being implemented by the work team coincided with peasants' perceived interests. Two cases each of "issue coincidence" and "issue divergence" are offered here. Issue coincidence for our purposes means that the policy being implemented by the work team coincides with the perceived interests of peasants. Where the policies being pursued by the work team run counter to the perceived interests of peasants, we refer to issue divergence. To support my earlier contention that whether or not a work team is carrying out a campaign is important for its receptiveness to peasant demand making, both "campaign" and "noncampaign" work team case studies are included in the following discussion.

146

The distinction between campaign and noncampaign work teams rests on the fact that only some work teams are charged with carrying out specific campaigns. Even if there is constant campaigning at the national level, not all activity at all levels is devoted to carrying out the campaigns. From 1962 to 1974, work teams were sent out to implement seven campaigns, as we saw earlier. They were not, however, sent to production teams and brigades for two other campaigns: the Three Loyalties campaign (*san-chung yun-tung*) in 1969, and the One-Hit Three-Oppose campaign (*yi-ta san-fan yun-tung*) in 1971.[25]

During this period, thousands of work teams were dispatched from all levels that had little to do with campaigns—commercial and sideline production work teams, public health work teams, leadership rectification work teams, and control work teams. These I have labeled noncampaign work teams. Because I have found no case of two work teams coming to a team or brigade at the same time, I infer that during campaigns, noncampaign work team activities, such as leadership rectifications or accounting control, are either suspended, or more likely, taken over by the campaign work team.

Issue Coincidence

Case Study 1: Campaign Work Team

Campaign work teams have put issues of cadre work style and their fitness for office on the agenda of production teams and brigades. In the case study that follows, taken from the Four Clean-ups campaign (1964–1966), the work team focused particularly on the issue of cadre corruption and the choice of new leaders, issues that were salient for peasants.

There is every reason to believe that by 1962–1963, cadre corruption had become a serious problem in rural China.[26] Lowering the unit of accounting to the production team gave production team cadres opportunities for graft that they had not possessed earlier, and they took advantage of the situation in many areas.[27]

Peasants were also interested in production team leadership selection, an issue dealt with by work teams. I have shown elsewhere that production team elections can have implications for peasants' interests.[28] Work teams were used to supervise production team elections during the Four Clean-ups campaign in some areas, although other places elected new cadres after the work teams had departed.[29] Even if work teams were successful in installing their preferred leaders in a production team, however, there is some question whether the new cadres could remain in office. At least one Four Clean-ups campaign work team, about which I have detailed information (my informant, a work team member, returned to the site of the work team's investigations some two years after the work team left), reported that "whomever the masses were dissatisfied with after the work team left were changed in subsequent elections."[30]

General accounts of work team behavior during the Four Clean-ups campaign have been offered elsewhere.[31] It is nonetheless useful to provide a case study to compare the methods and organizational behavior of this type with others.[32] My informant, Li, was a work team member sent to the countryside near Shanghai from July 1965 to June 1966 in a work team numbering fourteen people.

As soon as the work team arrived in the commune, a three-level cadre meeting (of team, brigade, and commune leaders) was called by the work team leader at the commune level. The Twenty-Three Points were studied and local cadres were told by the work team what was expected of them.[33] They were especially reminded that their attitude to the work team and to the work team's procedures was important. All agreed to cooperate willingly. The same procedure was repeated at brigade and team levels, where cadre-mass meetings were called, again led by the work team. Peasants mostly just sat and listened.

The work team members were sent to live in ten production teams (one per production team, with the remaining four—the work team leader, deputy leader, and two others—staying behind at brigade head-quarters). Li went to live with a fifty-year-old couple (surnamed Huang) whose grown children were away. He remained there for the duration of the campaign, working the required eleven days per month with them and sharing their meals.[34]

This household had been identified as an activist household during the "small" Four Clean-ups campaign, and had been assigned to the work team member.[35] Work team members in other places, however, have reported the difficulty of identifying a poor peasant household suitable to live with.[36] The Huangs proved to be a valuable source of information, particularly when Li asked them about members of their own production team.

Li visited every household in the production team, often several times, to complete the detailed information the work team required.

> We asked about the size of the household, the class background (ch'eng-fen) of its members, how long it had lived there, where it had come from if it had recently arrived, and what its situation had been there, the age of the members of the household, whether any of its members worked or went to school outside of the team, how many of the household participated in labor, and how well they participated, the number of workpoints each earned, and how many workpoints were earned by each annually, whether their standard of living was relatively high or low, what their grain situation was, what their attitude to the "small" Four Clean-ups had been, what

their income was, especially the sources of it, and the relationship between collective income and privately earned income. . . . We did this for each household.[37]

The production team cadres and their families were put under special scrutiny. In addition to the general information recorded for each household, Li made special trips to production team cadre households:

We looked at their workpoint income and their sideline occupations, and we compared these to their lifestyle, to see whether it was commensurate, or whether there was some disparity. We examined the cadre's distribution of workpoints, to see whether it was fair, and his distribution of work, his workstyle (whether he cursed or scolded people), and his relations with the "five bad elements."[38]

Li was thus preparing the groundwork for the work team's attack on cadre corruption. At this early stage, however, peasants were reluctant, even unwilling, to make accusations against their cadres. It was not that they approved of corruption but that the work team was seen as only a temporary presence, while the local cadres, the team members' neighbors, would remain long after the work team had departed. Little information on cadre corruption, then, came from team members at this stage. These household visits provided, nonetheless, a forum for the work team to probe the attitudes of production team members.

A major part of Li's time was spent poring over the records of the accountant, cashier, and storekeeper. In this, he was helped by three rural educated youths from the production team, who did the initial checking and found the initial discrepancies. Li chose these three youths himself, although using production team members in the investigation was a method first suggested by the work team leader in the brigade. As discrepancies in the accounts arose, they were checked against records in the brigade or commune, at, for example, the commune supply and marketing cooperative. Much of the initial information was based on data provided by the production team members during the household visits.

The first suggestions of corruption to emerge in Li's investigation were discrepancies in the team accountant's books. It appeared that he had often altered receipts received for production team purchases and pocketed the difference. When Li confronted him with these suspicions, however, the accountant hotly denied them. Other problems emerged from a close investigation of the accountant's records, all of which were denied.

During the next four months, Li continued to dig deeper into the problems of the accountant, but he was also investigating a 1962 grain theft, which had been partly uncovered by the "small" Four Clean-ups

149

campaign work team a year earlier. In the winter of 1962, it appeared, the team leader, deputy leader, accountant, and storekeeper, with five of their friends, had, over a period of several evenings, taken production team grain from the team warehouse and distributed it among themselves. Although this became obvious when accounts were compared, the cadres concerned denied it. The work team member's next move was important for the effect it had on the peasants' willingness to speak out to the work team, and so I quote from Li's account in detail:

> I told the work team leader in the brigade: I am only one person, and can do nothing [to get the cadres to confess], and I asked for his help. It was a very big problem, and 1962 had been a very bad year. I asked that a meeting of everyone in the production team be called, and that ten of the work team members from the brigade come to the meeting to support me. In the end, twelve came!

> I presented the case against the cadres at the meeting, and asked these nine people to cooperate with our work team. If not, I threatened them, then after the meeting each of them would be accompanied home by one of the work team members to discuss the problem until it was solved.

> The cadres got scared when they heard this. But they didn't say anything at the meeting. Immediately after the meeting each of us work team members took one of the nine and talked to him at length.[39]

In the end, the work team only got part of the story from each of the nine under suspicion. After discussing the situation with them (this lasted an average of two hours, but longer in some cases), the work team members met and put their various accounts together until they had a complete picture.

This incident had a large impact on the production team cadres, who came to see that they would have to tell the work team about any corrupt activities. The work team could keep them under semi-house arrest otherwise. Still some, like the deputy production team leader, resisted, only telling a small part of the story.[40]

The attitude of the cadres, specifically whether they were repentant, was an important determinant of the amount of restitution Li later decided they would have to make to the production team. It also affected their chances for reelection in the work-team-supervised elections that followed.

If the cadres' attitudes changed, even more did the attitude of the peasants, for they came to see that the work team, because it could detain and depose local cadres, had real power and they subsequently dared to speak out about cadre corruption. Still, the work team had to take the initiative, going to the peasants' houses and asking them about specific cadres:

They [the peasants] wouldn't say: "X is corrupt!" but might say "One day the accountant went to the store and he told me he was going to buy six books, but he returned with only five. This isn't right." They would say these things when I visited them in their houses. One time I was told by a peasant, "In May, the accountant's wife worked twenty-five days and earned X workpoints. I worked twenty-eight days and got fewer. Why is that?" I investigated, and there was trouble. I would look it up in the records.[41]

Peasants were now forthcoming about their attitudes toward various cadres and cadre corruption, and made demands that corrupt cadres be exposed and punished. These accusations now made up the bulk of those investigated by Li.

Evidence that peasants were concerned about cadre corruption comes from many peasant informants and work team members themselves. As one peasant informant put it:

Peasants like the work team "grasping" (kao) cadres because cadre corruption was exploiting the peasants. The money [they took] was the blood of the peasants![42]

And another informant:

When the work team came to the village, it was welcomed by the peasants, because it came to oppose corruption. Peasants disliked corruption because it was the exploitation of their money.[43]

A sent-down youth present during the Four Clean-ups campaign saw it this way:

The peasants didn't want to see the work team go! The work team had backed them up, protecting them from being cheated by the cadres, and they had brought the peasants a lot of good things, but the cadres hated them and were glad to see them go.[44]

If peasants disliked cadre corruption, they nonetheless tolerated a certain level of it, and came to expect that local cadres would take special

151

advantages. As one cashier, accused of corruption during the Four Clean-ups campaign, later said:

> People expected you to be corrupt in this kind of situation
> [being a cadre] without a doubt. There was no evidence, but it
> was something quite natural. No one talked about it, and it was
> considered better than stealing.[45]

While tolerating a certain level of corruption, then, the evidence strongly suggests that peasants were concerned about it.

For each instance of corruption, a detailed report was made by the work team. This was given to the work team leader in the brigade, who initialed it and returned it to the work team member, in this case Li. When the campaign was over, these reports were condensed into five or six pages each, a copy of which was sent to the work team leader and another to the commune. These reports presented a detailed account of the situation, including the attitude of the participants, how the participant was treated by the poor and lower-middle peasants, what peasant attitudes to him were, and finally, how the case had been handled.

The investigation of cadre corruption, although the chief purpose of the work team as Li saw it, still was not its only function. In addition, it cultivated activists, held elections of new local leaders, and set up a poor and lower-middle peasant association in the brigade.

The investigation into cadre corruption affected production. As a result of the criticism the cadres received, they became more reluctant to take any initiatives. Those with the worst attitudes, like the deputy production team leader, refused to accept leadership responsibilities at all. As the campaign wore on, then, production team members became more critical of the production team cadres, and this made unplanned interventions by the work team into the production realm necessary.

Especially after the 1962 grain theft was exposed:

> They [the production team members] were angry! Because the
> level of hostility was already so high, we did not pressure the
> cadres. But the peasants put pressure on them even though we
> advised against it. The cadres said to go and tell the work team
> if there was a problem—they were unwilling to continue in
> leadership roles.[46]

When the production team encountered a problem of insect pests, the team leader refused to take any action. "Go tell the work team!" he said, and Li finally had to lead the peasants in the application of insecticide. In such cases, work team members took the lead in production. It happened rarely, however, and resulted more from production team cadres abdicating their responsibilities than from work teams usurping them.[47]

If the work team acted as an institution through which peasants could pursue their interests—here, chiefly to discipline corrupt local cadres—it also acted to implement policies that ran counter to the interest of some, especially labor-rich peasants. This was because labor-poor households benefited from changes made in the incentive system by Li's work team.

Just before it departed, the work team introduced the Tachai workpoint system in the brigade, halting the use of piece rates, which had been common in this area previously. In addition, several inequities in the workpoint system were changed in the course of the work team's investigations. The number of workpoints received by cadres and their dependents was reduced; work assignments were more equitably distributed (the difficult job of harvesting cotton in November was rotated among more people); and, finally, the work team saw to it that rationed items, like cooking oil, were given in greater quantities to old people, whose workpoint incomes were low.

The campaign also had the effect of enforcing adherence to state production plans. Although virtually every production team in this brigade made some unauthorized alterations in their quotas, usually these were very minor adjustments in the plan. Yet this aspect of cadre behavior also received the work team's attention, with the result that one production team leader in the brigade was dismissed by Li's work team for not following the production plan during the Four Clean-ups campaign. In this team, the records were inaccurate:

> . . . they were all changed so as to hide what really was being planted. But the work team didn't "get" the accountant of this team. [Q.] Why not, if there were false records? Of course, he had false records, and, of course, he cooperated with the team leader in this. But *everyone in the team* cooperated to hide the real production. So, how could we "get" everyone in the team? The cadres would tell the production team members not to tell anyone about the changes. No one would talk.[48]

If the work team acted as a channel for peasants to express their dissatisfaction with corrupt cadres, it also acted to implement policies that many peasants were not happy with. Labor-rich households, in particular, could be expected to oppose the work-team-inspired changes in the incentive system, and the production team members as a whole may well have opposed the work team's clamping down on deviations from the plan. In this case, then, in the economic sphere, the work team did not act as an institution through which peasants articulated their interests. The work team may have acted in the interests of some team members, however, which is a different matter, not here under investigation.

After initial hesitation, peasants in this case used the work team to accuse their leaders, with the result that some production team leaders (the deputy team leader and the accountant) were dismissed from their posts by the work team, a result confirmed by a work-team-supervised election. The work team also made reports, including summaries of the attitudes of team members to local cadres, that were sent up through the work team chain of command, and to the commune. In both ways, the work team served as a channel for peasants to express dissatisfaction with deviant cadre behavior.

Even after work teams left the area, the work team presence lingered on in some cases. Peasants continued to have contact with some work team members after they left the area, and thus had an opportunity to continue to use this channel. One factory cadre who had been a Four Clean-ups work team leader in Hua county, Kwangtung, invited peasants from his Four Clean-ups "squatting point" to stay with him when they came to Canton, and they did. He thus kept up with the events in the brigade, although he denies ever intervening in brigade affairs after the campaign.[49]

When Four Clean-ups work team members were rural cadres from neighboring counties, it was easy for peasants to keep in touch with them. One informant reports that some peasants from her village made periodic visits to their former work team member friends who lived in villages nearby:

> Some people made good friends with members of the work teams, and went to the neighboring county to visit them once a year. Especially the people with whom the work team members lived. . . . Long after they had gone, peasants would talk about them.[50]

There was, thus, the opportunity to report changes in the brigade or production team, which tended to prevent a "reversal of Four Clean-ups verdicts" after the departure of the work team in some cases. How often this channel was used—or how effective it was—is not clear.

More formal procedures were instituted elsewhere. In several communes, for example, commune cadres had been stationed (chu) in the brigade on a long-term basis, since Land Reform. They were annually rotated and acted to supervise the implementation of commune policy at local levels. Because they were from the commune, they could be expected to see that the wishes of commune-level work teams were carried out, thus minimizing the instances of revenge taking, a worry of peasant and work teams alike.[51] Other communes sent out follow-up or lo shih (implementation) work teams in an effort to achieve the same results.[52]

This case study illustrates work teams acting as a structure through which peasants communicated their dissatisfactions over cadre corruption to higher levels. Peasants initially hesitated to make charges against local cadres either out of the fear of cadre retaliation, or because peasants felt cadre corruption was a local concern, not to be dealt with by outsiders.[53] In either case, the work team had to gain the confidence of the peasants, which, as we saw in the preceding example, came with the mass meeting to denounce the 1962 grain theft. Peasants came forward with their own complaints against cadres after that episode.

One result of the work team's drive against corruption was partly to paralyze local leadership. The production tasks that local cadres routinely dealt with, such as applying insecticide, were then taken up by the work team. Other issues were raised by the work team itself, in this case, incentive system issues, and while the work team was clearly acting in the interests of some peasants, particularly labor-weak households, it was not serving as a structure through which peasants articulated their interests on those issues, as I have used that concept here. It was implementing state policy.

The work team was made a vehicle for peasant grievances by the coincidence of interests between it and the peasants in disciplining corrupt cadres. Peasants did not formulate the policy that brought the work teams, however, but simply used them once they were there.

Case Study 2: Noncampaign Work Team

Work teams that are not sent out as part of a campaign, but come either on an ad hoc basis to make leadership changes at local levels or on a more regular, even routine basis to enforce production plans and correct production deviations, may serve as channels for peasants to articulate their interests.

This case study involved a new Party branch secretary in a Kwangtung brigade who had incurred the wrath of team cadres and members by putting cadres from minority lineages in the leadership positions of several production teams in order to suppress opposition to his policy of taking over production team sidelines—bamboo groves and fish ponds.[54] A work team was dispatched from the commune in 1974 as a result of commune-level concern about disunity in the brigade leadership group (several brigade cadres had opposed the new secretary's action on the team sidelines issues). The commune cadres had gradually learned of this problem through their own periodic visits to the brigade ("cadres coming down to lower-levels"), discussions with dissatisfied brigade cadres, and production figures (income from the affected production teams had fallen during the period of greatest disunity). The work team's purpose was to discover the causes of the lack of cohesion in the brigade, determine what influence this had on the production teams, and correct the situation.

The work team consisted of five commune-level cadres, three of whom lived in the brigade headquarters for one year during the investigation. They spread out to the production teams and investigated the relationship of the production teams to the brigade. After getting an initial briefing from the brigade secretary, the work team spent little time with him or other brigade cadres.

Unlike the Four Clean-ups campaign work team case reported earlier, this work team did not keep detailed records of each household in the brigade and made no effort to visit each poor and lower-middle peasant household. They did, however, learn of incidents which reflected badly on the new secretary (e.g., the time he cursed Old Wang, why he had done it, and who was at fault), and they talked directly to the peasants concerned.

Unlike the Four Clean-ups case, production team members were willing to talk to the work team from the outset. Although peasants did not take the initiative and seek out the work team members, they did not require a conclusive demonstration of work team power before they would speak out. This was probably because the work team members were not outsiders but were from the commune to which they would return when the investigation was completed. Also, the scope of the work team's investigation was much more narrowly circumscribed, limited in this case to a local issue, and this was reflected in the procedures adopted by the work team. Precisely because the investigation was not part of a mass campaign, peasants were more willing to speak out.

If revenge were to be taken against peasants who made accusations to the work team, it would have to be done by production team cadres, who controlled work assignments and influenced workpoint evaluations. But, as we have seen, in this case they stood to gain by allowing the peasants to express their dissatisfactions to the work team. Only the brigade secretary stood to lose. "There wasn't any revenge-taking in our team because of the bad relationship between the brigade secretary and the team cadres."[55]

No mass struggle meetings were held, although brigade party branch meetings, chaired by the work team, were held to criticize the new brigade secretary:

> He was frightened, and had no power. The work team had the power to manage production. The work team also chaired brigade meetings, not him. . . . If a production team had a problem, it went to the work team.[56]

The work team investigated brigade sideline production accounts and discovered several inaccuracies. The records were badly kept, and the accountant was taken briefly to the commune for questioning.

> Still no mass meetings were held, and no explanations given. Everyone knew there was disorder in the accounts, and *the*

156

peasants were dissatisfied about it. They told the work team how they felt.[57]

The progress of the work team was reported back to the commune Party committee by the two work team members who returned to commune headquarters each evening. After the year-long investigation, the commune decided that the new brigade secretary should be transferred out of the brigade (and back to the commune administration he had come from), the old brigade secretary be restored to office (he had been denounced as a follower of Liu Shao-ch'i during the Cultural Revolution), and the bamboo groves and fish ponds be restored to the production teams, a solution welcomed by the peasants.

This example makes clear the close connection between peasants' interests and the work team. Peasants of the dominant lineages in the production team, who had opposed the new brigade secretary (manifested by election results, as I have shown), demanded that action be taken to restore the original situation. The work team agreed and the production team cadres were restored to office, the brigade leadership changed, and production team sidelines returned. The work team's interest in restoring unity within the brigade thus coincided with the interests of production team members, making the work team receptive to peasant demand making. The more relaxed noncampaign atmosphere that characterized the work team's stay in the brigade also contributed to peasant willingness to speak out. They may also have been more intensely interested in the outcome of this dispute than in the cadre corruption case reported earlier. The work team here served as an interest articulation channel.

Issue Divergence

Work teams may be sent to teams and brigades to implement policies that peasants do not perceive to be in their interests. The following case studies show work teams in an essentially antagonistic (adversary) role to peasants' perceived interests.

Case Study 3: Campaign Work Team

The Study Tachai campaign saw work teams dispatched to many brigades in Kwangtung. In the following study, three cadres were sent from the commune in January 1972 to stay with the brigade and its production teams for one and a half months. They were sent to this particular brigade because it had been designated a model unit by the commune. The work team consisted of one commune cadre with responsibility for agriculture, one from the commune radio station, and a third from the commune *pao-wei tsu* (defense group). All were Party members. They did not live in peasant households but came daily from the commune.

Work teams were sent out to six of the fourteen best and worst brigades in the commune. In some backward brigades, the first task of the work team was replacing the leadership group in order to carry out the campaign:

> They wanted to change those people who were deficient in some way, and put those people with ability (*neng-li*) in the leadership group.[58]

As soon as the work team entered my informant's brigade, it called a meeting of all production team and brigade cadres to explain the meaning of the campaign. At the outset, a series of daily struggle meetings was held to mobilize peasants for the tasks of the campaign.

> The work team began struggling with people because some peasants wouldn't follow orders (*pu t'ing hua*). Some of these were middle peasants, some poor peasants. One peasant, for example, asked for leave from work due to illness, and the production team leader granted it and sent him home. Instead, he went to his private plot and took some watermelons to sell in the market—everyone saw him!! As a result, a meeting was called to struggle with him. Other peasants then were afraid to try it, and they all went out to work.[59]

These meetings were to prepare peasants for the agricultural construction work that was carried out under work team supervision during the campaign. The brigade opened up barren land, leveled existing fields, and made repairs to and extended the irrigation and drainage system during the campaign. In the informant's team, because it had no new land to open up, peasant time was spent leveling land. The work was very unpopular because, peasants grumbled, after leveling, water had to be pumped in and out of the fields by hand (they had no pumps), whereas before it drained naturally. Also, scraping the topsoil off some fields to put on others left some fields as patches of hard infertile clay. "Leveling land is useless—it just looks better," they complained.[60]

Previously, decisions about land leveling had been taken by the production team itself. It had done a little at a time, from 7 *fen* to 1 *mou*.[61] But the work team decided leveling should be extended first to 5 *mou* and then to more than 30 *mou*. Each person now worked longer hours, cutting into time for private sideline production. Incomes from that sector subsequently fell.

> Peasants were unhappy. They could not disobey and go on strike, however. Some, though, secretly did not go out to work,

but went to their sidelines instead. Others officially "at work," just sat around and told stories.[62]

Peasants did not dare to verbalize their dissatisfaction with the campaign to the work team. They did work longer hours, but without enthusiasm. When the work team left a month and a half later, however, the agricultural construction work, which had been the focus of the campaign, abruptly stopped.

Many areas did not have work teams for the Study Tachai campaign and other informants reported that they came at various times.[63]

The issue in this case study was how labor was to be allocated. Peasants, according to my informant, maximized their short-term interests and only grudgingly set out to achieve the objectives of the campaign. They had no choice, however, as one production team leader pointed out to his fellow team members:

> Now the commune wants us to study and, moreover, has sent people down—we all must study. And the commune defense group cadre has also come. If you don't go out to open up new land, perhaps we will struggle with you. Don't say I didn't warn you![64]

The policy the work team was charged with implementing clearly ran counter to the perceived interests of these team members. In such cases of issue divergence, work teams are not receptive to peasant demand making and, as in this case, peasants can do little except bide their time and carry out the campaign. They could not use the work team as a channel through which to articulate their interests because the issues being pursued by the work team were opposed by most peasants in the team.

Case Study 4: Noncampaign Work Team

Noncampaign work teams, charged with implementing a policy not perceived by peasants as in their interests, can also block peasant use of work teams to articulate their interests. Work teams sent to enforce production plans are an example, as peasants in one Kwangtung production team learned.[65]

Located in T'ai-shan County, the production team was famous for its fruit and sugarcane. The team sold sugarcane produced by peasants from other production teams in the area in the market as their own, a service for which they received a daily commission from the other production teams. The peasants who actually did the marketing paid 1 yuan per day to the production team, and pocketed the rest (usually 0.8 yuan per day). They also received workpoints from their production

159

team. At this time, the value of the production team's workpoints was quite low (0.5 yuan per labor day). Still, individual peasants and the production team cadres thought there was no problem because most families in the production team gained under the scheme.

Later, however, the commune discovered that those selling sugarcane in the market were all from one production team. Moreover, they found that this team had failed to complete its obligations to repair water conservation works. The commune Party committee was annoyed when it learned that most of the team's labor power was being sent to market the sugarcane, and a work team was organized to go to the production team.

The work team, consisting of eight people sent to the production team for a short period, conducted "rectification and struggle," stopped the marketing, and departed.

This case illustrates not the procedures used but the reasons for sending out such a "control" work team. The issue here was whether sideline production was going to be allowed to interfere with the collective economy, an issue of direct concern to peasants. In this case, the work team came down against the perceived interests of most peasants in the team (but favoring those few families in the team who did not participate in private sugarcane marketing), enforced production norms, and carried out state policy to implement production plans.

Although work teams are sometimes sent to enforce state planning directives, as in this case, they have been sent to lower production quotas as well. In 1963, for example, a Kwangtung County sent out a work team to discover why Hung-p'o brigade had failed to fulfill its quota. The work team discovered that the commune had arbitrarily raised the brigade's rice quota, although it had little land suitable for rice cultivation. The quota was then lowered by the work team: "The commune Party committee corrected the original unrealistic demand."[66]

In May 1972, a work team from Che-cheng County Party committee (Shangtung) discovered that peasants in a brigade were criticizing the production plan for that year. The county had increased *kao-liang* (sorghum) acreage based on the previous year's successful performance at the expense of sweet potatoes and millet, creating peasant dissatisfaction. This action, the work team discovered, did not suit local conditions, and the plan was changed accordingly.[67]

Noncampaign work teams deal with a wide variety of issues, as these examples have indicated. The press has reported highway snow-damage control work teams, public health, medical, and sanitation work teams, work teams to make loans, to change labor norms, to supervise the repair of farm tools, and to change production plan quotas.[68] They come to lower levels either in a time of crisis—that is, on an ad hoc problem-solving basis—or at regular intervals to undertake routine checking and control operations, as well as to gather information.

Conclusions

Where peasant and work team interests have coincided, work teams have acted as structures through which peasants can articulate their interests. Whether a work team was receptive to peasant demands, then, depended in the first instance on the policy the work team was implementing, which we have seen could be carried out either as part of a nationally inspired campaign or as a locally inspired task.[69] Peasants were more likely to use work teams to make demands during noncampaign periods. First, we have seen that whether a work team was implementing a campaign affected the composition of the team. Campaign work teams, like those of the Four Clean-ups, were more likely to be composed of outsiders, who were unfamiliar with the local situation, either because they were not peasants themselves, had no rural experience, or were unfamiliar with the language and customs of the area. These problems had to be overcome before the work team could act as an interest articulation structure in a campaign setting.

One procedure devised by the Party to facilitate local work by outsiders has been the Three Togethers (eating, living, and working together with the masses), the practice that in the first case study went some way toward breaking down the barriers between the work team and the peasants. The Three Togethers increases the contact points between work team members and peasants. Work team members are then in a position to receive demands, because they make household visits, work with peasants, live with a host peasant family, and use the services of some peasants (rural youth in the case study) to carry out their duties. Although practicing the Three Togethers is neither a necessary nor sufficient condition for peasants using work teams to articulate their interests, it does increase the likelihood of peasants using this structure under campaign conditions, simply because it increases the points of contact. Campaign work teams that do not use the Three Togethers, such as the work team implementing the Study Tachai campaign in the case study reported earlier, seem to be signaling to peasants that they are not interested in receiving peasant demands.

Noncampaign work teams, usually composed of local (e.g., commune) cadres, are more familiar with local conditions and are less in need of practicing the Three Togethers to carry out policy.

Second, the campaign setting made it less likely that peasants took the initiative to make demands of work teams or were willing to speak out to them at all. The sanctions that a work team brought with it to local levels, more obvious to peasants during campaigns, affected the atmosphere of the campaigns in a team or brigade. As we have seen, work teams replaced local leaders; controlled inputs such as fertilizer, seeds, mechanization, electrification, and building materials; changed local production quotas; and detained and struggled with team members and local cadres, all obvious manifestations of their power. These changes could drastically affect the livelihood of team members. In the case studies, I have provided evidence that work teams sometimes used these sanctions to carry out policies, from agricultural construction to cleaning up corruption. A work team was more likely to use these sanctions during a campaign, if only because of the need to mobilize all team members to produce quick results. The outsiders usually making up campaign work teams needed clear demonstrations of their authority, which the use or threatened use of these sanctions could provide.

There were, however, important limits to work team authority: The practical limits of the scope of the work team's activities (noncampaign work teams had more narrowly defined targets), the internal cohesion of the work team, to be discussed later, and the temporary nature of the work team all imposed limits on the permanence of work-team-supervised change. Work teams, further, could not dismiss a member from the Party, nor could they pass sentence on, execute, or beat detainees. That the real limits on work teams were so few, however, was one demonstration of their power.

Campaign work teams were more likely to use methods such as struggle meetings and detaining cadres or peasants, activities that tended to inhibit peasant demand making. We have seen that peasants were much less willing to make demands to work teams during campaigns. This may have occurred because the stakes were smaller during noncampaign periods—the risks for peasants were smaller, simply because the scope of noncampaign work team activity was more narrowly defined. To make demands during a campaign was to run the risk of impeding the campaign, thus inviting the wrath of work team members as well as local cadres.

This situation found its most extreme form in "key points" during campaigns. In an earlier study, I found that work teams in key points tended to take over all leadership duties from local cadres and make decisions without consulting either local cadres or peasants.[70] Three Togethers procedures were practiced, if at all, in a peremptory manner, and new local leaders were imposed on local production units. These circumstances tended to decrease the likelihood that work teams would be used by peasants as an interest articulation channel.[71]

The internal cohesion of work teams also affected the likelihood of peasants using this mode of pursuing their interests. Splits within work teams, based on personal ties, occupation, unit of origin, or level of origin, were sometimes used by peasants to make demands of work team members.

In one Four Clean-ups work team stationed in Shansi (May 1964), for example, the split between peasant cadres and university students making up the work team became so fierce that the work team was unable to supervise the election of new local cadres. Without preparation, a

162

production team mass meeting was called by the peasant cadre work team member stationed in one production team. At the meeting, it became obvious that several peasants were vying for leadership posts. One poor and lower-middle peasant representative, with "no respect among the masses," according to my informant (a university study work team member), was particularly adamant:

> He and the work team member argued fiercely causing the meeting to break up without a decision. The work team leader came from the brigade and only then was this poor peasant's temper cooled down. Afterwards, another poor peasant was elected to be team leader, but this person was changed very quickly because he had no ability, and no education.

> Finally, the former production team deputy leader was made the team leader, and the poor peasant who had argued so fiercely was made the deputy team leader.[72]

This case contrasts sharply with other cases of elections supervised by work teams. In the more common pattern, although commune members were consulted, it was never in doubt that the final selection of new cadres would be taken by the work team. Several meetings and several reelections were unnecessary. Yet in the case just presented, because the work team was badly split, its authority in the eyes of the peasants was low. It could not simply decree that a particular peasant would be the new team leader. The ensuing fracas was the result of the badly split work team in this production team.

Politics within the work team, then, may influence the way peasants' interests are articulated to them. Splits in the work team may make it more likely that peasants' views are transmitted upward as they become issues in disputes within the work team. Also, failure of the work team to agree on a solution may permit peasants to make their own view known— as the disgruntled poor peasant did in contesting the production team leadership position in the case just cited. Since work teams composed of members from different backgrounds are more likely during campaigns, when large numbers of cadre resources are required, the conclusion that campaign work teams are less likely to act as interest articulation structures must be modified. Uncohesive campaign work teams may give peasants greater opportunities for pursuing their interests than cohesive campaign work teams.

How reliable were work teams as interest articulation structures? Because campaign work teams are intended chiefly as policy implementation devices, the dispatch of such work teams depends on elite decisions. They have not, for example, been sent out with every campaign. Whether in any particular campaign peasants can predict that they will come at all remains doubtful. Indeed, when asked, peasant informants denied that they could predict the arrival or departure of work teams at all.

There is, however, an element of predictability in the dispatch of noncampaign work teams. When serious leadership disputes arise, as in the case study just presented, it may be expected by peasants that a work team will come down to the team or brigade. How it will handle the dispute, though, rests entirely in elite (work team) hands.

Second, brigades and production teams that experience radical production output changes and natural disasters, and also those units designated as models or key points (whether backward or progressive), can expect frequent work team visits.

Hua-kao-chia brigade in Te-ching County, Chekiang, for example, reported a drop in production in 1968, with the result that "many persons went down to basic levels" to reduce leftist deviations, the alleged cause of the drop in production. In 1969, there was a bumper harvest. More problems developed, however, with local cadres becoming "arrogant and complacent," resulting in another bad production year in 1970 (production fell 16 million catties in the county). As a result, sixteen work teams were organized and sent down to the countryside.[73]

This case ties the sending of work teams directly to the drop in production. Any perceptive observer of production output figures might have predicted the arrival of a work team when the figures were made known. In the same way, natural disasters and other crises, of both natural and human origin, may prompt the sending of work teams. Although there was some predictability in the sending out of these noncampaign work teams, whether or not the interests of the work team coincided with those of local cadres and peasants lies largely in the hands of elites.

The data suggest that the policies implemented by work teams from 1962 to 1974 can be seen as either political or economic. Political goals or policies are those that take leadership changes or control functions as their primary aim. The Four Clean-ups work teams had a political goal orientation because their primary objective was disciplining corrupt local cadres. Politically oriented work team goals here mean those involving changes in the structure of power, the rectification and change of personnel and leadership positions, education and propaganda, and control of planning and of class enemies.

The Study Tachai campaign work teams, on the other hand, took economic goals as their objectives because their primary aim was to make changes in basic agricultural construction or changes in production techniques or the use of mechanized inputs. Economically oriented goals here mean those involving the development of collective and private production as well as changes in production technique and in the incentive system.

Both Four Clean-ups and Study Tachai work teams were campaign work teams. If we classify work teams according to their *setting*, whether they were implementing a campaign, and their *goal*, whether political or economic as used here, work teams from 1962 to 1974 can be placed in Table 7-1.

Table 7-1

Work Teams Classified by Setting and Goal

	Setting	
Goal	Campaign	Noncampaign
Political change	Socialist Education Four Clean-ups Cultural Revolution Criticizing Lin Piao and Confucius Rectify and Rebuild the Party	Leadership and control
Economic change	Study Tachai	Commercial side-line production, public health, etc.

Work teams deal with personnel changes, cadre work style, corruption, public and private sideline production, changing the unit of accounting, labor norms, technical improvements, and agricultural plans and investments, as we have seen. Oversimplifying, we can lump these issues under two general headings—leadership issues and output issues. The issues dealt with by the work teams are shown in Table 7-2.

Table 7-2 does not tell us whether peasants will articulate these issues to work teams but rather which issues will be placed on the agenda of brigades and teams by the work teams. Work teams will be most likely to respond to peasant demand making on these issues. That is, campaign political work teams will put leadership change issues on the agenda, and peasants will have an opportunity to make demands on this issue. Campaign-economic work teams, such as work teams sent out for the Study Tachai campaign, put both leadership and output issues on local agendas, but as we have seen—at least in Case Study 3—they were not responsive to peasant demand making, chiefly because the policies they were advocating in these issue areas did not coincide with the majority of peasants' perceived interests in the brigade.

Table 7-2

Issues Dealt with by Work Teams

Goal	Setting	
	Campaign	Noncampaign
Political	Leadership	Leadership and output
Economic	Leadership and output	Output

Noncampaign-political work teams, such as the work teams to rectify local cadre deviations and to carry out routine control functions, such as checking accountants' records, put leadership and output issues on local agendas. Again, whether peasants will use these work teams to make demands depends on the coincidence of work team and peasant interests.

Noncampaign-economic work teams, of which there are no case studies reported in this chapter, put output issues on local agendas. Work teams sent to develop local sideline production or to develop commerce in teams and brigades are examples.

Knowing which issues will be placed on local agendas is important, for work teams will be most receptive to peasant demand making on these issues. Work teams may themselves articulate the interests of some or all peasants in local units on these issues as well, activity that goes beyond the scope of this chapter.

I have argued here that work teams can be seen either as facilitating or blocking peasant interest articulation, and have presented evidence in the form of case studies of these two kinds of relationships. Rarely in practice, however, are work teams and peasant interest either totally issue-coincident or divergent. Work team and peasant interests should rather be seen on a continuum from most coincident to most divergent, with most work teams coming down someplace in the middle. I have sought to demonstrate the relationship between peasant interest articulation and work teams by focusing on the more extreme ends of that continuum.

I have argued that where work team policy and peasant interest coincided, work teams were most likely to act as structures for peasant interest articulation. Conclusions beyond this can be stated briefly: Noncampaign work teams were more likely to be used by peasants to articulate their interest because of these work teams' local composition and the more relaxed atmosphere of noncampaign periods. The difficulty for peasants of using campaign work teams as interest articulation channels was, however, reduced when the Three Togethers procedures were used or when the work team lacked cohesion. Cohesive campaign work teams that did not practice the Three Togethers were the least likely to act as peasant interest articulation channels.

Finally, whether or not to dispatch work teams, their policies, and their procedures were all decisions in the hands of higher levels over which peasants had no control, nor could the peasants predict the frequency, scope, or nature of the work teams if they were dispatched.

NOTES

I wish to express my gratitude to the director and staff of the Universities Service Center in Hong Kong, where the research and writing of this chapter was undertaken, and to Thomas Bernstein, Victor Falkenheim, Andrew Nathan, William Parish, Lynn White, Martin Whyte, and S. L. Wong for reading earlier drafts of the chapter and providing many useful suggestions for its revision. Needless to say, all errors are my own responsibility.

1. See, for example, Amitai Etzioni, *A Comparative Analysis of Complex Organizations* (New York: Free Press, 1975).

2. Anthony Downs, *Inside Bureaucracy* (Boston: Little, Brown & Co., 1967), p. 112.

3. Ibid., p. 126.

4. Work teams are to be distinguished from production teams (*sheng-ch'an hsiao-tui*), the lowest-level rural production units. Approximately ten production teams, consisting of from twenty to forty households, make up a brigade (*sheng-ch'an ta-tui*), and ten or so brigades make up a commune (*jen-min kung-she*). There is considerable variation in the size of these units.

5. For a discussion of work team activities during Land Reform, see Peter N. S. Lee, "The Land Reform Movement of the Chinese Communist Party in the Civil War Period 1945–49: The Mobilization Process and Class Structure" (master's thesis, University of Indiana, 1968), and William Hinton, *Fanshen: A Documentary of Revolution in a Chinese Village* (New York: Monthly Review Press, 1967). For work teams in the Four Clean-ups campaign, see Richard Baum, *Prelude to Revolution: Mao, the Party, and the Peasant Question, 1962–1966* (New York: Columbia University Press, 1975), passim, especially pp. 68–76.

6. Interest articulation here means that process of individuals and groups communicating their perceived interests to decision makers. See Michel Oksenberg, *A Bibliography of Secondary English Language Literature on Contemporary Chinese Politics* (New York: East Asian Institute, Columbia University, n.d.), p. xxx, and Gabriel Almond and G. Bingham Powell, Jr., *Comparative Politics: A Developmental Approach* (Boston: Little, Brown & Co., 1966), p. 73.

7. See Baum, *Prelude*, p. 19 for a discussion of *san-t'ung* ("the three togethers"—living, eating, and working together with the masses).

8. See ibid., pp. 61–83, for a discussion of key points during the Four Clean-ups campaign (1964–1966). This campaign was carried out as part of the Socialist Education campaign (1962–1966), and was designed to discipline corrupt local cadres for sloppy accounting practices, warehouse losses or thefts, and for misappropriated assets and workpoints. Politics, economics, organization, and ideology all were to be cleaned up.

9. See Michel Oksenberg, "Methods of Communication within the Chinese Bureaucracy," *China Quarterly* 57 (January–March 1974):24–28, for a discussion of an investigation team's activities in Kwangtung. Informants CN5 and KP1 have suggested to me that investigation teams are to be distinguished from work teams on the basis of the latter's power to make on-the-spot changes. CN, KP, and NM are notations indicating informants interviewed in Hong Kong from May 1975 to October 1976. CN

indicates a sent-down youth informant; KP, a cadre informant; and NM, a peasant informant.

10. See C. S. Chen and C. P. Ridley, *Rural People's Communes in Lien-chiang* (Stanford: Hoover Institute Press, 1969) for an exception to this general rule.

11. Mao Tse-tung, "Oppose Book Worship," *Selected Readings from the Works of Mao Tse-tung* (Peking: Foreign Languages Press, 1967), pp. 33–41.

12. Ibid., p. 40.

13. Mao Tse-tung, "Some Questions Concerning Methods of Leadership," *Selected Readings*, p. 235.

14. For a discussion of Mao's concept of mass line, see James R. Townsend, *Political Participation in Communist China* (Berkeley: University of California Press, 1969), pp. 72–74 and 94–95.

15. See Mao Tse-tung, "On the Question of Agricultural Cooperation," *Selected Readings*, p. 321, for the importance of checking up on local levels.

16. See Robert F. Miller, "The Future of the Soviet Kolkhoz," *Problems of Communism* (March–April 1976), pp. 34–50. Inter-*kolkhoz* association chairmen are drawn from outside.

17. Lowell Dittmer, *Liu Shao-ch'i and the Cultural Revolution* (Berkeley: University of California Press, 1974), pp. 123–126.

18. Liu Shao-ch'i, *Collected Works of Liu Shao-ch'i, 1945–1957* (Hong Kong: Union Research Institute, 1969), p. 120.

19. Dittmer, *Liu Shao-ch'i*, p. 80.

20. The Socialist Education campaign (1962–1966) was initially aimed at persuading the peasantry to abandon "spontaneous capitalist" tendencies. By 1964, however, the campaign had been turned into the Four Clean-ups campaign, which sought to discipline corrupt local cadres (see n. 8). The Cultural Revolution (1966–1969) was a campaign led by Mao to rectify the Party at its highest levels. Its impact on the countryside, particularly in more remote areas, was negligible. The Clean Up Class Ranks campaign (1969–1970) was designed to restore order after the Cultural Revolution, and was used by those local leaders who had been attacked during the Cultural Revolution to punish their detractors. The Rectify and Rebuild the Party campaign (1970) had as its purpose the strengthening and consolidation of Party organization. The Criticizing Lin Piao and Confucious campaign (1973–1975) sought to explain Lin Piao's demise without damaging party unity, and in the process linked his attitudes and behavior to Confucius. The Study Tachai campaign (1969–1974) encouraged local rural production units to emulate the national model Tachai brigade.

21. Mao Tse-tung, "Talk on the Four Clean-ups Movement," in *Miscellany of Mao Tse-tung Thought* (Washington, DC: Joint Publications Research Service, no. 61 269-2) (20 February 1974), p. 443. This originally appeared as *Mao Tse-tung ssu-hsiang wan-sui* [Long Live Mao Tse-tung Thought].

22. Dittmer, *Liu Shao-ch'i*, pp. 79–80.

169

23. See Ch'en Yung-kuei, "Thoroughly Criticize the 'Gang of Four' and Bring about a New Upsurge in the Movement to Build Ta-chai Type Counties throughout the Country," *Hung-ch'i* [Red Flag] 1 (7 January 1977) in *Survey of China Mainland Magazines* 910 (7 February 1977), p. 69, where it is charged that the Gang of Four prohibited the sending out of work teams after the First Tachai Conference on Agriculture.

24. See Chen and Ridley, *Lien-chiang*, pp. 105–106 for reports of peasant attitudes to the "household contracting" system in 1961–1962.

25. The Three Loyalties campaign (1969) sought to propagate loyalty to Chairman Mao, his thought, and his proletarian revolutionary line. The One-Hit Three-Oppose campaign (1971) attacked counterrevolutionaries who were sabotaging production, and opposed corruption and theft, speculation and profiteering, and extravagance and waste. There is conflicting evidence in my data on the Clean Up Class Ranks campaign (1969–1970), some informants saying that work teams came to their teams and brigades, others denying it.

26. See Chen and Ridley, *Lien-chiang*, pp. 196–197. But informant NM9 reported that he was unaware of any cadre corruption in his production team (in NM9A-21).

27. NM9A-21.

28. See John P. Burns, "The Election of Production Team Cadres in Rural China: 1958–74," *China Quarterly* 74 (June 1978):273–296.

29. NM9A-19. See also NM8D-3 and Richard Madsen interview WW 14/12.

30. CN4B-5, 8.

31. Baum, *Prelude*. Also Byung-joon Ahn, *Chinese Politics and the Cultural Revolution* (Seattle: University of Washington Press, 1977), pp. 89–122.

32. See my interviews with NM9, NM8, and NM4 for similar case studies.

33. For the significance of Mao's Twenty-Three Points, see Baum, *Prelude*, pp. 127–135, and Ahn, *Chinese Politics*, pp. 113–115.

34. CN4A-1.

35. The "small" Four Clean-ups, conducted locally, preceded the "large" Four Clean-ups campaign and was in general an unsuccessful attempt by commune cadres to clean up brigade and production team cadres' corruption. See Baum, *Prelude*, pp. 61–83.

36. Initial suggestions were usually made by brigade and production team cadres, often of households loyal to them. This would be discovered by conscientious work team members, who then sought out "reliable" poor peasant informants. False accusations made by some householders or uncomfortable living conditions were grounds for moving even into middle peasant accommodation, although it was forbidden for work team members to practice the Three Togethers with cadres in this campaign. See KP2A.

37. CN3A-1. Another account from a former work team member in Shansi during the Four Clean-ups campaign states: "Each work team member had a notebook. On the upper part of the first page you wrote the person's name, class background, number of

people in the family, the family head's name, etc. On the second page you wrote the household's kinship relations. This was to see if the household had any ties to cadres or landlords. . . . The third page was to record relationships between households. Who said what about this household, and what they said good or bad about them, etc. I recorded it all with the date. I recorded it in detail. The interviewing varied from household to household, but finally we could verify the truth. We investigated their sources of income as well" (CN4A-1).

38. CN3A-2. The "five bad elements" were landlords, rich peasants, counterrevolution-aries, rightists, and bad elements (usually criminals).

39. Ibid.

40. From the cadre's point of view, the situation looked grim: "I'll remember this until the day I die!! It [the work team] treated me like a landlord! Beat their hands on the table, looked like they were going to beat me. Cursed me! What a fierce group!" Richard Madsen interview. WW 17/2.

41. CN3A-3.

42. NM11E-6.

43. NM9A-20.

44. Richard Madsen interview WW 14/8.

45. . NM4C-4.

46. CN3F-12.

47. Here team cadres tended to abdicate, but in key points it was more a case of work teams simply taking over cadre duties and decisions.

48. CN3D-2.

49. NM10.

50. Richard Madsen interview WW 17/3.

51. NM8D-12.

52. CN2.

53. Fear of cadre retaliation was not an idle fear. See a letter written by a peasant to the Lu-cheng County Party Committee telling of brigade cadres taking revenge against peasants in 1964. Another work team was dispatched to the brigade to deal with the problem. Radio Shansi, 3 December 1964, in *News from Chinese Provincial Radio Stations* (Hong Kong: British Regional Information Service) 86 (10 December 1964), pp. 33–34.

54. For more details of this case, see Burns, "Election," pp. 292–294.

55. CN11D-3.

56. Ibid.

57. CN11D-3; emphasis added.

58. CN5K-1.

59. Ibid., p. 10.

60. Ibid.

61. One *mou* equals one-sixth of an acre. There are 10 *fen* in each *mou*.

62. CN5K-7.

63. See NM9B-33.

64. CN5K-10.

65. CN5J-12.

66. *Nan-fang Jih-pao* [Southern Daily], 3 March 1963. This case and the next are really instances of "issue coincidence" but are included here because they bear on the quota issue.

67. Radio Shantung, 16 May 1972, in *Foreign Broadcast Information Service* (Washington, DC: Department of Commerce) 99 (May 1972), p. C7.

68. References to these work teams appear in: Radio Hupei, 11 January 1966 in *News from Chinese Provincial Radio Stations* 141 (20 January 1966), p. 17; Radio Kwangtung, 5 December 1969 in *Foreign Broadcast Information Service* 237 (9 December 1969); Radio Kwangtung, 3 May 1966 in *News from Chinese Provincial Radio Stations* 157 (12 May 1966); Radio Hupei, 25 December 1964 in *News from Chinese Provincial Radio Stations* 88 (30 December 1964), pp. 21–22; Radio Anhwei, 18 July 1963 in *News from Chinese Provincial Radio Stations* 16 (25 July 1963), p. 12; *Southern Daily*, 15 March 1963.

69. Locally inspired campaigns implemented by work teams also exist but are not considered here.

70. See John P. Burns, "The Election of Production Team Cadres in Rural China: 1958–74," a paper prepared for the Workshop on the Pursuit of Political Interest in the People's Republic of China, Ann Arbor, Michigan, August 1977, pp. 39–57.

71. This conclusion is based mainly on the Four Clean-ups campaign work team cases.

72. CN4B-2.

73. Radio Chekiang, 28 August 1972 in *Foreign Broadcast Information Service* 170 (30 August 1972), p. C2.

IV. Conflict Resolution

Conflicts and contradictions are very much a part of China's process of societal transformation. One of the legitimate ways in which the system encourages citizens to bring conflictual issues to the attention of the public for resolution is the letters to the editor column in the press.

Godwin Chu and Leonard Chu analyze the letters in the official *People's Daily* over a twelve-year period, covering 1967–1968 during the Cultural Revolution and 1976–1978 in the aftermath of the Gang of Four. The different political climates apparently affected the functioning of the letters column. Instead of a tone of restraint as in the Cultural Revolution years, now the Chinese are speaking out in unprecedented numbers, and with unprecedented candor. Tens of thousands of Chinese, from peasants to middle-echelon cadres, each month write to the editor. They raise policy issues, complain of human rights violations, argue ideological points, and criticize local officials. In this sense, the letters column in the *People's Daily* has become a forum for public discussion. Through this channel the central leadership orients itself toward the divergent views and conflictual issues at the grassroots level.

Resolution of local conflicts, which used to be mediated through the clan networks, now follows a different route. Mitch Meisner uses the Tachai case to illustrate how local cadres like Ch'en Yung-kuei might appeal to personal prestige, acquaintance connections, and other types of local loyalties to forge horizontal channels of communication. These channels are then used as a basis for political alliance to counter hierarchical disposition of power during periods of political conflict. In the Tachai case the internal solidarity among the peasants enabled Ch'en to take a stand against the county hierarchy. Recent revelations about false production records and abuse of power have ended the stellar status that Ch'en once enjoyed during the days of the Gang of Four. However, the importance of informal, horizontal communication to counterbalance the official vertical channels, as illustrated by the Tachai experience in its early days, deserves further study.

8

Mass Media and Conflict Resolution: An Analysis of Letters to the Editor

Godwin C. Chu
Leonard L. Chu

Conflict, according to Simmel, is a form of social life in the sense that no group can be entirely harmonious.[1] Any group will show harmony and disharmony, association and disassociation. The question is, how are these two types of social processes structured in a society either to maintain cohesion or to foster disruption?

Elaborating on the theoretical writings of Simmel, Coser has suggested that social conflict may serve to establish the identity and maintain the boundaries of a society, and thus may be functional instead of dysfunctional.[2] This proposition rests on one basic assumption: That the social structure will provide adequate institutions through which conflict may be channeled and resolved in a socially sanctioned manner without serious disruptive consequences. Such institutions of conflict resolution, Coser points out, should be distinguished from what are generally known as safety-valve institutions.[3] The latter have the function of diverting hostility onto substitute targets or providing a mechanism for tension release, and thus may alleviate or postpone conflict. They do not, however, necessarily provide a socially recognized channel through which conflict may be expressed and resolved.

Even though the pursuit of conflict and conflict resolution following regulated social patterns may be considered a functional prerequisite, the manner in which this function is fulfilled would appear to vary with the nature of the social structure. In other words, structural alternatives would exist in different social systems.[4] In a society like the United States, for instance, a number of such structural mechanisms permit the expression of rival claims and opposite views by the free press system, by town hall meetings, by debates in legislative councils, and, in the sixties, by the behavioral enactment of dissent.

Such structural mechanisms are apparently not developed to the same extent in a country like the People's Republic of China. Following Simmel and Coser, however, we assume that some mechanisms must exist for the pursuit and resolution of conflict. In this chapter we shall attempt to demonstrate that the "Letters to the Editor" column in the

People's Daily, the official newspaper of the People's Republic, provides such an institutionalized mechanism.

This thesis is inspired by the pioneering work of Inkeles on the Soviet system of mass media.[5] Inkeles and Geiger took note of the letters published in *Pravda* and other major newspapers in the form of *samokritika*, that is, self-criticism. The purpose of the letters, according to Inkeles, was to expose errors in the work of others as well as to acknowledge one's own mistakes and learn from them. Inkeles appeared to regard the letters more or less as a safety-valve institution for releasing tension and channeling aggression toward permissible targets. Inkeles' model was followed in Yu's analysis of the media system of the People's Republic, in which he made references to letters published in Communist Chinese newspapers.[6]

We recognize that some of the letters could serve the latent function of releasing tension, and seek supporting evidence in our analysis of the letters in the *People's Daily*. Our primary thesis, however, is that the letters are not merely safety valves but an institutionalized mechanism for the pursuit and resolution of conflict. Through the letters column, we hypothesize, individuals in China are allowed a channel to express some of their claims to status and resources over and above those of their rivals, although such conflicts may be veiled beneath petty grievances and complaints.

The Letters Column

The letters column in Chinese newspapers is a recognized channel between the Party and the people.[7] In the *People's Daily*, this column may occupy either a full page or a dozen square inches. In terms of editorial display, the column usually appears on page 2 or 3 of the six-page edition (expanded to eight pages since 1 January 1980). Occasionally it may be given front-page treatment.

Letters from readers are handled by the *Hsin Fang Tsu* (Letters and Visits Section)[8] which belongs to the *Chun Chung Kung Tso Pu* (Department of Mass Work), one of the five major departments of the *People's Daily*.[9] The number of letters received and published seems to have fluctuated with political events. For instance, during 1967 and 1968, when the Cultural Revolution was at its height, a total of 182 letters was published. When the tide of the Cultural Revolution subsided in the following years, the number of letters published also decreased. In 1969, 1970, and 1971, only 108 letters (23, 20, and 65, respectively) were published. In 1972 and 1973, however, the number of letters published increased to 124 and 105, respectively, as a result of the anti–Lin Piao and anti-Confucius campaign. In 1974, 1975, and 1976, the number of letters published dropped to 19, 52, and 27, respectively. Nevertheless, after the arrest of the Gang of Four in October 1976, letters began to bounce back. As many as 8,000 letters were received in one month by the *People's Daily* in 1977. In March 1978, the number went up to 20,000 and in June to 40,000.[10] In October 1978, the *People's Daily* was receiving more than 3,000 letters a day.[11] The number of letters published in the *People's Daily* also exceeded those in previous years. From October 1976 to September 1978, a total of 375 letters were published.

In the *People's Daily*, the letters appear either alone or together with the comments of the editor and/or the investigations of the complaints. Responses to the charges made in the letters are often published, sometimes together with the accusing letter and sometimes after an elapse of time. Letters disagreeing with the responses or the editor's comments may also be published. There were times when the *People's Daily* sought clearance from a higher unit of the accused party before a letter was published.[12]

Methodology

The letters analyzed in this study were those published in the *People's Daily* during 1967 and 1968 as well as those published from October 1976 through September 1978. The years 1967 and 1968 were chosen for a number of reasons. The Cultural Revolution started in the summer of 1966. By January 1967, the outcome of the power struggle began to crystallize when revolutionary committees took over the various regions. As a whole, the years 1967 and 1968 represented a gradual transition from the violent upheavals of late 1966 to a consolidation of power by the radical group. During this period, the Party not only encouraged the mass of people to participate in a nationwide campaign against Liu Shao-ch'i and his followers, but also allowed the expression of rival claims and grievances of a minor nature. Letters published in the *People's Daily* during the two-year period were thus considered likely to shed light on the research problem we have proposed.

The letters published in the *People's Daily* from October 1976 through September 1978 were chosen for several reasons. Chairman Mao Tse-tung died in early September 1976. Within a month, his widow Chiang Ch'ing and her three most trusted associates were arrested as the Gang of Four. The following two years represented a transition from the ideological and behavioral norms of the Cultural Revolution to those advocated by the new leaders under the Four Modernizations. The mass of the people were not only urged to join a nationwide campaign against the Gang but also encouraged to expose the errors and mistakes of cadres. Thus, letters published in the two years after Mao's death are also pertinent to our research problem.[13]

All the 182 letters in 1967 and 1968 as well as the 375 letters in October 1976 through September 1978 were analyzed and discussed under the categories of (a) characteristics of letters; (b) kinds of groups in conflict with each other; (c) nature of conflict; (d) modes of conflict resolution; and (e) orientation of letter content. For convenience, we have grouped all the letters into four periods: Period Ia covers 1967; Period Ib, 1968; Period IIa, October 1976 through September 1977; and Period IIb, October 1977 through September 1978. Periods Ia and Ib will be referred to as the Cultural Revolution years; Periods IIa and IIb, as the post-Gang years. Comparisons will be made to see whether any change has occurred.

Characteristics of Letters

Cultural Revolution Years

Most of the letters published during the Cultural Revolution years (60 in 1967 and 66 in 1968) were classified under the Conflict category, in the sense that they expressed rival claims to scarce resources, status, or ideology (Table 8-1). Of all the letters we analyzed, only 8 in 1967 and 2 in 1968 were classified as Safety-valve letters that sought release from personal frustration, defined as being unable to reach an individual goal, or from minor grievances, defined as being treated with unfairness.

The remaining 46 letters (about one-fourth) were classified under Others, most of them providing or seeking information or expressing support of the Party policy. Although these letters will not be further discussed, a few examples will clarify their contents. Some told of the use of cheap materials as substitutes for ink and paste in writing *tatzupao*.[14] Another reported how workers had applied Mao Tse-tung's thought in operating a train locomotive.[15] In a letter seeking information, one Peking Red Guard inquired about the killing of some 100 college students in Rangoon, Burma.[16] Three letters by soldiers of the People's Liberation Army asked their parents to join the Cultural Revolution and support the Party.[17]

Of all the letters, more than half were unsigned. Their writers were identified simply as "A Reader," "A Worker," "A Soldier," and the like. More than 10 percent of the letters were written by groups of people, for instance, "A Group of Revolutionary Workers," and were classified under collective authorship.

Of those writers whose characteristics we could identify, workers, soldiers, and peasants were the most numerous categories (Table 8-2). In 1967, when the Cultural Revolution was still going on, 16 letters were attributed to Red Guards who were mostly students, compared with only one in 1968. Party cadres appeared somewhat less frequently as letter writers than did workers, peasants, and soldiers. Institutions, such as a commune or a production unit, were attributed 4 letters, and another 6 were written by the correspondence sections of some units. In nearly 32 percent of the letters (59), the characteristics of the letter writers could not be determined.

The individuals and groups referred to in the letters appear to fall into

178

Table 8-1

Identity of Letter Writers

	Safety Valve				Conflict				Others				Total	
	Period I		Period II		Period I		Period II		Period I		Period II		Period I	Period II
	a	b	a	b	a	b	a	b	a	b	a	b		
Signed	3	0	2	22	16	27	70	118	6	7	22	43	59	277
Unsigned	5	2	1	1	34	29	5	16	18	12	2	0	100	25
Collective	0	0	0	1	10	10	12	22	2	1	14	24	23	73
Total	8	2	3	24	60	66	87	156	26	20	38	67	182	375

Notes: Letters attributed to any group or institution, such as a commune, a report section, a municipal bureau, etc., are classified as Collective. Letters are classified as Signed when names are given, Unsigned when names are not given.

Period I: Cultural Revolution years—(a) 1967; (b) 1968.

Period II: Post-Gang years—(a) October 1976 to September 1977; (b) October 1977 to September 1978.

Table 8-2
Characteristics of Letter Writers

	Safety Valve				Conflict				Others				Total	
	Period I		Period II		Period I		Period II		Period I		Period II		Period I	Period II
	a	b	a	b	a	b	a	b	a	b	a	b		
Red Guards	0	0	0	0	12	1	1	0	4	0	0	0	17	1
Intellectuals	0	0	0	4	1	1	1	15	0	0	2	3	2	25
Students	0	0	0	1	0	0	2	2	1	0	1	2	1	8
Teachers	0	0	1	0	2	1	3	2	3	1	0	1	7	7
Workers	4	0	1	3	10	13	6	12	2	5	3	4	34	29

Peasants	1	1	0	0	4	8	5	8	1	4	3	2	19	18
Soldiers	0	0	0	1	5	7	10	10	6	3	2	9	21	32
Cadres	2	0	0	1	4	6	22	37	3	1	1	4	16	65
Correspondence or report section	0	0	0	0	5	1	4	2	0	0	8	0	6	14
Institutions	0	0	0	1	1	3	9	20	0	0	6	23	4	59
Unidentified*	1	1	1	13	18	27	24	49	6	6	12	19	59	118
Total	8	2	3	24	62†	68†	87	157†	26	20	38	67	186†	376†

*Unidentified refers to those whose characteristics could not be ascertained from either the attribution of authorship or the content of the letter.

†Subtotals are greater than the number of letters included in the category because some letters were coauthored by individuals of different class backgrounds.

Table 8-3

Individuals and Groups Referred to in Letters*

	Safety Valve				Conflict				Others				Total	
	Period I		Period II		Period I		Period II		Period I		Period II		Period I	Period II
	a	b	a	b	a	b	a	b	a	b	a	b		
Red Guards	0	0	0	0	2	2	2	0	4	0	0	0	8	2
Intellectuals	0	0	0	1	3	5	6	20	2	2	1	8	12	36
Students	0	0	1	0	8	9	6	4	2	2	2	2	21	15
Teachers	0	0	1	6	4	12	9	6	0	3	1	1	19	24
Workers	3	0	1	6	16	34	16	29	4	11	16	23	68	91
Peasants	0	0	2	3	10	31	30	24	15	7	11	4	63	74
Soldiers	0	0	0	1	1	13	9	5	6	2	10	7	22	32

Cadres	2	0	1	5	20	15	59	129	5	2	23	33	44	250
Clique/factions†	0	0	6	0	8	1	61	79	0	0	21	27	9	194
Capitalist roaders‡	0	1	0	0	15	38	9	8	10	1	0	1	65	18
Collectivity	1	2	0	0	6	10	0	0	1	9	1	0	29	1
Revolutionary mass	2	0	1	5	21	10	15	48	4	1	5	12	38	86
Others	0	0	0	3	8	2	18	13	3	0	6	1	13	41
Total	8	3	7	36	122	182	240	365	56	40	97	119	411	864

*Calculation was based on the frequencies of mention for each category of people in letters. One letter may refer to several categories.

†Cliques/factions in Period II refers to the Gang of Four.

‡Capitalist roaders in Period I were the targets of criticism. These leaders were disgraced during the Cultural Revolution. This term was infrequently used in Period II to refer to followers of the Gang.

the same categories as the letter writers (Table 8-3). Peasants, workers, and Party cadres were the more numerous categories. In both 1967 and 1968, a large number of letters referred to "capitalist roaders" as a source of conflict, whereas "revolutionary mass" was often cited as a source of support. While soldiers wrote many letters, they were not referred to in letters written by others as frequently as workers and peasants.

The relatively high frequencies in which peasants and workers appeared as letter writers and as the parties in conflict suggest that these two groups were both the holders of preferred status and contenders for scarce resources. In comparison, teachers and students appeared to hold lower status. Soldiers, while holding relatively high status, seemed to express contention less frequently than workers and peasants. When they were referred to in the letters, they were generally presented as models of behavior or groups who helped resolve conflict, but hardly ever as a party involved in conflict. As far as we could tell, only two letters seemed to be written by individuals whose names suggested that they were women. In no case did the content of any letter indicate that the writer might be female.

Post-Gang Years

Most of the letters (64.8 percent) published during the post-Gang years (87 in Period IIa and 156 in Period IIb) were classified under Conflict. Only 3 in Period IIa and 24 in Period IIb were Safety-valve letters (7.2 percent). The remaining 105 letters (about 28 percent) were classified under Others, which provided or sought information, or expressed support of Party policy (Table 8-1). Compared with the letters published in 1967 and 1968, the distribution of letters over the three categories was similar.

We found that more than half of the letters (54.6 percent) written in Period I were unsigned. For the post-Gang years, however, only 25 (6.7 percent) were unsigned. This increase in the number of signed letters suggests that the Party's call for exposing the errors of the Gang met good response from the readers. Compared to ten years earlier, the unsigned letters now contained more information, that is, that the writer was a technician, a worker in a certain factory, or a poor or lower-middle peasant of a particular brigade.

While cadres, workers, soldiers, and peasants continued to be the more frequent letter writers as was the case ten years previously, institutions, such as a commune, or a Party or administrative unit, were writing more letters, as were intellectuals. Another difference noted was the single letter by a Red Guard, no longer a privileged class.

The individuals and groups referred to in the letters appear to fall into the same categories as the letter writers (Table 8-3), except for the high frequency of mentioning the Gang of Four, as opposed to "capitalist roaders" ten years before.

184

In Period I, there was a high frequency of mentioning *chi ti* (collectivity) compared to only one mention in letters of the post-Gang years, reflecting the change in ideology. The frequencies with which peasants, workers, and cadres appeared as letter writers and as parties in conflict remained high. The increase in the number of intellectuals as letter writers suggests a shift away from previous policies. Soldiers continued to hold high status and presented themselves in the letters as reporters of conflicts rather than participants.

The post-Gang years found 11 letters written by women. Whether this implies a significant change in women's status and role in society, however, needs further verification.

Kinds of Groups in Conflict

Cultural Revolution Years

During the Cultural Revolution, the letter writer frequently did not place himself directly in a conflict situation, but rather played the role of an observer by reporting on a conflict involving others. His own position in the conflict, however, could be clearly inferred. For instance, a letter writer would describe a current practice, such as Party cadres using year-end surplus funds to make woolen work uniforms.[18] Instead of directly objecting to this practice, he would quote Chairman Mao Tse-tung to indicate that such use of public funds was not proper. Our analysis regarding the groups in conflict, therefore, is not necessarily based on the relationship between the letter writer and the parties referred to, but on the situation as we could assess it from the content of the letter.

Table 8-4 summarizes the results for 1967 and 1968. For both years, the largest number of conflict situations involved "class enemies and capitalist roaders." We found peasants, workers, intellectuals, and the "revolutionary mass" all attacking "class enemies and capitalist roaders" along the line of the Party's sixteen-point directives.[19] More significant, however, was the finding that in 1967, Party cadres were frequently in conflict with workers and peasants. In most of these cases, the workers and peasants were expressing dissenting views and disagreeing with the Party cadres over either the allocation of material resources or the use of labor. One example was the letter written by a worker of the Peking People's Bus Company. Citing Mao's instruction on "grasping revolution and promoting production," this worker said some of the section leaders held different views, and because of this, some workers wanted to replace them. In some sections, he said, the disagreement almost led to a fight.[20]

Also noteworthy were the conflicts between workers and intellectuals, mostly because the workers did not agree with the way the intellectuals were handling things concerning them. This can be seen in a letter written by Lin Hsun-lung, a worker in Peking's Third Steel Mill. Lin

Table 8-4

Kinds of Groups in Conflict*

	Red Guards	Intellectuals	Workers	Peasants	Cadres	Soldiers	Class enemies, Capitalist roaders	Revolutionary Mass	Cliques/Factions
Red Guards	2/0†	0/0	0/0	0/0	0/0	0/0	0/2	0/0	0/0
	0/0	0/0	0/0	0/0	0/0	0/0	0/0	0/0	2/0
Intellectuals		6/1	7/1	0/6	1/0	0/0	5/7	0/0	0/0
		0/0	0/0	0/0	1/16	0/0	0/0	0/0	11/7
Workers			4/3	0/1	5/2	0/1	0/23	0/0	0/0
			0/0	0/0	5/8	0/0	0/0	0/0	9/1
Peasants				5/5	5/4	0/0	6/12	0/0	0/0
				0/0	21/25	0/0	0/0	0/0	5/0
Cadres					2/7	0/0	0/4	2/1	0/0
					10/24	0/1	0/0	12/27	4/6

Soldiers	0/0	0/0	0/0	0/0
	0/1	0/0	0/0	1/0
Class enemies, Capitalist roaders		0/0	7/7	0/0
		0/0	0/0	0/0
Revolutionary Mass‡		0/0	0/0	0/0
		0/0	0/0	6/5
Cliques/Factions§			9/1	
			0/0	

* It was frequently difficult to ascertain what groups were in conflict because the letters were not always specific about the parties involved. This table includes only those groups in conflict that could be clearly identified.

† All figures should be read as follows:
   Period Ia/Period Ib
   Period IIa/Period IIb

For example in the first column, under Red Guards vs Red Guards, 2/0 means there were two mentions of conflict between Red Guards and Red Guards in Period Ia but none in Period IB. For Periods IIa and IIb, 0/0 means no such conflicts were mentioned.

‡ In Period II, Revolutionary Mass became Mass of People in 99 percent of the letters.

§ Cliques/Factions refers to the Gang of Four in Period II letters.

told of a case where an expert came to his factory with a group of newly graduated technicians to install a plastic pipe for acid discharge. Workers in the factory offered advice, which was ignored. The result was disaster.[21] This kind of conflict appeared less frequently in 1968 than in 1967.

In 1967, there were frequent references to cliques and faction fights, clearly a reflection of the Cultural Revolution. It is significant that soldiers were presented in a conflict role only in one case in 1968 and not at all in 1967.

Post-Gang Years

In general, letter writers were now more blunt in presenting the conflicts, unlike the tendency to beat around the bush ten years earlier. For instance, a branch Party secretary wrote that he could no longer stand the many meetings he was required to attend. He said that during the first season of 1977 he had to attend meetings on forty-seven days, leaving him no time for his regular duties.[22] A Shanghai resident complained that he had been bothered for more than ten years by the noise from a fan installed in a restaurant next door. His request for correcting the situation was ignored again and again in spite of promises from the restaurant's management to reduce the noise. In making this complaint, the letter writer was to the point.[23]

Table 8-4 shows the groups in conflict that could be clearly identified. For both Periods IIa and IIb, we found no cases of "class enemies or capitalist roaders" being attacked by other groups, a sharp contrast with the results in letters of 1967 and 1968. Cadres, however, continued to be in frequent conflict with workers, peasants, the mass of the people, and among themselves. In most of these cases, like ten years before, the workers and peasants expressed disapproval of the cadres' allocation of material resources or management styles. One example was a letter indicating that some local cadres had insisted on implementing the "three plantings and three crops" without taking different local soil and weather conditions into consideration.[24]

Conflicts among the cadres themselves were numerous, suggesting contentions among different units or between higher and lower units. For instance, a letter from three cadres of a Chi-lin machine factory said that they had to receive and entertain all kinds of inspection groups during the year, leaving them little time to perform routine duties. They suggested that inspections from the various units be integrated into a single group and conducted only twice a year.[25]

Another difference noted was the conflict between cadres and intellectuals, especially during Period IIb. While ten years earlier intellectuals had been faced with criticism, they were now contending with cadres who still clung to practices discriminating against intellectuals. For instance, a technician working as a laborer in Ma Wei

188

Shipyard of Fukien Province wrote that 53 percent of the college graduates at the factory were still working as manual laborers. Though technicians ought to have been restored to their original posts, their requests for transfer were ignored by the factory's cadres.[26]

While attack on "capitalist roaders" was characteristic of Period I, the trend in Period II was to direct criticism against the Gang of Four or their followers. As mentioned, soldiers were rarely presented in conflict roles. Reference to "cliques and faction" fights, typical of the Cultural Revolution, was absent in letters of the post-Gang years.

Nature of Conflict

The nature of conflict as indicated in the letters was classified into three categories: (1) allocation of resources, both human and material; (2) attainment of high status and exercise of leadership; and (3) ideological differences. The results for both the Cultural Revolution and the post-Gang years are presented in Table 8-5.

Human Resources

Cultural Revolution Years. Some of the conflicts over the allocation of labor had to do with inefficient management. For instance, two members of Chuan Shui People's Commune, Peng Chi County, Liaoning Province protested the numerous meetings that were taking up the time of cadres as well as commune members. In March 1968, only two of the commune's twenty-three cadres were working in the commune. The others spent most of their time attending meetings. Whenever there was a "broadcast rally," all commune members had to stop work and attend the rally, which would last anywhere from four to eleven days. After they returned to their commune, they would attend more meetings to "thoroughly study" what they had learned at the rally. Sometimes two weeks would be wasted in such a way. Citing Chairman Mao, the two suggested fewer meetings and shorter meetings. If a broadcast rally were necessary, it could be held in the evening.[27]

Other cases of conflict arose from differing philosophies of the purpose of education or labor training. A young worker at Peking's Third Steel Mill said that even though Chairman Mao had told them that the objective of education was to serve the proletariat by labor, all he was told to do in school was to get good grades and pass entrance examinations. When he became a worker after high school, he found that the things he had learned from books had no connection whatsoever with his job. He demanded a change in the education system.[28]

In 1967 and 1968, many conflicts could be traced to rival claims regarding whether top priority for labor utilization should go to production (or, in the case of Red Guards, returning to school for their education), or to continued participation in the Cultural Revolution.

Table 8-5

Nature of Conflict*

	Period I		Period II		Total Period	
	a	b	a	b	I	II
Human Resources						
Management-bureaucracy	3	4	32	29	7	61
Education-training	6	5	9	12	11	21
Revolution vs production	8	18	10	1	26	11
Revolution vs education	5	3	9	1	8	10
Material Resources						
Against waste	10	9	12	28	19	40
Distribution of rewards†	5	8	2	26	13	28
Status and Leadership						
Leadership	10	4	10	22	14	32
Clique/faction	9	1	4	0	10	4
Class conflict	3	14	0	0	17	0
Ideology						
Individual	3	1	0	11	4	11
Collective	9	11	23	21	20	44
Human rights	0	0	0	13	0	13
Total	71	78	111	164	149	275

*A considerable number of letters in both periods covered several kinds of subject matter. Thus, the total reported here is greater than the 126 letters included in the conflict category for Period I (a and b) and the 243 letters for Period II (a and b).

†Distribution of rewards in Period II includes the distribution of farming machine parts or other scarce materials (such as houses, material supplies, etc.).

Several letters from peasants objected to the practice of organizing the commune members into political propaganda teams in the name of "grasping revolution." Also in the name of revolution, some cadres loaded the peasants into buses and transported them to rallies or demonstrations several hundred miles away. In both cases, production suffered.[29]

Toward the end of 1966, after Chairman Mao had reviewed millions of Red Guards in Peking, most Red Guards were urged to go back to school. Some Red Guards evidently refused to do so and claimed that they should stay away from school to "thoroughly stir up revolution." A number of letters attacked this position and urged the stray Red Guards to return to school.[30] None of the letters supported the countermovement of "thoroughly stirring up revolution."

Post-Gang Years. As mirrored in the letters, conflicts over the allocation of workers in this period were similar to those during the Cultural Revolution, except that there was more criticism of bureaucratic and nepotistic management. One major area of conflict was the assignment of commune members to nonproductive duties, such as office work or propaganda activities, at the expense of local productivity. One letter said that the Ta Si Chuang brigade of Kwang Lin County, Shansi, had 47 percent of its labor force engaged in nonproductive work while other commune members had to share their work burden and contribute to their income.[31]

The problem of labor wastage existed in factories as well. Kai Yuan Paper Mill was an example. Located near a commune, this paper mill recruited rural laborers for "special projects," which did not exist. Furthermore, workers in the factory took advantage of these "special projects" to get jobs for their own relatives in the villages.[32] A poor and lower-middle peasant of Ku Cheng Commune's Chao Village brigade, Yang Kao County, Shansi, said that his brigade had at least seventy members doing next to nothing, and the brigade's fur factory had its staff inflated from fifty to eighty. This practice, he said, had affected rural production.[33]

Too many meetings continued to be a serious problem confronting the cadres and the people alike. Again and again, cadres, soldiers, and workers pleaded for "fewer meetings, shorter meetings." A Party branch secretary in Peking said that during the first three months of 1977, he spent thirty-two days in meetings and another fifteen days for regular study sessions, leaving only thirty-one days for work and labor duties.[34] A worker in Shantung said everywhere he went there were meetings, sometimes five or six a day. The meetings were long because every leader had to say something, usually a repetition of platitudes.[35]

Other cases of conflict had to do with the function of education. Three Party members urged that the Party strengthen the education and discipline of leadership cadres.[36] A worker wrote that more popular books on science and technology be published and courses be organized to help elevate the technical skills and knowledge of workers.[37]

Two teachers urged that the teaching of basic knowledge be given equal emphasis with political education. They said that some teachers were still apprehensive about teaching basic knowledge for fear they might be accused of ignoring political education. The two said this policy of the Gang of Four needed to be corrected.[38] Several students of Kwangtung Chung San Medical College wrote that they were required to go to a political course every Thursday, to attend a political study session on one afternoon, to participate in Party and League activities another afternoon, and to be present at a class affairs meeting one evening. Their regular study activities, they said, were greatly affected. They had pleaded to no avail for a reduction in such political activities.[39]

In Shantung, an import-export artcraft company had a similar problem. One letter revealed that in 1977 the company had to devote the afternoons to political studies for one-third of the year. In January 1978, the company reserved all the afternoons for political studies and two full days for meetings. The writer said that political sessions were nothing more than reading newspapers, announcing documents, or chattering. To make up the lost labor during political studies, each year the factory had to hire some 1,300 temporary workers. The writer considered the practice a waste and wondered whether the factory should devote so much time to political studies at the expense of production.[40]

Material Resources

Cultural Revolution Years. Most of the conflicts over allocation of material resources had to do with wasteful practices. For instance, two readers in Honan Province wrote separate letters opposing the demand by their cadres that each family hoist a red flag in front of its house, because it would cost the commune both money and clothing rations to comply with this rule. Another wasteful practice found objectionable was the use of production vehicles for sightseeing tours across the country. For instance, on 2 July 1967, at 5 p.m., one resident of Peking counted more than thirty such vehicles parked in front of the Peking Revolutionary Museum. "This resulted in tremendous waste of public gasoline," he wrote.[41] Another wasteful practice occurred at harvest time. A reader in Anhui Province wrote that some production units were holding big feasts using collective funds.[42] In Wuhan, when revolutionary committees were being organized, different units competed with each other in staging parties.[43] In other areas, besides holding celebration rallies, parades and the exchange of gifts were common practice, which resulted in waste of both human and material resources.[44]

Another source of conflict was the distribution of rewards in the form of bonuses. Almost unanimously, the letter writers expressed objection to the bonus system, which was apparently widely practiced, judging by the diverse geographical locations the letters came from.[45] This conflict had not abated by 1968.

Post-Gang Years. Most of the conflicts over the allocation of material resources in these years were very much the same as before and in quite a few cases were more serious in tone and substance. Overall, there seemed to be a genuine concern about waste of material resources. One example is a letter from a bank cashier in Shao Hsing, Chekiang.[46] The Party's district committee had ordered a refrigerator for its own mess hall for a sum of 7,400 yuan. When the disbursement notice reached the People's Bank branch office at Shao Hsing, the bank employees had a discussion. The cashier refused to pay the amount for the following reasons:

1. The refrigerator was ordered presumably to look after the "welfare" of the mass of the people. Did it mean the welfare of the people was neglected if the district committee's mess hall did not have a refrigerator? No public restaurants in Shao Hsing currently had a refrigerator. Why should the Party's district committee be different?
2. Where did the Party's district committee get the 7,400 yuan? Why did the provincial government approve it? With this kind of leadership, how could the bank exercise its function as controller of national funds?

The cashier asked the *People's Daily* for advice because in refusing to pay the amount he was running a risk. If his action should be considered wrong, he would be punished either by criticism or administrative discipline.

Along with the letter was the editor's comment: The cashier was completely right in refusing payment. The Party's district committee had accepted criticism from the people and had given the refrigerator to a hospital in Shao Hsing. Even though a refrigerator was a small matter, said the editor, leadership cadres should exercise caution in the use of public funds. The bank should take its responsibility seriously, as did the cashier in Shao Hsing. All cadres should accept criticism from the people with an open mind.

Another letter criticized a practice among many offices of spending public funds for nonessential purchases or travel toward the end of the fiscal year.[47]

In 1977, three cities in Heilungkiang formed themselves into a unit of intramural competition known as *tui k'ou sai* ("compete mouth-to-mouth," or race neck-and-neck). The various organizations of the three cities exchanged visits in order to learn from each other's experience. This started a stampede of travel and feasts, with gongs and cymbals, firecrackers, welcoming *tatzupao*, and endless banquets. The letter writer, himself a cadre, said there was resentment among some cadres. It was indeed "compete mouth-to-mouth," but in eating rather than working, said the letter.[48]

The Provincial Party Committee investigated and found the charges to be true.[49] The so-called exchange of visits was merely an excuse for sightseeing tours, all paid for by the state. For instance, when the Finance and Trade Representatives of Chi Hsi visited Ho King, they had a feast for three days, during which no two dishes were the same. Even the pastries bore the special greeting, "Warm Welcome." The three cities did not compete in production but tried to outdo each other in wasteful spending and extravagance. In his comment, the editor condemned the three cities and praised the letter writer for exposing what was apparently a common practice.[50]

Another wasteful practice had to do with management that stressed "face" more than "substance." In Shansi Province, a poor and lower-middle peasant wrote that from 1972 to 1975 his brigade used some 10,000 yuan and engaged some 30,000 workers to build three reservoirs and an around-the-mountain aqueduct. All the projects failed; efforts and money were wasted.[51] Another Party member urged local cadres not to engage in blind building of reservoirs.[52] In all these cases, the cadres cared more about showing off their projects than paying due attention to the projects' endurance.

The distribution of rewards in the form of bonuses, a major source of conflict in letters of 1967 and 1968, was no longer mentioned in the letters of 1976–1978. The focus of concern now had moved to the allocation of scarce materials, such as tractors, machines, bicycle or radio parts, houses, and so on. Perhaps the more serious cases had to do with the distribution of parts for farming machines. In Feng Si County of Shansi Province, 72 of the 102 tractors could not operate for the lack of batteries. Many important parts for other machines were also lacking. The cadres complained that they simply could not get the parts no matter how hard they had pleaded.[53]

Status and Leadership

Cultural Revolution Years. Conflicts over status were classified under leadership, fights between cliques and factions, and class conflict in general. In 1967, frequent references were made to faction struggles in which different groups within the Party fought for control of their units. Generally, no details were given.

The attainment and exercise of leadership were another major source of status conflict, particularly in 1967. One letter writer pointed out that at Lung Chang Commune, Liao Yang County, Liaoning Province, some cadres were given more important assignments after the establishment of the revolutionary committee and acted as if they were officials. He reported how a conflict between the public and the private had been created by the behavior of these cadres; that is, they should serve the interest of the public, not assume private importance as officials.[54]

In other cases, the position of cadres was challenged because they failed to provide leadership in production.[55] The seriousness of such conflicts was indicated by an incident at a Peking shirt factory, where prolonged disputes were reported over the appointment of a deputy director. Only after careful study of Mao Tse-tung and related newspaper articles and discussion among the workers was the conflict finally resolved.[56]

While class conflict in general received relatively little mention in letters published in 1967, many letters in 1968 attacked "class enemies and capitalist roaders," that is, followers of Liu Shao-ch'i.

Post-Gang Years. Most of the conflicts over status cited in this period similarly had to do with the exercise of leadership. There were now only four mentions of fights among cliques (criticisms against the Gang of Four), and no mention at all of the class conflict manifest during the Cultural Revolution.

Many of the conflicts over the exercise of leadership involved the bureaucratic practices of cadres. For instance, a poor and lower-middle peasant in a Hopei commune said that cadres were doing nothing but empty talk. He gave a portrait of those "relatively few cadres."

> A cup of tea,
> A lighted smoke,
> A newspaper for over half a day.
> Their voices are loud at meetings.
> When it comes to hard work they vanish.

Most of these cadres stayed in the office, the letter said. When they occasionally got down to the field for inspection known as *tun tien* (squat at a point), they simply walked around, pointing to this or that. They blamed the village cadres for being too conservative, but whatever they themselves proposed was usually impractical. They were very good at formalism, or knowing how to present a good case. They told lies and made false reports.[57]

Some cadres at the local level invented their own regulations. A commune member in Shansi said that in his region, some cadres used food rationing control as a punishment. For instance, a family's food rations would be reduced if the wife failed to obtain her IUD, if the family did not raise pigs, if the family failed to deliver the required number of eggs, or if somebody failed to show up at a meeting. "How can we live without food?" the writer asked. He wanted this practice stopped.[58]

In another commune, workpoints were reduced if a person was late at a meeting. The doorway was the dividing line. Anybody who arrived outside the doorway at the time the meeting started was punished with a reduction of workpoints. The peasants shuddered whenever they heard there was to be a meeting, said the writer. Even after the purge of the Gang of Four the commune cadres were reluctant to do away with the "doorway" policy for fear that nobody would come. The policy was finally abolished in September 1978.[59]

An employee of a petroleum service station in Shansi complained that the deputy director of the Business Bureau refused to follow gasoline sales regulations. "Does it mean that our system does not apply to the deputy director?" he asked. Both the district Party committee and the editor issued statements criticizing the deputy director.[60]

Four letters were classified under "cliques and factions," all directed against the members of the Gang of Four.

Perhaps the most significant letter on the conflict over leadership was the one by Yang Hsi-yen, who accused the Peking Municipal Party Committee of covering up in spite of the downfall of the Gang of Four. He urged that more truth be revealed.[61] This letter preceded the dismissal of Peking's Mayor Wu Teh by several months.

Ideology

Cultural Revolution Years. Ideological conflicts mentioned in 1967 and 1968 were classified into two categories. Some letters referred to individual deviance, in which the writer pointed out differences either between his previous and present ideological positions, or between his own ideological position and that of others. In both 1967 and 1968, only a few cases of such individual ideological deviance were published. Although these letters amounted to an admission of error, their publication did imply the existence of rival ideology among the people.

Most letters on ideological conflict took a collective tone, in which the writers exposed the then-erroneous ideological positions of "others" (who were generally not clearly identified) and demanded their rectification. Another kind of collective ideological conflict was between the thought of Mao Tse-tung and traditional Chinese fatalism. A commune member in Feng Jen County, Hopei Province reported that some members in his commune would rely on "heaven" for rainfall instead of working on irrigation canals. He told how he used Chairman Mao's ideology to convince them and overcome their reliance on heaven's rainfall.[62]

Post-Gang Years. Ideological conflicts in this period were classified into three categories—individual, collective, and human rights, the third a new category not present in the letters of 1967 and 1968.

In the post-Gang years, there were only eleven cases of individual ideological deviance. For instance, in a letter entitled "Teachers, Please Forgive Us," a former student recalled how during the days of the Gang, his school was total chaos. He himself often quarreled with his teachers, using abusive language appropriate only for enemies. "During those days there were no teachers in my eyes." Now he had come to repent, to realize the poisoning influence of the Gang.[63]

Most of the letters took a collective tone in expressing concerns about the erroneous ideology and thinking that had spread among the people when the Gang of Four was in power. These conflicts were over the cadres' general lack of concern for the welfare of the people,[64] the leaking of Party secrets,[65] and the lack of respect for intellectuals and education,[66] and so on.

Hatred stood out in some of the letters that criticized the ideology of the Gang. A worker said the Gang's claim that they supported the proletariat was simply a lie.[67] Four Party members in the Hopei Military Region noted an attitude among some cadres, that since what the Gang of Four did was so absurd, it was not even worth criticizing. This attitude was wrong, said the four writers. The Gang of Four and their followers must be thoroughly criticized.[68] Another Party member said that with the purge of the Gang, "a big, heavy stone has been lifted from our hearts. Now democracy can be restored to the Party."[69]

The poor peasant administrative committee in an elementary school in Shantung said the Gang of Four nearly destroyed China's education and popularized the attitude that "school is useless."[70] An educator in Hupei said the Gang of Four used to call teachers "flies swarming around stinky, rotten fish," the "worms" and "garbage" of society. They did everything possible to persecute teachers.[71]

Several letters, all by Party members, emphasized the need to reestablish Party discipline after the damage caused by the Gang of Four.[72] One letter specifically advised against using Party membership as an incentive for work performance.[73]

These ideological conflicts differed from those identified in letters of 1967 and 1968, when such conflicts focused on the study of Mao's thought or on Mao's ideology and Chinese fatalism. Letters published since October 1976 concentrated on the errors of the Gang.

The thirteen letters classified as ideological conflict over human rights were mostly about people being persecuted because of their family backgrounds. All these letters appeared in Period IIb. This concern with human rights was a previously unheard of area of contention. A commune member outside Peking challenged the Party's policy on class background and won a major concession.[74] Wang Yi, a girl who in her words "was born in the new society and raised under the red flag," had gone to Chaoling-chuang brigade for rustication and permanent settlement upon graduation from junior high school in 1968. Her father had a "serious historical problem," which she hated. After she had settled down in the village, she severed all relations with her father. In 1970, she became engaged to Ma Feng-chun, the leader of her production team. Ma informed the Party branch office of his engagement to Wang, and

197

emphasized that no relationship would be maintained with her father. After they got married, however, Ma's name was removed from the list of alternate members and he was dismissed from his post as a production team leader. As the Party's branch secretary put it, he had to choose between his wife and the Party. In her letter to the *People's Daily*, Wang asked: Why?

The Party's branch secretary had said that Ma could have his alternate Party membership restored if he left his wife. Ma appealed his case to the commune, but got the same answer. Now, seven years later, Wang asked the *People's Daily* to help. The *People's Daily* endorsed her request. The consciousness of an individual, commented the editor, is not inherited from the parents. Class background is a factor, but not the only determining factor. "In our country all people who are willing to contribute to the socialist reconstruction, including those of undesirable backgrounds, have a bright future.[75]

The result was immediate. Ten days after the *People's Daily* published Wang's letter of complaint, the Party restored her husband's membership retroactive to May 1967 and destroyed all the "erroneous records of the past."[76] On the same day this was announced, the *People's Daily* published a letter by a factory worker in Nanking, in which the writer criticized Wang for severing all relations with her father. If her father had a sinful background, Wang should *hua ching chieh hsien* (draw a clear ideological boundary between herself and her father), and should criticize and even struggle against her father, the better to help the Party reeducate the undesirable elements. However, said the letter, parent-children relations were objective facts, and children had the responsibility of supporting their parents. Wang's letter might unintentionally encourage other young people to cut all relations with their parents of sinful historical backgrounds. They might even do this as a demonstration of their loyalty to the Party. This, said the letter, was against the Party's policy.[77]

The problem of family background similarly haunted Wang Chiang, a student sent down to a farm in Liaoning Province for rustication. Wang told the editor that she was born in a landlord family. Her father, because of his history, had been classified an "enemy of the people." He had gone to a faraway place when she was born, and they hardly saw each other. She had a happy childhood. In high school, she was active in sports—basketball, ping pong, and long-distance running—and she liked mathematics, chemistry, and physics as well as literature. She was a propagandist for her class and took part in many activities. Every year she was elected a model student.

Before her graduation she applied for membership in the Communist Youth League. She was permanently rejected because she belonged to the "five black classes." Some of her classmates observed: "What a pity! Once you are born from the wrong womb, your whole life is finished." She had the first sleepless night in her life. On another occasion, during a physics experiment, she put together a radio set that could get Peking. Excitedly, she tried every station. Suddenly came a chilling remark from a classmate: "No use doing well in physics. Better have a good father." She felt as if she had been floored. She had another sleepless night. Still she wanted to contribute to socialism. Without consulting anyone, she volunteered to go to a remote village to work and learn from the peasants, to prove her loyalty. Now, with the downfall of the Gang of Four she had finally been allowed to join the Communist Youth League.[78]

A soldier of the Liberation Army told the editor his experience. Chiao Liang's parents, both long-time Party cadres with no undesirable historical backgrounds, had been purged seven years before by the Gang of Four and given the label "diehard capitalist roaders." Because of this, Chiao was dismissed by the junior high school in which he had just enrolled, even though he had been a model student and a leader of the Young Pioneers in school. From then on, all his classmates, his teachers, and his friends avoided him as if he was an ill-omened, contaminated object. A young worker who still befriended Chiao was disciplined for "fooling around with the son of a capitalist roader." Chiao said he could not understand this sudden change, and could only blame himself: Why did you end up with the wrong parents! He later left home, became a coal miner, and eventually joined the Liberation Army. Even though he himself had been vindicated, Chiao wanted the *People's Daily* to speak up for all others who suffered similar treatment.[79]

Another letter demanded legal rights.[80] Wang Ying-ping was a machinist in Peking with a worker's family background. On 4 April 1976, the day before the Tien-an-men Square riots, he posted four poems to pay tribute to Premier Chou En-lai. Because of this, he was branded a counterrevolutionary and arrested on 26 April. While in prison, he refused to admit any crime. After the purge of the Gang of Four, he was released on 3 December. At that time, he said, the Public Security Bureau of Peking was still under the control of "that black vanguard" of the Gang of Four. The security men used every possible means to find fault with him and others who had to be released. In Wang's case, the new charge was that he had once read Tolstoy's *Anna Karenina*, considered to be "yellow literature," that is, pornography. They "caught his tail" (that is, to maliciously catch someone on the most nitpicking of charges, if no grounds can be found for more serious charges). Even after his return to his original factory, he continued to be harassed by the leadership who had previously persecuted him.

Later, after *Anna Karenina* had been officially cleared and re-published, Wang went to reason with his leadership. But now a new charge was brought against him. Because Wang had once written short stories touching on the theme of love, he had authored "yellow literature." The Security Bureau seized his short stories and burned them. When he went again to the Public Security Bureau to reason, he was shown out. Now he appealed to the *People's Daily* for justice.

The editor responded with a lengthy comment condemning the practice of "catching a tail."[81] The editor revealed a few variations of the same practice.

One arrested demonstrator became so excited when the news about the purge of the Gang of Four reached his jail that he started shouting, "victory, victory." He was reprimanded: "Don't get excited too early. You opposed the Gang of Four, but you did it prematurely. You upset the game plan of Chairman Mao. It's like going to a battle. You fired a shot before everything was ready. You simply alerted the enemy."

For another person, the "tail" caught upon his release from jail was: Why did you notice the problem of the Gang of Four when other people did not notice it at all? Therefore your opposition to the Gang of Four was against the Party's organizational principle. It was erroneous, and must be seriously examined so that you can learn a lesson.

Another example: The Gang of Four then held the posts of vice-chairman and members of the Political Bureau. Yet you opposed them, and that was just like pointing your spear at Chairman Mao. This was a serious political mistake.

Or this example: When you voiced your dissatisfaction with the Gang of Four, you were actually attacking the Great Proletarian Cultural Revolution and the socialist system.

All these "tails," said the editor, were absurd.

A letter by six workers in Liaoning Province complained about the local police. They were riding on a bus and, when passing a traffic policeman, one worker made a joking salute. The policeman was furious, got in a car, and chased down the bus. Even though the worker repeatedly admitted his mistake, the policeman was not satisfied. He slapped the worker in front of a crowd, and brought him to the station. Other policemen approved the slapping, calling it "corporal education." The police fined the worker 5 yuan and said sarcastically: "You could have saved the 5 yuan for going to a restaurant. What a pity!" The workers wanted the editor to tell them which article in the Constitution specifies this kind of "corporal education."[82]

In his comments, the editor noted that he had received many similar letters, some involving far more serious violation of the human rights.[83] All these letters had been forwarded to the Party secretaries and appropriate agencies in the areas for their attention. Along with the letter by the six workers, the *People's Daily* published a statement by the Public Security Bureau of Shenyang City.[84] Blaming the Gang of Four, the Bureau had taken the following actions: (1) The policeman involved and his superiors had been reprimanded and criticized; (2) they also went to the factory to apologize to the victimized worker, and returned the fine;

(3) leadership cadres of the Public Security Bureau later visited the factory and listened to workers' opinions on how to improve relations with the citizens.

Modes of Conflict Resolution

We analyzed the letters to see whether the conflict reported had already been resolved, and if so, what were the predominant modes in which the conflict resolution had been achieved (Table 8-6).

Cultural Revolution Years

In more than half the cases, the conflict mentioned in the letters of 1967 and 1968 had been resolved. The predominant mode of conflict resolution mentioned was relatively open discussion, in some cases over a lengthy period, between the parties concerned. Two kinds of discussion were noted. Sometimes discussion seemed to have taken place directly between the parties in conflict without a mediator. At one production brigade, for instance, the poor and lower-middle peasants had organized "big meetings, small meetings, and in-the-field meetings" among themselves, and their conflict over the distribution of their crop was resolved.[85]

Discussions were carried out through the mediation of a third party in nearly half the cases. Often the mediator was a unit of the Liberation Army. At one middle school, two Red Guard organizations were involved in a "civil war" scale conflict. With the help of the Liberation Army in charge of the school's military training, the two groups engaged in lengthy talks and the conflict was resolved.[86] At West Ta Tun Commune, Han Tan County, Hopei Province, the Liberation Army's "support agriculture team" was reported to have helped the poor and lower-middle peasants resolve their conflict between "grasping production and stirring up revolution."[87]

There were also cases in which both the Liberation Army and the local revolutionary committee mediated between conflicting parties. At Sun Chang First Middle School, Fukien Province, various revolutionary organizations contended for more office supplies and administrative expenses. A letter reported that the Liberation Army unit at the school and the revolutionary committee organized all teachers, students, and workers to hold discussions and study sessions. The conflict was resolved and the school had been practicing austerity in its supplies ever since.[88] In nearly all cases reported in which the parties in conflict had a chance to exchange views, discussions had led to a resolution of the conflict. In only four cases was conflict resolution not mentioned following discussion between the parties concerned, but the tone of the letters implied that the conflicts no longer existed.

Another prominent feature of the modes of conflict resolution was

Table 8-6

Modes of Conflict Resolution*

	Mao's Guidance Mentioned				Mao's Guidance Not Mentioned				Total	
	Period I		Period II		Period I		Period II		Period I	Period II
	a	b	a	b	a	b	a	b		
Mediated Discussion										
resolution	12	15	7	1	0	0	7	14	27	29
no resolution	0	1	0	0	0	0	0	1	1	1
Nonmediated Discussion										
resolution	9	15	2	0	0	0	0	1	24	3
no resolution	1	2	0	0	0	0	0	0	3	0
Others										
resolution	3	15	9	2	0	0	7	11	18	29
no resolution	26	14	26	8	9	4	29	118	53	181
Total	51	62	44	11	9	4	43	145	126	243

*Whether there was resolution or not was determined by the letter's report of the resolution, by the content of the response letter, or the editor's comments. "Others" include letters that did not report whether there had been discussions or not.

the guidance of Mao Tse-tung's thought. As shown in Table 8-6, the guidance of Mao was mentioned in nearly 90 percent of the letters for both 1967 and 1968. Generally, in cases where conflict was resolved, the teachings of Mao were given credit as the guiding principle that led the parties involved to reach a compromise. In cases where the letter only described a conflict, quotations from Mao were cited to indicate the preferred manner of resolution. No persistent patterns could be ascertained about the kinds of conflict in which the teachings of Chairman Mao were or were not cited. It may be noted, however, that in those few cases where Mao's guidance was not mentioned, none of the conflicts were resolved.

About half the letters in 1967 and one-fourth in 1968 only presented the conflict without reporting its resolution. Most of these letters had to do with the struggle between different factions or between the revolutionary mass and "capitalist roaders." These were problems that had prevailed all over the country during the turmoil of the Cultural Revolution.

Post-Gang Years

Except for a few cases, the modes of conflict resolution identified in these years were quite different. Ten years earlier, letters often mentioned the intervention of the local Party secretary, the local cadres, or the military unit. Now we found only two letters that mentioned the mediating role of the local Party secretary in resolving conflicts.[89] Instead, the mediators now were usually cadres from higher units. The military played no role at all in the conflict resolution mentioned in both Periods IIa and IIb.

Another difference noted was that there were fewer references to the guidance of Mao's ideology. In the later years, only 22.6 percent of the "conflict" letters mentioned Mao's guidance, compared to 90 percent ten years before. The difference was particularly pronounced in Period IIb. In Period IIa, the number of letters with or without Mao's guidance was about equal—44 and 43, respectively. In Period IIb, however, of 156 letters, only 11 mentioned Mao's guidance, whereas 145 did not. Nineteen letters referred to Chairman Hua Kuo-feng's instructions.

Ten years earlier, more than half the letters mentioned the resolution of conflicts, but in Periods IIa and IIb, only 25.1 percent, or 61 letters, mentioned resolution. The other 182 letters merely exposed conflicts and requested their resolution. In all the cases reported, conflicts were resolved through investigations by the People's Daily and/or the units concerned, usually involving higher units. In cases where the resolutions were not satisfactory, sometimes more letters were sent to the newspaper protesting the way the conflicts had been handled. Two examples will illustrate.

A worker at the Wuhan Steel Mill had translated an article on science and technology for a magazine. The article had been accepted, and the magazine was ready to pay him a fee. Some of the cadres at the steel mill told him, however, that doing translation during his spare time was like "working on the private plot," an indication of "seeking fame and profit." It revealed a "tendency of self-motivated capitalism," something that had frequently been the focus of criticism in the past. The writer asked two questions: (1) Was doing translation during one's spare time like "working on the private plot," and a "tendency of self-motivated capitalism"? and (2) What should he do when he received the fee from the magazine?[90]

The National Bureau of Publications, to which this letter was referred, answered as follows: Doing translation on science and technology during one's spare time after one's assigned duty has been accomplished should be encouraged. It contributes to development of science and technology, and should not be regarded as "working on one's private plot," or a "tendency of self-motivated capitalism." The translation fee is a reward for the translator from the Party and the people. The translator has the right to do whatever he pleases.[91]

This statement, however, elicited a protest from a commune member in Hunan, Fang Tien-yi, because it implicitly equated "working on the private plot" with a "tendency toward self-motivated capitalism." The new Constitution, said Fang, specifically stated that commune members are allowed to work on small private plots and engage in family sideline production. Just as doing translation in one's spare time contributed to science and technology, working on the private plot or engaging in family sideline production in one's spare time could also be a contribution to the socialist construction. I should have been given encouragement, not condemnation.[92]

Another case was the protest against the evasion of responsibility. One of the Hwai-nan coal mines was flooded on 22 October 1977. The Hwai-nan Mining Bureau immediately went to the Nanking Metal Machinery Company for equipment and materials to stop the flooding. The company, however, would sell the materials only on condition that the Mining Bureau sold them eight tons of coal. The Mining Bureau did not have that much coal. Receiving the complaint, the People's Daily investigated. On 29 March 1978, the People's Daily published a letter of complaint from the two cadres of the Mining Bureau, its own investigation report, and the reply by the Nanking Metal Company, which merely made a perfunctory criticism of its "selfish attitude" and promised to improve in the future.[93] A month later, the People's Daily published four more letters protesting the way the case had been handled by the Nanking Metal Company and the newspaper itself. The People's Daily, in an editor's comment, admitted its oversight and asked the readers to continue criticizing its work.[94] About two months later, two more letters were published. One letter from the Hwai-nan coal mine detailed what had happened on the day of flooding. Another from the Nanking Metal Company thanked the protest letters for "awakening them from numbness and making them recognize their mistakes." It admitted that the company had tried to evade its responsibility.[95]

Sometimes the mere exposure of conflict in the People's Daily seemed able to exert pressure to get the conflict resolved. In the case of Ma Feng-chun mentioned earlier, it was only ten days after his wife's letter was published that his Party membership was restored.[96]

In other cases, though resolution was not reported, the writer's desire for resolution was obvious. For instance, many letters indicated that cadres did not heed the villages' urgent need for farm machine parts. The People's Daily would write a comment urging that the cadres take active responsibility for supplying the parts.[97]

As indicated earlier, most of the letters (182, or 75 percent) presented only the conflicts without reporting the resolutions. These letters had to do with complaints about inadequate supplies of spare parts for farm machines, assignment of easy jobs to cadres or their relatives, and general confusion over educational policies or ideology as a result of the Gang of Four. These were problems that apparently prevailed in the country and might require a longer time for resolution. This pattern was different from that of ten years earlier, when most of the letters reporting conflicts without resolutions had to do with the power struggle between different factions.

Orientation of Letter Content

Our analysis indicated three different orientations: (1) individual orientation, where the letter was related to individual problems; (2) primary collective orientation, where the letter was oriented to problems involving the local collectivity of which the writer was a member, such as his commune, his factory, and so on; (3) secondary collective orientation, where the letter was oriented to a broader collective beyond the individual's own group, for instance, the nation, the socialist revolutionary movement, or the educational system (Table 8-7).

Cultural Revolution Years

All letters in 1967 and 1968, including those individually oriented, made some reference to national objectives or the goals of the socialist revolutionary movement. Only a few were individually oriented. An overwhelming majority of the letters were oriented toward either primary or secondary collectivities. The few individually oriented letters voiced minor complaints, such as walking several miles to find a store closed[98] or being kept awake by the loud noise from propaganda trucks.[99] None of these letters referred to individual material concern.

Primary-collective oriented letters usually dealt with problems of the

Table 8-7
Orientation of Content

| | Safety Valve | | | | Conflict | | | | Others | | | | Total | |
| | Period I | | Period II | | Period I | | Period II | | Period I | | Period II | | Period | Period |
	a	b	a	b	a	b	a	b	a	b	a	b	I	II
Individual	7	1	1	18	3	0	2	34	6	0	0	20	17	75
Primary Collective	0	1	1	4	34	30	37	68	11	8	9	30	84	149
Secondary Collective	1	0	1	2	23	36	48	54	9	12	29	17	81	151
Total	8	2	3	24	60	66	87	156	26	20	38	67	182	375

local units, either to call attention to the existence of certain conflicts of general concern or to recount how certain conflicts had been resolved.

Secondary-collective oriented letters generally referred to unidentified authorities and were couched in the prevalent radical ideology. Most of these letters assumed a more critical tone than either individually oriented or primary-collective oriented letters. This pattern implied that it was safer for the writer to direct criticism against authorities or institutions if they were not identified. For instance, one letter blamed certain "capitalist roader" cadres for evading their responsibilities as leaders and said their threat to resign was only a means to "sabotage the Cultural Revolution and production." This letter further stated:

> We want to warn all cadres who have made mistakes that giving up their responsibilities was a crime. You must listen to the criticism of the mass people and at the same time assume solid leadership in production so that you may redeem your offense. Those who have committed serious mistakes must also continue to work their best so that your crime may be redeemed.[100]

The tone was harsh. Nevertheless, the letter referred only to "certain units" instead of any specific organization, and the writer identified himself as "a reader" of Ching-chin Mines, Hopei Province.

Post-Gang Years

In the post-Gang years, 20 percent of all letters were individually oriented. However, the proportion was greater in Period IIb, when 29 percent were individually oriented, compared to only 2.3 percent in Period IIa. Furthermore, these letters were quite specific in presenting the conflicts. Ten years before, almost all the letters had used sweeping praise to mask individual concerns. This shift toward a more straightforward presentation of conflict suggests that the Chinese people were responding to pledges by the new leaders that they would right the wrongs done during the Cultural Revolution.

Another difference noted was that there were letters expressing concern about personal material well-being, which had been absent from letters ten years earlier.

Those letters classified as primary-collective oriented dealt, as they did in the previous period, with problems of local units. Some of them were authored by the units concerned in response to criticism or complaint presented in letters from readers. This kind of letter was also absent in the Cultural Revolution years.

Like those of ten years before, secondary-collective oriented letters generally referred to unidentified authorities or the whole nation. Unlike them, however, the later secondary-collective oriented letters did not necessarily assume a more critical tone than either the individually or primary-collective oriented letters. Also, the percentage of secondary-collective oriented letters decreased from 60.9 percent in Period IIa to 29.6 percent in Period IIb, suggesting that after a year of adjustment following the purge of the Gang of Four, the people became more open in their criticism.

Most of the secondary-collective oriented letters had to do with the general lack of discipline among cadres or Party members, and discrimination against politically "bad" classes, and intellectuals. The contents of these letters were also different from those of 1967 and 1968, all of which referred to conflicts only in the vaguest terms.

Safety-Valve Letters

As we have already mentioned, only a few letters in 1967 and 1968 were classified under the category of Safety Valve, in which the writer either sought release of personal frustration or voiced minor complaint against unfair treatment. For instance, an old peasant of Ming-sui County, Heilungkiang Province complained about his unit's co-op store still being closed well beyond nine o'clock in the morning. He had to walk some seven *li* (about two miles) to get a new hoe.[101] A factory cadre in charge of audit complained about being unfairly labeled a "bourgeois reactionary." After some serious study of Mao's thought, he was able to clear himself of the charge.[102] These letters were all punctuated with quotations from Mao.

Safety-valve letters in the post-Gang years were also few. Unlike those of ten years earlier, however, they no longer cited quotations from Mao. A few examples will illustrate the change. A teacher in Kiangsu Province complained that the noise of several loudspeakers had interfered with each other as well as with the regular conduct of teaching.[103] A student reported the poor service at a Peking department store, where she saw three clerks chattering and directing a customer to a wrong counter.[104] A technician in Liaoning was looking for a savings office on a Sunday, the only day he was free from work, but all savings offices in the city were closed. Could the savings offices take another day off?[105] He got two replies. The city propaganda department thanked him for bringing up an important problem. The city bank said that from that moment on, all savings offices in that city would be open year around.[106] Two months later, the People's Bank National headquarters issued a statement in which it endorsed the practice of keeping the savings offices open year around in principle, but asked the various branches to work out appropriate schedules to suit local needs.[107]

A letter from a steel-mill worker in Sinkiang, who called himself Dumb Cow, revealed some interesting examples of *tsou hou men* (entering through the back door), which were resented by the people.[108] One morning he went to the market to buy fish. He got in line but noticed that the fish being sold were small and rotten. When his turn came, he saw a salesgirl stuffing large fresh fish into a cabinet under the counter. Other customers were furious but dared say nothing. Then another salesman came over. He opened the cabinet, took two bags of dried shrimps, left three yuan, and walked away. "This was *tsou hou men* in front of the public," Dumb Cow said.

Apparently the sales personnel in different stores—confectioneries, bakeries, can stores, seafood stores, tobacco and liquor stores, cloth shops, meat stores, vegetable stores—formed a league. Whenever good supplies were available, the employees from these stores just walked in through the back door and took their pick. Even restaurants followed this practice. "If you are known to them, or if you work in one of the stores, you get twice as much for the same price." Dumb Cow gave what he called an absurd example. Sinkiang Restaurant had a special dish made of rice, carrots, and oil. Every morning, when this special rice was cooked, all the cooks, waiters, and employees would eat their fill. Then they took what was left, mixed it with white rice left over from the previous day, and sold it to customers for 35 cents a dish. The same situation existed in the grocery markets as well. Good vegetables were sold to friends, *lao hsiang* (individuals from some sales personnel's native province), and the several hundred employees of supply stores. For the tens of thousands of workers' families, there were only leftover or rotten vegetables.

The writer said that he had nothing against the store employees personally, but he thought this was something the leadership would like to know. He would appreciate it very much if the editor would refer his letter to the district Party committee.

The editor had this note: "Upon Dumb Cow's request, we sent his letter to the Sinkiang Autonomous District Party Committee and asked them to investigate. The committee found what he said was essentially true, and said the letter could be published in the *People's Daily*. We hope comrade Dumb Cow's letter will alert all business departments and related leadership to pay attention to this problem. The masses of people want this problem not only recognized, but also more importantly, corrected."[109]

Processing Letters

Since the purge of the Gang of Four, letters to the editor have increased manifold. In the eight months preceding June 1978, letters received by the *People's Daily* increased thirty times.[110] Though some organizations took an evasive attitude and simply let the letters pile up, creating dissatisfaction among the people, others seemed to treat the letters seriously, resulting in the decrease of complaint letters.[111] Futhermore, the *People's Daily* advised in an editorial that all letters of complaint be referred to the agency one step above, not to the same agency in which the letter writer was located, and never to the cadre who was the cause of the complaint. Any cadre who attempted to retaliate against a letter writer would be brought to face "the discipline of the Party and the law of the state."[112]

Letters sent to the *People's Daily* sometimes received attention from the highest authorities. One example was reported on the front page on 18 July 1978.[113] In January that year, Lo Hsiu-ying, a Miao tribe actress in a dance troupe in Peking, returned to her home district in Kweichow for a visit. She found that improper practices were still common among the cadres even though the Gang of Four had been purged. For instance, many tribal families were not raising chickens, but the cadres ordered them to buy chickens and eggs for delivery to the state. If the chickens and eggs were not delivered within five days, the case would be treated as not showing support for Chairman Hua Kuo-feng. Lo assured the Miao tribal members that this could not have been Chairman Hua's idea.

When she visited some of the homes of the poor and lower-middle peasants, she found that they had very little food. Many peasants told her that this was because the commune and brigade cadres had themselves pocketed the food and cloth subsidies from the state and filed false reports. The peasants did not even see the subsidies.

This letter, first published in an internal publication of the *People's Daily*, received the attention of Hua,[114] who ordered an investigation. The responsible officials of Kweichow provincial government took immediate action. The original letter by Lo was reprinted in the *People's Daily* along with a report that corrective actions had been taken following Hua's instruction.[115]

A similar example concerned the poor service in railway trains. A reader wrote to the *People's Daily* about the rude manner of the conductor and the disorder he saw on the train from Harbin to Shenyang. The letter was published first in the internal publication of the *People's Daily*. Hua read the letter and instructed the Ministry of Railways to improve the service.[116]

The more genuine concern with the resolution of conflicts reported in the letters of the post-Gang years was also evident in the *People's Daily*'s disclosure of letter-processing procedures in an article entitled "How a Criticism Letter Was Handled."[117]

In February 1978, the *People's Daily* received a letter signed by a peasant of Hsiao Hsi Kuan brigade, Ti Chia County, Honan, which revealed how a cadre of the brigade, currently deputy director Liu Wen-hao of the county's trade bureau, had staged a lavish wedding for his son. The *People's Daily* referred the letter to Ti Chia County and its superior Hsin Hsiang District for investigation. An investigation team sent back the following report to the *People's Daily*:

1. Liu Wen-hao was one of the old cadres victimized by the Gang of Four and thus deserved appropriate treatment.

2. He used a vehicle from the trade bureau only one and a half days for the wedding, not ten days as alleged in the letter.
3. He arranged a purchase of 140 catties of pork and five packages of pork products for the wedding, not 300 catties and ten packages as alleged.
4. He had a wedding party of about sixty tables, not "nearly 200 tables."
5. He received case contributions of 1,000 yuan, not 1,300 yuan.
6. He did receive high-quality blankets, clothing, and other gifts, but there was no evidence that these items were worth "upwards of several thousand yuan."
7. He hired cooks and other help totaling more than forty persons, not "just cooks nearly thirty" as alleged.
8. The charge that the District Office tacitly supported Liu was not true. The County secretary did criticize Liu for the waste, but Liu did not call off the wedding feast.

The District Office put through a call to the *People's Daily* to acknowledge that most of the charges were essentially true, but in view of the fact that Liu was an old cadre previously victimized by the Gang of Four, asked the *People's Daily* to refrain from publishing the letter.

The *People's Daily's* response was that being victimized by the Gang of Four was no excuse for special treatment. Even though the county Party secretary said he had criticized Liu, nothing had been done to stop the lavish waste. Furthermore, the investigative report, which tried to find minor inconsistencies with the original letter, amounted to a cover-up. The *People's Daily* sent all the documents to the Provincial Party Committee of Honan. Replies from both the Honan Provincial Party Committee and the Hsin Hsiang District Committee were published. The provincial committee said that the district office had made an error in trying to defend Liu.[118] The district committee admitted that its attempt to find a way out for Liu was a mistake.[119]

Nearly two months later, the *People's Daily* ran a special editorial, entitled "We Want Revolution, We Don't Want Officials Protecting Each Other." Since its publication of "How a Criticism Letter Was Handled," said the *People's Daily*, it had received more than 500 letters from all over the country. Many praised the poor peasants for speaking up; others condemned the Party cadres for attempting to protect their peers. "Officials always protect each other" (*kuan kuan hsiang hu*) was a rotten habit of the reactionary old society, and must be stamped out, said the editorial. Party cadres must not continue to follow this practice, even though the individual involved is a *laotung shih* (old colleague) or a *lao pu hsia* (old subordinate).[120]

Three of the letters were published along with the editorial. A navy staff officer said: "After I read 'How a Criticism Letter Was Handled', the excitement in my heart remained unabated for a long time. With the downfall of the Gang of Four, our people have finally dared to speak up!"[121]

A worker said he finished reading that story with mixed feelings of elation and anger. He was elated because a new political spirit was born with the purge of the Gang of Four, but he was angry because there were still cadres like those on the Hsin Hsiang District Committee or the one who did the cover-up investigation.[122]

A political cadre in the Liberation Army said that even though someone had been victimized by the Gang of Four before, it would be wrong to cover up that person's mistakes.[123]

Three official statements were published on the same day. The Ti Chia County Committee said severe disciplinary actions would be taken against Liu for the lavish wedding party for his son.[124] The cadre who conducted the initial investigation confessed to his error.[125] A circular from the county committee said Liu had been ordered to return all the gifts and to submit to a public investigation.[126]

Not all letters ended that well. Chai Chen-hsueh, a young worker, experienced prolonged persecution because of a letter he had sent to Shansi Daily. The following is a report by a Hsinhua correspondent, published in the People's Daily.[127]

Chai, a junior high school graduate with a lower-middle peasant family background, worked in the purchasing department of Yu Meng Cement Works, Yun Cheng County. He disagreed with the county's practice of banning the rural free market, and in October 1977 wrote a letter to the People's Daily. In November 1977, upon reading an article in the People's Daily that criticized the Gang of Four's opposition to the rural free market, Chai wrote a letter to the Shansi Daily. The county's ban on the rural free market, Chai said, was in support of the Gang of Four, and therefore must be abolished.

The Shansi Daily referred his letter to the Yun Cheng County Party Committee. The deputy secretary of the committee considered the letter a "vicious attack," and sent it to the standing committee for action. On 4 January 1978, two cadres from the county visited Chai's factory for an investigation, to see whether there was somebody behind his letter. The following day, these cadres visited with Chai, pretending that they were reporters from the Shansi Daily. The real motive, said the Hsinhua correspondent, was to find out if anyone behind had engineered the letter. There was no one. Right after that visit, Chai was arrested.

In a report submitted to the county committee after Chai's arrest, the Party branch committee in his factory found "the content of the letter reactionary, the language vicious, and the approach base and mean. It was a spear pointed toward the Party's central leadership, toward Tachai . . . in short, toward socialism." A special committee was formed in the factory to investigate Chai. All the employees and cadres in the factory took part in a criticism movement. Mass criticism rallies, medium-sized groups, and small groups were organized to criticize him "till he stunk." During his detention, Chai went through seven such prolonged criticisms, in addition to other criticism meetings held in his absence. Eventually, Chai was released and returned to his work, but his case had been classified as a conflict "between the enemy and the people," a serious charge. When the Hsinhua correspondent visited him, Chai was very nervous, and was reassured only after the reporter showed his identification card. The comment at the factory, said the reporter, was, "Who could have imagined that you could get into such big trouble just because you wrote a letter to a Party newspaper to express your views?"

Conclusion

Comparative Analysis

Compared to those of 1967 and 1968, the letters published in the 1976–1978 period raised points of contention in a far more direct manner. Reference was usually made to the evils of the Gang of Four. This done, the letter writer proceeded to ask pointed questions without mincing words. Unlike the earlier letters, which only occasionally blamed individual cadres, letters in the later years openly faulted the bureaucracy. There was undisguised criticism of the leadership for failing to serve the people. "Whole-heartedly serve the people" was an ideal Chairman Mao himself advocated time and again. Now the letter writers reemphasized it in the context of practical needs.

The kinds of conflicts expressed were different too. In 1967 and 1968, the radical group was still grappling with Liu Shao-ch'i's supporters for control of the country, and there were many accounts in the letters of fights between local factions. Ten years later such accounts were scarcely to be found. On the other hand, there was unanimous condemnation of the Gang of Four. Conflict between workers and intellectuals was very much in evidence in the letters of 1967 and 1968, but none was mentioned in the post-Gang period. There was much talk about class conflict then, but ten years later not a single letter referred to class conflict.

A good many letters in 1967 and 1968 discussed ideological conflict, either making personal confessions of ideological errors, or attacking unidentified others for failing to live up to the canons of Chairman Mao's ideology. These letters were all phrased in general terms without specifying the content of the ideology or the nature of the errors. There were no such letters at all in the recent period. Instead, some letters directly challenged a cornerstone of the radical ideology, namely, the perennial importance of class background as a basic index of ideological purity, extending even to the third generation. The experience of Ma Feng-chun was a case in point.

Other letters in the recent period raised issues that were largely ideological in substance, but not presented in ideological terms.

Examples were human rights and legal rights, issues that had never been discussed publicly in the Chinese media before.

Rising individual aspirations mark another major difference between the post-Gang years and ten years earlier. The relevance of education provides an illustration of the different perspectives. In Period I, a worker wrote to complain that the education he received in school was not suited to the revolutionary atmosphere of work in his factory, and demanded a change in the educational system. In Period II, workers complained that their current assignments did not fulfill the personal aspirations they had acquired through schooling, and demanded a change of jobs.

The modes of conflict resolution in the two periods were vastly different. In Period I, ideological conflicts were resolved by reaffirmation of Chairman Mao's doctrines, and local conflicts were resolved by discussions within or between groups, always following the guidance of Mao's teachings. Ten years later, hardly any squabbles among local groups were reported in the letters, nor were there theoretical debates on ideology. Chairman Mao was mentioned only in a few letters. Resolution of conflict in the post-Gang era, as indicated by the letters, was by concrete actions, often speedy and sometimes by top level leaders, to redress bureaucratic shortcomings.

One more major difference needs to be mentioned. In 1967 and 1968, the letters came from various localities and discussed many diverse issues, but hardly any letters referred to those previously published on the same topic. Each letter writer sought the attention of the public via the *People's Daily* on his or her own. No one intended to support the positions taken by other letter writers. Ten years later, an issue raised in one letter would sometimes touch off a national echo, with hundreds of letters pouring in from all over the country in support of the original writer. Sometimes, a few letters were selected by the editor and published to give an indication of the public sentiment. Quite often, responses from the official agencies involved were published along with the complaint. In this sense, the letters column in the *People's Daily* had come close to becoming a forum for public discussion.

In the context of these major differences, the similarities seem to be all but lost. In Period II as well as Period I, there were complaints about too many meetings taking up too much of one's time, about incessant loudspeakers, about extravagance by Party cadres, and about poor services of various sorts. These complaints were apparently expressed regardless of the political climate.

Integrative Functions

Letters to the editor for articulating conflict and seeking a resolution have become a major institution in China. In a system as closely coordinated as China's, in which dissent does not receive active encouragement, the letters column provides a legitimate channel for citizens to send messages to the central leadership. Through this channel the central leadership orients itself toward the divergent views and conflictual issues at the grassroots level. By airing minor grievances, the letters serve as an outlet, or safety valve, for releasing some of the latent tension before it accumulates to an intolerable degree. But more importantly, the letters help focus public attention on substantive areas of contention and conflict that must be resolved in order to maintain the adequate functioning and viability of the system.

The importance of this channel as a link between the Party and the people was clearly recognized by the Party authorities, both before and after the purge of the Gang of Four. This is evidenced in official statements in the theoretical journal of *Red Flag* and the *People's Daily*. For instance, an article in the October 1971 issue of *Red Flag* said:

Handling the letters and visits by the people is an important task of mass coordination and ideological indoctrination. Party committee members and revolutionary committees at the various levels must do the job seriously and do it well, because the letters provide a close link between the mass people and the Party and government, and contribute to the solidarity of the proletariat rule. . . . Letters written by the people are the best research materials. They provide information you don't hear around the conference table, nor can you get it in written reports. They are important sources of references for leaders at the various levels to enable them to grasp the overall situation and coordinate their work.[128]

Our analysis shows, however, that the radical group in power during the Cultural Revolution paid only lip service to these principles. Letters published in those years appeared to be more a chorus than a genuine expression of public concern. The new leaders are now relying heavily on letters and visits from the people to expose the misdeeds of cadres and to correct them. "Doing a good job in letters and visits from the people is a long-term political duty. It is an important channel linking the Party and the mass," said *Red Flag* in October 1978.[129] Article after article re-iterated the important functions of letters and visits and demanded that cadres at all levels pay serious attention to the complaints and dutifully correct the mistakes.[130]

Smashing the wicked wind and establishing the right wind, like doing other work, must motivate the mass and rely on the mass. Being the victims of the wicked wind, the mass of people can see more clearly. Leadership at all levels must pay serious attention to the opinions and requests of the mass of the people, handle seriously letters and visits from the people and patiently accept the mass's supervision. . . . Repression, hindrance, and reprisals will absolutely not be permitted.[131]

But as one reads these letters, one cannot help pondering one question: Why do the Chinese have to write to the *People's Daily* in Peking to seek redress of such local problems as working hours of a savings office? Why can't they communicate directly with the local authorities instead of having to rely on the *People's Daily* to get the message across? The answer is provided in part by the worker in Shansi who tried to express his views on the local policy of banning the free rural market. Chances are that messages sent to the local authorities directly will probably be ignored (as experienced by Dumb Cow of Sinkiang), or worse still, provide grounds for harassment (as happened to the worker in Shansi).

This phenomenon is a prolonged manifestation of the traditional Chinese bureaucratic practice known as *kuan-kuan hsiang-hu* (bureaucrats tend to protect each other). Some may argue that this practice is not uniquely Chinese but universal. If so, then the question is: What social institutions are available in a system to provide a measure of checks and balances? In China, where such social institutions are not yet fully developed, the letters to the editor have come to assume the important function of filling the gap.

The practice of writing letters to air grievances and resolve conflicts reveals a curiously traditional inadequacy of the Chinese social system, that is, the reliance on *jen-chih* (personalized rule) instead of institutionalized rule. In the past, when a person had a major grievance for which no reparation could be found because no *yamen* office would bother, he or she would seek (and usually waylay) an official of rare integrity to present the case. The tales of Judge Pao are familiar examples. The most extreme case would be for the person to lie in wait for the emperor to catch his royal attention—a favorite fantasy in traditional Chinese novels, known as *kao yu chuang*, which bore no resemblance to reality. The very popularity of these tales bespeaks an unspoken yearning for some institutionalized mechanism by which grievances could be heard and conflicts resolved. That *Hai Sui Dismissed* should have become such a popular play in the late 1950s was not without its historical and social background. The letters to the editor column in the *People's Daily* has gone a long way toward fulfilling this yearning, albeit partially. In this sense it may become an essential mechanism of societal integration in China.

NOTES

1. George Simmel, *Conflict*, trans. Kurt H. Wolff (Glencoe, IL: Free Press, 1955).

2. Lewis Coser, *The Functions of Social Conflict* (Glencoe, IL: Free Press, 1956), pp. 33–39.

3. Ibid., pp. 39–48.

4. For a discussion of functional prerequisites and structural alternatives, see Robert K. Merton, *Social Theory and Social Structure* (Glencoe, IL: Free Press, 1957), pp. 19–84.

5. Alex Inkeles, *Public Opinion in Soviet Russia* (Cambridge, MA: Harvard University Press, 1962), pp. 197–203, 207–222. Alex Inkeles and Kent Geiger, "Critical Letters to the Editors of the Soviet Press: Areas and Modes of Complaint," *American Sociological Review* 17 (1952):694–703. Alex Inkeles and Kent Geiger, "Critical Letters to the Editors of the Soviet Press: Social Characteristics and Inter-relations of Critics and the Criticized," *American Sociological Review* 18 (1953):2–22.

6. Frederick T.C. Yu, *Mass Persuasion in Communist China* (New York: Frederick A. Praeger, 1964), p. 164.

7. "The *People's Daily* and Letters from Readers," *China Reconstructs* 10 (October 1978):3.

8. Ying Tse, "A Visit to the *People's Daily*'s Letters Unit," *Tong Hsiang* [the Trend], 5 (February 1979), pp. 25–27. *The Trend* is a monthly magazine backed by the Chinese Communists and published in Hong Kong.

9. James C.Y. Chu, "The PRC Journalist as a Cadre," *Current Scene* 13 (11) (1975):1–14.

10. "*People's Daily* and Letters from Readers," p. 4.

11. Yang Yi, "18 Days of Journey to the North," *Ming Pao Daily*, Hong Kong, 2 November 1978.

12. For instance, in Hsin Hsiang District of Honan Province, a poor and lower-middle peasant wrote the *People's Daily* a letter accusing the district trade bureau's deputy director of staging a lavish wedding for his son. The *People's Daily* forwarded the editor's comments, together with the response letter of the District Party Committee and the paper's investigation reports, to the Provincial Party Committee for clearance before publishing the documents. See "How a Criticism Letter Was Handled," "Response from the Chinese Communist Party's Honan Provincial Committee," "Response from the Hsin Hsiang District Party Committee," *People's Daily*, 15 May 1978.

13. Letters signed by reporters of the *People's Daily* were not included in the analysis. These letters by reporters would fall under what we would commonly call investigative reporting. About two dozen letters grouped under "readers, writers and editors" and published on the literary page, called *Chan Ti* (Battlefield), were excluded because they were concerned exclusively with the content of this weekly

217

page, either to show like or dislike for some articles or to suggest the publication of certain authors' works. Three letters written by foreigners were not analyzed. One was written by a West German associated with the Peking Foreign Languages Institute. He complimented a bank clerk for returning the two cents he had been overcharged while cashing his bank draft. "I Shall Keep This Two-Cent Coin," *People's Daily*, 14 February 1978. The second was by a Canadian student at Nanking University who suggested the inclusion of both negative and positive Chinese figures in dictionaries. "Suggestions for the New Four-Digit Index Dictionary," *People's Daily*, 31 August 1978. The third was by the publisher of the *Pittsburg Post-Gazette*, who complained about the traffic noise in Peking and suggested some remedial measures. "Please Use Automobile Horns Correctly," *People's Daily*, 26 September 1978.

14. A Soldier, "Using Yellow Mud as a Substitute for Paste," *People's Daily*, 15 June 1967. A Fighter, "In Writing Big Character Slogans, Attention Must Be Paid to Saving Paper"; Anonymous, "Use Cheap Materials to Make Substitute Ink," *People's Daily*, 30 July 1967.

15. Support-Left PLA Soldiers Stationed at Engineering Section, "Chairman Mao's Red Railway Workers," *People's Daily*, 21 April 1968.

16. A Red Guard, "The Bloodshed of the Reactionary Government of Newin Five Years Ago," *People's Daily*, 7 July 1967.

17. Chang Ho, "Struggle China's Khrushchevs until They Stink"; Hsueh Yu, "Down with Advocators of 'Three Tzu's and One Pao' "; Kwang Yu, "Refute the Absurdity of 'Exploitation Is Rescuing Others' "; *People's Daily*, 29 July 1967.

18. A Store Clerk, "Don't Be Fooled by the Small Handful of Bad People," *People's Daily*, 17 January 1968.

19. "Decision of the Central Committee of the Chinese Communist Party Concerning the Great Cultural Revolution, adopted on August 8, 1966," *Peking Review* 9 (33) (12 August 1966):6–11.

20. A Worker, "Don't Bring Deviation into Production Work," *People's Daily*, 25 August 1967.

21. Lin Hsin-lung, "The Working Class Vows to Be the Stalwart of Educational Revolution," *People's Daily*, 12 December 1967.

22. Liu Kuei-tang, "I Am Occupied with Too Many Meetings to Work," *People's Daily*, 12 May 1977.

23. Ting Chun, "The Motor's Noise Bothered Us for More Than Ten Years," *People's Daily*, 30 November 1977.

24. Li Ming, "Don't Insist on Three Plantings and Three Crops," *People's Daily*, 28 September 1978.

25. Liu Shu-lin et al., "Thousands of Threads from Above, But One Needle Below," *People's Daily*, 25 July 1978.

26. A Technician, "How Much Longer Shall We Wait?" *People's Daily*, 6 May 1978.

27. Tsui Cheng-yao and Heh Kwang-shan, "Fewer Meetings and Shorter Meetings in Busy Times," *People's Daily*, 26 April 1968.

28. A Young Worker, "Thoroughly Repudiate the Old Educational System," *People's Daily*, 12 December 1967.

29. Yueh Shan-hung, "Do Not Travel Far to Visit during Busy Seasons," *People's Daily*, 20 October 1967.

30. A Red Guard, "We Are Heading on the Right Road!"; A Revolutionary Teacher, "Correctly Recognize the Situation and Resume Education While Stirring Up Revolution," *People's Daily*, 9 December 1967.

31. "Strengthen the Labor Force on the Rural Front Line," *People's Daily*, 15 March 1977.

32. Chiu Shih, "This Gate Is Being Guarded Well," *People's Daily*, 25 March 1978.

33. "The Cadres of Our Brigade Have Taken the Lead," *People's Daily*, 26 April 1977.

34. Liu Kuei-tang, "I Am Occupied with Too Many Meetings to Work." Also see 1 February 1977 for other examples.

35. A Worker, "Make Up the Mind and Condense Meetings," *People's Daily*, 22 June 1977.

36. Ting Po-chai et al., "Strengthen the Party's Education and Supervision of Cadres," *People's Daily*, 7 December 1977.

37. "We Workers Need to Study Culture and Techniques," *People's Daily*, 11 November 1977.

38. Tung Chia-wu and Chu Ming-hsu, "The Teaching of Basic Cultural Knowledge Courses Needs to Be Stressed," *People's Daily*, 30 March 1977.

39. "We Students Want a 'Five Sixth'," *People's Daily*, 5 July 1978.

40. Ming Li-hsin, "Cleanse This Remaining Poison of the 'Gang of Four'," *People's Daily*, 2 May 1978.

41. A Peking Resident, "Don't Use Production Vehicles for Long-Distance Sightseeing," *People's Daily*, 17 July 1967.

42. A Reader, "In Harvest Time, Do Not Forget Austerity," *People's Daily*, 23 June 1968.

43. A Soldier, "This Practice Shall Not Be Allowed," *People's Daily*, 25 November 1967.

44. A Soldier, "Fewer Celebration Rallies during Busy Seasons," *People's Daily*, 15 June 1967.

45. Letters came from Honan, Shenyang, Shensi, Shansi, etc. Wei Keh, "Smash Counter-Revolutionary Economism," and "Don't Be Fooled by the Small Handful of Bad People," *People's Daily*, 17 January 1968.

46. Wei Fu-an, "Leadership Units Spend Lavishly: I Can No Longer Resist It," *People's Daily*, 20 April 1978.

47. Wen Yu and Choh Fang, "Prevent Lavish Spending at Year's End," *People's Daily*, 19 December 1977. See also editor's comment and a report from a correspondent on the same page.

48. Li Hsiang-ming, "This Is Not Competition in Working, But Competition in Eating," *People's Daily*, 11 December 1977.

49. Heilungkiang Provincial Party Committee's Investigation Section, "The Mass Has Sounded the Alarm for Us," *People's Daily*, 11 December 1977.

50. Editor's comment, "Know the Mistakes and Correct Them," *People's Daily*, 11 December 1977.

51. "Plan Seriously," *People's Daily*, 5 November 1977.

52. Wang Ping-ho, "Don't Seek 'Grandeur'," *People's Daily*, 15 December 1977.

53. Bureau of Farming Machines, "The Supply of Parts Is in Urgent Need," *People's Daily*, 3 April 1978. For other letters that indicated the urgent need for farming machine parts in rural areas, see issues of 19 March 1977, 25 March 1977, 12 May 1977, 29 May 1977, and 3 April 1978.

54. Liao Hsiang-yang, "Always Serve the People," *People's Daily*, 28 May 1968.

55. A Cadre, "Lower Level Cadres Should Lead Boldly in Production Work," *People's Daily*, 13 March 1968. A Cadre, "Wheat Harvest Must Be Tightly Grasped," *People's Daily*, 6 June 1968. Both letters reported the hesitation of cadres in fulfilling their duties as leaders in Hopei and Honan, respectively.

56. A Cadre, "Let Revolutionary Cadres Grasp Revolution and Promote Production," *People's Daily*, 27 October 1967.

57. "We Welcome Cadres Who Do Work," *People's Daily*, 29 October 1977.

58. Lien Chun-hsian, Liu Chuan Commune, Hsin Chiang County, Shansi, "Indiscriminate Reduction of Food Rationing Should Be Stopped," *People's Daily*, 5 September 1978.

59. Jen Chin-ta and Chou Yung-hsiao, " 'Doorway Points' Have Been Abolished," *People's Daily*, 15 September 1978.

60. Chao Chin-yao, " 'System' Does Not Apply to the Bureau Director," *People's Daily*, 19 June 1978.

61. Yang Hsi-yen, "Who Is Covering Up?" *People's Daily*, 30 July 1978.

62. A Commune Member, "Spearhead in Politics to Overcome Dependence on Heaven," *People's Daily*, 16 February 1968.

63. Keng Hua-chin, "Teachers, Please Forgive Us," *People's Daily*, 19 February 1978.

64. See, for example, letters published on 11, 13, and 18 February 1977.

65. See, for example, letters published on 14 February and 28 March 1977.

66. See, for example, letters published on 19 March and 13 December 1977, and on 29 June 1978.

67. Chu Kung, "Strip Off the Skin of So-Called 'Placing an Equal Sign with the Laboring Mass'," *People's Daily*, 19 November 1976.

68. Chao Lien-tung, Wang Hung, Chang Yu-lin, and Liu Cheng-po, "The Thinking of 'Stink without Criticism' Must Be Conquered," *People's Daily*, 31 January 1977.

69. Party Secretary, Tou Wen brigade, Liu Sha Commune, Pu Ning County, Kwangtung, "Seriously Edit a Good Column on the 'Active Democratic Living within the Party'," *People's Daily*, 16 May 1977.

70. Poor Peasants Committee of Chao Lin Elementary School, Ping Liu Commune, Chang Lo County, Shantung, "Study Culture and Shoulder the Heavy Burden of Revolution," *People's Daily*, 1 December 1976. See also 2 April 1977 for similar letters.

71. Hung Keh, "Uncover the Gang of Four's Conspiracy of 'Pressing Down the Ball'," *People's Daily*, 30 March 1977. "Pressing Down the Ball" means intellectuals must be kept suppressed, otherwise they will "float up" again, like a ball in the water once you lift the pressure. Also see letters of 19 March 1977.

72. Shih Chi-ming, "Strengthen the Party's Education in Discipline," *People's Daily*, 6 February 1977. See also issues of 14 February 1977, 21 March 1977, and 2 December 1977.

73. Liu Hsiao-ming, "Party Membership Should Not Be Used as an Incentive to Stimulate Progressiveness," *People's Daily*, 27 June 1977.

74. Wang Yi, "The Distress of Ma Feng-chun after Marriage," *People's Daily*, 9 August 1978.

75. Ibid.

76. Wang Yi and Ma Feng-chun, "Ma Feng-chun's Problem Has Been Solved," *People's Daily*, 24 September 1978.

77. Chiang Wei, "No Need to Sever All Connections with One's Father," *People's Daily*, 24 September 1978.

78. Wang Chiang, "The Party Has Rejuvenated Me from Decadence," *People's Daily*, 26 August 1978. See issues of 22 January and 29 March 1978 for other letters.

79. Chiao Liang, "The Party's Policy Has Warmed My Heart," *People's Daily*, 26 August 1978. Two more letters of the same nature were published on the same day.

80. Wang Ying-ping, "Talk About My 'Tail'," *People's Daily*, 3 August 1978.

81. Kao Fang, "Comments on 'Catch the Tail'," *People's Daily*, 3 August 1978.

82. Wang Chin-hsueh et al., "Does the Constitution Contain Any Statute on 'Corporal Education'?" *People's Daily*, 25 July 1978.

83. "Response from Shenyang Public Security Bureau," *People's Daily*, 25 July 1978.

84. Ibid.

85. Poor and Lower-Middle Peasants, "Remember Our Revolutionary Endeavor," *People's Daily*, 7 July 1967.

86. A Red Guard, "Three 'Talks'," *People's Daily*, 20 September 1967.

87. Yung Wei-tung, "On Political Basis, Fight a Good Battle in Busy Summer," *People's Daily*, 21 June 1968.

88. Revolutionary Committee of Sun Chang First Middle School, Fukien Province, "For Revolution, Take Good Charge of Financial Management," *People's Daily*, 14 March 1968.

89. Peng Yen-chiang, "Insist on Diligence and Frugality," *People's Daily*, 2 February 1977; also Liu Sun-chuan, "We Have Bean Curds Again," *People's Daily*, 28 January 1978.

90. Fei Kwong-ming, "Is Translation in Spare Time 'Working on One's Private Plot'?" *People's Daily*, 25 July 1978.

91. Ibid.

92. Fang Tien-yi, "The Comment Is Incorrect," *People's Daily*, 24 August 1978.

93. *People's Daily*, 29 March 1978.

94. *People's Daily*, 23 April 1978.

95. *People's Daily*, 11 June 1978.

96. Wang Yi, "The Distress of Ma Feng-chun after Marriage"; Wang Yi and Ma Feng-chun, "Ma Feng-chun's Problem Has Been Solved."

97. Letters in 3 April 1978 *People's Daily*. Please note that letters to the editor are sometimes published in an "internal publication" of the *People's Daily*. For example, see 11 June 1978, and 18 July 1978.

98. An Old Poor Peasant, "Co-op Stores Should Provide the Mass with Convenience and Help with Production," *People's Daily*, 12 May 1968.

99. Letters from Revolutionary Masses, "The Mass of People Demand that the Use of Broadcast Trucks and Loudspeakers Be Discontinued," *People's Daily*, 16 June 1967.

100. A Reader, "Deal a Heavy Blow at Those Who Threaten to Resign," *People's Daily*, 10 February 1967.

101. An Old Poor Peasant, "Co-op Stores."

102. A Cadre, "Carefully Audit Every Expense," *People's Daily*, 1 September 1967.

103. Huang Tao-yi, "High-Pitch Loudspeakers Have Interfered with Our Studies and Rest," *People's Daily*, 3 September 1977.

104. Keng Hsiao-mei, "I Want to Speak for the Mass Consumers," *People's Daily*, 17 April 1978.

105. Hsu Tsu-tung, "When We Rest, They Rest," *People's Daily*, 9 April 1978.

106. Propaganda Department of Chang Wu County Party Committee and Savings Division of Chang Wu County Bank, "Responses," *People's Daily*, 9 April 1978.

107. Chinese People's Bank, "Pay Attention to Letters from the Mass and Improve the Savings Service," *People's Daily*, 5 June 1978.

108. Tsun Niu [Dumb Cow], "This Kind of Business Practice Must Be Corrected," *People's Daily*, 5 July 1978.

109. Ibid.

110. "Grasp the Handling of People's Letters and Visits as a Big Matter," *People's Daily*, 12 June 1978.

111. Ibid.

112. Ibid.

113. Lo Hsiu-hing, "May the Leadership Send Somebody to the Miao District," *People's Daily*, 18 July 1978.

114. "Materialize Chairman Hua's Instructions, Firmly Grasp the Realization of Policies," *People's Daily*, 18 July 1978.

115. Lo Hsiu-hing, "May the Leadership."

116. "Chairman Hua Made Important Comments on a Letter from the Mass," *People's Daily*, 11 June 1978.

117. Editor, "How a Criticism Letter Was Handled," *People's Daily*, 15 May 1978. See also 31 March and 1 June 1978 for other reports on letter-processing procedures.

118. "Response from the Honan Provincial Party Committee Secretary," *People's Daily*, 15 May 1978.

119. "Response from Hsin Hsiang District Party Committee Secretary," *People's Daily*, 15 May 1978.

120. Staff Commentator, "We Want Revolution, Not 'Officials Protecting Officials'," *People's Daily*, 10 July 1978.

121. Yang Yung-hsian, "The People Now Dare to Speak," *People's Daily*, 10 July 1978.

122. Chian Hsiao-ko, "With This Kind of People, No Fort Cannot Be Pierced," *People's Daily*, 10 July 1978.

123. Chang Chen-hai, "Really Care for the Cadres," *People's Daily*, 10 July 1978.

124. "Response from Ti Chia Party Committee Secretary," *People's Daily*, 10 July 1978.

125. Ma Ming-hsi, "Response from Ti Chia County Party Committee Secretary," *People's Daily*, 10 July 1978.

126. " 'Notice' of Ti Chia County Party Committee Secretary" [Excerpts], *People's Daily*, 10 July 1978.

127. Wu Chun-hsiao, "Criticism of the Abolishment of Market Trading in Violation of Policy Results in Chai Chen-hsueh's Persecution by Some People of the Yun Cheng District Party Committee," *People's Daily*, 11 September 1978. For other cases of persecution, see letters published on 24 September 1978, and cases reported in "A Visit to the *People's Daily*'s Letters Unit," p. 26 and "*People's Daily* and Letters from Readers," p. 3.

128. Tu Chien, "Attention Must Be Paid to Letters and Visits from the People," *Red Flag*, no. 11 (1 October 1971):67, 69.

129. "Pay Close Attention to and Do Well in Handling Letters and Visits from the People," *Red Flag*, no. 10 (October 1978):75.

130. For examples: Brief Commentary, "Treat the Mass's Criticism in the Right Way," *People's Daily*, 25 April 1977; Editor's Note, "Dutifully Handle Letters from the Mass," *People's Daily*, May 29, 1978.

131. Hsieh Tso, "Wicked Wind Must Be Suppressed," *Red Flag*, no. 4. (1 April 1978):94.

9

Horizontal Mobilization and Communication for Conflict Resolution: The Tachai Case

Mitch Meisner

Contemporary approaches to the study of modernization, with their focus on national integration, tend to place special emphasis on transforming the local rural communities within the larger society. To secure such change, appropriate use of communication means may aid political authorities in the search for wider and more effective national identity.

An approach to development that examines communication patterns in relation to problems of centralization and decentralization can provide a framework particularly useful for viewing conflict and change in an "active" society like China, with its immense, diffuse rural sector. The expectation is that, in the course of guided change, the cultural and political "small world" of communal symbols, intimate attachments, and local elites of the village will be integrated into the "great world" of the urban-centered, cosmopolitan-aspiring, centrally led nation. Emphasis on centralization is common to most modernization and development literature, including Marxist and contempory neo-Marxist variants. Most writers stress the necessity of establishing a high degree of "stateness,"[1] and the burden of change usually falls on the village or other preexisting local community.

Specific experiences in the Chinese case, however, beginning with the impact of rural setting on the revolutionary experience itself, have suggested that the top-down model of societal integration for development might be subject to modification. For example, Vivienne Shue suggests a relationship "between the localities and the center in which both sides assume some unpleasant burdens, and both accept some restrictions imposed by the other on the range of legitimate actions available to them."[2] Some of my work on the political history of the model Tachai brigade in Shansi Province suggests a similar rethinking. In this chapter, I shall demonstrate the existence of horizontal and vertical linkages, alliances, and channels of communication to describe potential patterns in Chinese political activity that may serve to offset the dominance of centralizing political hierarchies. The primary focus is on discovering instances of solidarity within basic-level communities (especially the production brigade) or large rural locales (especially the *hsien* or county) that may play supplementary or countervailing roles in relation to the national political system.

The immediate subject of study is a series of incidents in the political history of Tachai and some other brigades and communes in surrounding Hsiyang County. In 1963–1964, Tachai was boosted to extraordinary national prominence as a model for rural development and remained in that position until 1980. Obviously, Tachai brigade and its leadership, including ex-Party Branch Secretary Ch'en Yung-kuei, have not had a typical career. Their successes in raising and diversifying output in the particularly bad conditions of the east-central Shansi Taihang mountain region were at one time considerable. Tachai carried out a number of radical institutional reforms, including establishing management and accounting at the brigade level (against the national trend in 1960), abolishing private plots, and implementing an egalitarian system of "self-assessment and public discussion" in workpoint and basic grain distribution. These policies were subsequently instituted in brigades throughout Hsiyang County.[3] Partly because of their much-publicized status and unorthodox practices, they became at times targets for adverse political maneuvers not always evident on the surface. Since its status as an advanced unit went back to the mid-1950s, Tachai was in the spotlight for some time, and, especially because of the activism of its Party secretary, was embroiled in a number of conflicts, most notably with authorities at county and prefectural levels, and in later years, when the Tachai brigade rose to national prominence, with provincial and national representatives as well.

Tachai's experiences in conflict situations were undoubtedly skewed by its reputation and by its later symbolic importance. But its early efforts to fend for its own views were real and comprehensible. Some aspects of emergent patterns shed interesting light on the Chinese political process. A relatively large amount of information is available on Tachai and Hsiyang County, from visitors as well as official publications. I would like to explore some of Tachai's history here in order to examine the horizontal linkages and communication patterns in political conflict. It should be made clear that I attempt to look at the "real Tachai" as much as possible—this is *not* a study of the Tachai model as officially reconstructed prior to the downfall of the Gang of Four.

I shall first look at internal relations in Tachai village during the mutual aid team era in the 1940s and at patterns of leadership and group contact that worked to establish horizontal solidarity among the worse-off village strata. Here conflict involved divisions within intravillage social and political groupings over specific interests perceived to be affected by the mutual aid program. The developing ties became the political basis for Ch'en Yung-kuei's leadership. They also served as a basis for the solidarity of the Tachai community later, during external conflict with county or higher-level authorities.

In the second section of this chapter I shall deal with an instance in the late 1950s, after the formation of the People's Communes, in which the Tachai brigade dealt with problems arising from vertical linkages due to its model status. Tachai was subjected to pressures from county and prefectural levels to conform with a vertical system of communication designed to further the emulation of development policies. In this case, Tachai was faced with demands from the radical programs of the early stages of the Great Leap Forward.

In the final part of the chapter I shall analyze a period of outright conflict with Hsiyang County leadership during the several years immediately preceding the Four Clean-ups campaign in 1964 and that movement itself. This conflict demonstrates possibilities for horizontal alliances among dissenting groups against the vertical Chinese political hierarchy.

Focusing on such horizontal linkages is particularly revealing, because it is during periods of crisis and shattering of routine that deeper-lying structures may emerge to view. An opposition group of county and basic-level cadres centering around the prestigious but low-ranking Ch'en Yung-kuei acted to oppose certain policies. Later, conflict was heightened and shifted to new ground during the Four Clean-ups period of the Socialist Education movement. This led to a pattern of horizontal defense links fostered by Ch'en Yung-kuei, who made use of intra-Tachai village solidarity and contacts with other local cadres to resist the powers vested by the Four Clean-ups campaign in the externally organized work teams that carried out campaign activities in Hsiyang County from 1964 to 1965.

The epilogue summarizes events since the purge of the Gang. The latest accusations revealed that once Ch'en gained position and influence, he fell into the same patterns of fabrication of production figures and abuse of power that he fought against so hard when he was an informal leader in a small production brigade.

Communication and Group Affiliation: Mutual Aid in Tachai

As part of an area in Shansi liberated relatively early, Tachai village undertook "mutual aid" in 1946. In this first state of cooperation, it enjoyed some political advantages, in that it had a nucleus of politically experienced members who had been through long years of war and underground organization. Economically, however, the situation was not promising. Its bad land and climate, a perennially low and unstable agricultural product, and its war-wounded economy have become proverbial in many accounts of the Tachai success story. One problem that colored the significance of early experiences with mutual aid and cooperation was Tachai's diminished and uneven supply of full-strength farm labor. In 1940, the Japanese occupation army massacred more than forty village men and youths. In addition, about twenty-five able-bodied peasants had left to fight with the revolutionary forces by 1945. The village as a whole was depleted of labor, possessed little working capital, and a number of households were seriously weak in relation to others. Once land was distributed, both the absolute and relative impact of the labor shortage became a significant factor in the economic future of this manual labor community.

The subsequent growth in Tachai in many ways was established by developments during this period. It centers around the successful attempt by the militant ex-farmhand Ch'en Yung-kuei (around thirty years old, and to become Tachai village Party branch secretary in 1952) to organize a mutual aim team among ten families with low labor power (out of about seventy households in Tachai at this time) and, cooperatively against great odds, to raise production. His mutual aid team (MAT), consisting mostly of old men and teenage or subteenage youths, became known as the Old and Young Team. By dint of enormous striving over several years, they were able to outproduce another team consisting of a number of the most prosperous and labor-rich families. Composed of members of the dominant Chia lineage, this team was nicknamed the Stalwarts.[4] Ch'en's team cooperated well and stayed together while the other floundered, and eventually members of the original Stalwarts and other households joined a unified team under Ch'en's leadership, swelling its membership to forty-nine households by 1949—more than two thirds of the total number of families in Tachai. The forty-nine member mutual aid team several years later incorporated itself in its entirety as a lower-stage agricultural producers' cooperative.

Several factors in Tachai's mutual aid experience are of interest to a study of the patterns of internal communications and group affiliation in this prominent example of China's rural development. They involve issues of leader-mass relations, group affiliation within a changing economic and political structure, and the ideological form and context of communication in the transformation of internal village solidarities.

The beginnings of mutual aid in 1946 in the base areas set in motion a process in each village that not only provided for economic transformation but set conditions for potential conflicts as choices were made within a new institutional form. In Tachai, lines of conflicts were twofold: class conflict between richer and poorer, distinguished especially by available labor; and inclusion or exclusion from new collective networks and power within them on the basis of clan affiliation. Thus, Ch'en's achievement, by making a success of the risky Old and Young Team, was to win support for a leadership that cut across the exclusiveness of the dominant lineage group already strongly represented in the Party core. It also identified with the needs and economic potential of less prosperous Tachai residents, whose positions ultimately stood only to be aided by a collectivist developmental path.

The reorientation of village leadership to a more inclusive and broadly based alliance took place during economic transformation and growth. This provided an economic attraction which meant that the poorer members in the village, recent immigrants to Tachai, and People's Liberation Army and families were joined by participants in mutual aid from among the better-endowed Tachai residents. This in turn swelled the economic potential of the enlarged mutual aid team and in the long run provided a more substantial base for greater economic solidarity in the village. The resulting solidarity, which showed its vigor during the next decade of growth that brought model status to Tachai, was based on two major appeals—the welfare of the poorest members of the community (a rural class unity); and the mobilization of all energies, including the resources of better-off villagers, for the economic advancement of the whole (mass unity).

The conflict in Tachai's early years over the leadership and group affiliation in mutual aid was characterized in part by the continued Chia clan dominance within new forms of agrarian organization. Clan loyalties figured in conflict over village leadership as well as in economic organization.[5] But the issues and resolution were interpreted by Tachai's leadership as being rooted in class relations and not primarily kinship rivalries. When members of the Stalwarts Team ridiculed the Old and Young Team in public, Ch'en remembered the taunts as containing a class animus.

Sentiments against sharing labor and resources with a wider group of households were seen as being strictly based on feelings against risking cooperation with the poor. Ch'en explained that his own unwillingness to work with the better-off Chias and his desire to help some of the badly off families were based on "class feeling." In a 1971 interview with William Hinton, Ch'en gave some hint of the changing patterns of communication in the transitional village that demonstrated the way class came into play to order the new universe.[6]

Asked about his motives for forming the Old and Young Team, Ch'en recalled that as he listened to the worries and grumbling of labor-short families too poorly equipped to benefit from their newly distributed land, he considered his choices.

> At that time *I didn't think in terms of political line.* I thought: "These are poor peasants and I am a poor peasant. They suffered in the old society and so did I. These difficulties are not just theirs. They are mine too. The road we take must solve all difficulties, why not theirs?" I came to this through class feelings not through any recognition of two lines.[7]

Ch'en withdrew from the Stalwarts and stated that he organized the Old and Young Team because of his class sentiments. However, he did not explain his motives on that level:

> I was a strong young man. When the labor-short families heard that I was doing this they were very happy. They didn't see it was a class feeling. *They were concerned about their very survival.* They loved me because I was strong and good at farming. The Stalwarts, on the other hand, laughed at us. "That Ch'en is crazy," they said. "Such a strong laborer getting together with old people and children! He really is out of his mind."[8]

When Hinton asked Ch'en why the other Old and Young Team members thought he wanted to work with them, he answered:

> They just welcomed it. They had never dreamed of such a thing. They didn't say I was stupid. If they said that, I might leave them. The Stalwarts said I was stupid, but not those families. . . .
>
> Gradually the Old and Young began to understand why I stayed with them. They discussed this problem behind my back. "Why does Yung-kuei, so strong and able, stay with us? Why does he take all the hard work on himself? He is protecting us. He does the work of two or three." They thought I had a soft heart. But after the rich peasants started to slander us, saying, "In the fall, there'll be quite a scene to see," they began to see the difference between the two classes.[9]

Ch'en suggested, in effect, three contexts of meaning that provide a framework for understanding changing social relations. One is the theoretically informed, programmatic, and authoritative understanding of the policy design that emanates from the political center. Ch'en alluded to this context when he referred to understanding the *line*. A second context is derived from experiential understanding originating in actual practice but capable of a new orientation toward the nature and resolution of social conflict. This is the level of *class feeling*. Finally, there are the immediate *practical sentiments* of the villagers in relation to their perceived needs (common sense), which have only a partial sense of Ch'en's broader motivational context. In fact, the villagers protected their fortunes for a time by not asking questions. However, with the experience of opposition from others in the village, plus a lot of discussion, Ch'en Yung-kuei allowed members of his mutual aid team, over time, to approach the broader context of class relations. By his admission, he worked only between the second and third levels. The context of line was not accessible—nor does its lack seem to have been important.

At this stage in Tachai's development, the rising leader Ch'en Yung-kuei worked at a point of communication that was not linked directly to the political center.

One noteworthy aspect of the Old and Young Team's success, later to become an integral and widely emphasized part of the Tachai experience, was the close connection that Ch'en maintained with the rest of the team in all aspects of farmwork. This allowed for maximum use of their slim collective resources and for maximum interchange among the members. In this way, economic progress and an increased popular understanding of the mode of change could develop in a unified cycle.

In retrospect, a major question of the mutual aid period in Tachai involved the nature of the links between the newly forming Party organization and the masses in the village in the course of institutional transformation tightly connecting economic and social change. The resulting mutual aid linkages of both class unity and eventually greater village mass unity in Tachai persisted in the 1952 attempt to establish an enlarged village cooperative that eventually won the approval of a reluctant higher Party leadership.[10]

In addition, the inclusive nature of the settlement Ch'en made helped to establish the tradition of a unified leadership in the village that subsequently saw very little internal change—with the exception of generational circulation—in thirty years.[11]

Refusing to Exaggerate: Withdrawal from Centralizing Communication

The enormous enthusiasm and pressures for achievement during initial stages of the Great Leap Forward brought from many units disturbing embellishments upon the truth of increases in production. A situation that occurred in Tachai in response to these pressures is instructive in revealing another facet of the interplay between regime-centered and local unit-oriented communication activity. The setting was a large-scale emulation meeting called by the central Shansi district in the fall of 1958, in which "advanced units" were to report Great Leap increases in agricultural yields. As Ch'en Yung-kuei reported it, he went proudly to present Tachai's increase of over 200 catty/*mou*[12] in 1957–1958 only to find that other units were advancing yields of astronomical proportion: "One 'sputnik' brigade reported 33,000 catties per *mou*. There was a 1,000 catty county and a 10,000 catty commune."[13]

Ch'en was informally urged by members of the Hsiyang County Party committee and district officers at the meeting to take Tachai's yield figures and revise them quietly upward to 2,000 catty/*mou*. Ch'en thought it over but felt that such lying would only play into the hands of village conservatives who could easily debunk such exaggeration. The ordinary peasants with whom he generally kept counsel would know from experience that he was making things up. Ch'en's professed standard of truth and response to authorities obviously originated in the milieu of the local collective and did not come from the context of the centrally organized emulation conference.

Ch'en was concerned with maintaining credibility, and not threatening the viability of internal village solidarities built up through long effort, and conversely, not adding to the potential for crosscutting leadership appeals by opponents of his village regime. The decision lends credibility to a self-reliance posture based on local solidarities and achievement.

Refusing to exaggerate, Ch'en incurred the anger of Hsiyang County leaders; he was forced to "learn from" a group of "advanced units" that had reported such extremely high yields.

> Some of the supposedly backward units had much respect for these "advanced" units. They studied them enthusiastically— how they plowed, how they planted, how many seeds, etc. But I had *ch'ing hsu* (I felt upset). I didn't ask anything. I just sat with head back and kept my eyes shut.[14]

Ch'en reported that representatives of the "advanced" units at this meeting were asked to go to a "heroes meeting" in Peking, a further incentive tying into centralizing linkages. Their units also got material rewards including trucks and tractors. Ch'en continued:

> To comfort the "backward" units who were left behind, a get-together with city workers was organized—a *kung-nung lien-huan*. They elected me as head of the peasant delegation to go and celebrate with the workers. I wouldn't go. I wanted to be on the delegation that went to Peking to see Chairman Mao, but our merits were not enough.[15]

Finally, Ch'en reported the following incident. One of the cadres who was a member of the county Party committee, recognizing Ch'en's dispiritedness after this, tried to "reason" with him.

> "You shouldn't be so disgruntled. Those units have achieved things, that's why they were chosen.
>
> I said, "It's all false."
>
> "Don't say that," he said. "You'll mess things up."
>
> I knew him well, so I said, "Well, I'm only telling you. Don't tell anyone else."

Clearly, I didn't always resist wrong things as well as I should have.[16]

Tachai's refusal to exaggerate yields was based on internal standards derived from experience. To some extent, Tachai leaders also made use of information from informal horizontal links with other units. For example, Ch'en told of one brigade in another commune in their county that reported a yield in oats of over 3,000 catty/*mou*. They styled themselves the Oat Kings.[17] But Ch'en had a sister in that brigade. Inquiring casually, he found out that their actual yield was more like 240 catty/*mou*.[18]

Emulation campaigns, meetings, conferences, on-the-spot visits, exchanges of experience, rewards and honors, and the like may all be understood as part of a communication repertoire utilized by central leaders and designed to encourage basic-level producers to initiate and sustain greater efforts, to perceive new possibilities, and to learn new methods. In the case of the "exaggeration meeting" of fall 1958, Ch'en's action as a Tachai leader was striking. Though he did not engage in active protest against an apparently corrupt exercise in centralizing communication, he did refuse to participate in a number of expected ways—to exaggerate Tachai's own yield statistics, to "learn from" advanced units, and to attend a consolation celebration. In this particular instance, Ch'en withdrew from participation in certain aspects of a system of centralizing communication (centered around the emulation conference). Instead, he viewed the local community as a separate source of relevant messages about their real experience in production.

The salience of the local communication context was to be even more pronounced in the political interplay of the early 1960s, when local solidarities and horizontal linkages provided a basis for active protest against authoritative behavior. Given the primacy for Chinese rural development of the intensified vertical linkages with local units, it is my intention to affirm the importance of local initiatives, or at least demurrals from general policies, for agrarian transformation.

In looking at the case of Tachai, we have seen that the nature of the collective unit in its founding states, though based on a universal model (mutual aid teams), was stamped in character by perspectives and initiatives generated within the local milieu. Local initiatives are often complementary to centralized direction, but at times have reached the point of outright conflict or opposition to actions by the state. Oppositional politics from the local units, however, pose threats to the perspective of integrated national development. Such instances within Chinese experience bear some discussion. The demonstration of the existence of such significant, locally generated and horizontally linked political activity may also be a useful supplement to communication analysis of the People's Republic system that concentrates on communication activity as a centralizing, national-integrative phe-nomenon.

The following discussion focuses on a critical and exceedingly conflictual period of Chinese rural politics, the early and mid-1960s: the post–Great Leap years that included the Socialist Education movement and led up to the impact of the Cultural Revolution on rural jurisdictions.

In this instance, representatives of basic units involved themselves in political alliances along horizontal lines from community to community. Basic-level cadres in particular were active, operating from community-level perspectives rather than as representatives of the central system. Such political linkages, extensions of channels of information, planning, and intensified sharing of political identifications may be thought of in terms of modes of communication activity, thickly involved with political power.

Given the nature of the pattern I am sketching here, it must be understood that available data are sparse and merely suggestive of an area of rich complexity. Actual instances of face-to-face contact between local cadres are rarely documented but can often be inferred from episodic descriptions of the general course of events. Further information from a variety of cases would be necessary to make more conclusive statements about the role that informal, horizontal political linkages and channels of communication play in reference to the vertically integrated organization of authority in political conflict situations. In this case specifically, looking at some relatively revealing data on conflict with Hsiyang County in the early and mid-1960s, I will argue that horizontal linkages among basic-level cadres, that is, brigade and commune cadres, reinforced by the special role played by "local notable" Ch'en Yung-kuei, were important in generating political discussion and opposition to certain activities of higher-level authorities, sometimes during the course of severe conflict.

The following discussion will draw on experiences from two different periods, the first centering on intra-Hsiyang County conflict in 1961–1963,[19] and the second involving broadened conflict in 1964–1965, during attempted implementation of the ssu-ch'ing yun-tung (Four Clean-ups campaign) in Tachai and neighboring units.

Conflict and Political Alliances: 1961–1963

A major change of political regime in Hsiyang County in 1961 set the stage for some internecine political skirmishing that lasted well into the early part of the Cultural Revolution. It was resolved only when Ch'en and a group of allies came into power in the spring of 1967. In 1961, a new secretary for the Hsiyang County Party committee was appointed. The former secretary, who had held the post for some twenty years and was closely affiliated with local cadres, was transferred to another jurisdiction. The move may have been part of a planned shake-up intended to eliminate the effects of mistakes made during the previous years in the economy and to implement policies designed to strengthen the growth in agriculture. As we now know, important aspects of agricultural revitalization policies during 1960–1962 were attacked by leftist critics as threats to the socialist character of rural institutions. At any rate, the new Party secretary did not prove popular with a large number of local cadres. Many Hsiyang cadres appear to have had fondness and feelings of loyalty toward the former incumbent of the post.[20]

After 1961, moves to reexamine local developments dating from 1958 threatened reputations and wounded local feelings, leading to a certain measure of grumbling and, eventually, opposition by grassroots cadres. Ch'en himself mentioned several situations including the so-called three check-ups in 1961, in which the new Party secretary sent a work team to Tachai to check the accuracy of reported figures on land, output, and amount of grain sold to the state. According to Ch'en, the new secretary tried to force Tachai into revising their per-unit output figures downward, but in response Ch'en threatened to take a countercase to higher levels via the help of a "sympathetic journalist" with the *Shansi Daily*. This journalist passed the message on to Party leaders in Shansi and the local demands on Tachai were dropped at the time.[21]

Another example mentioned by Ch'en was that of a fight he had with the new secretary over the proposed alienation from county use of a reservoir built by mass labor during the Great Leap Forward. Ch'en mentioned that a group of local cadres arrayed with him on the issue had gone to consult with the former Party secretary (working in a nearby county) on the reservoir problem.

Another informant in Hsiyang stated that a group of Hsiyang County cadres from different units led by Ch'en Yung-kuei wrote letters of protest during this period to the Party committees of the province and district. They were protesting a directive issued by the county secretary stating that individual households should reclaim land on an assigned basis to be added to their already-cultivated private plots. For this, the protesting cadres were labeled "anti-Party agents."[22]

Local opposition, mobilized horizontally and enjoying the aid and support of the prestigious though low-ranking Ch'en Yung-kuei, so threatened the county secretary that he branded a group of 180 or so of them an anti-Party clique. Many of these were severely struggled against, expelled from the Party, or otherwise disciplined during the work team phase of the Four Clean-ups movement in the fall of 1964.

Local antagonisms between a number of cadres from Hsiyang County and the new county secretary led to severe recriminations. They also provided partly successful examples of linked resistance to external pressures and discipline concentrated during the 1964 Four Clean-ups phase of the Socialist Education movement, which will be discussed shortly. I would like now to explore the context of operations faced by the Hsiyang County official after assuming his position in 1961.

The new secretary came into office during a time of consolidation and retrenchment from the trouble-ridden Great Leap period. Given the nature of his responsibilities, and worries about protecting his reputation by performance in the new post, the relatively radical image of the Tachai experience would likely have troubled him. He may have been wary of allowing Tachai's prestige to inspire concrete, radical, and misplaced emulation that would lead basic-level cadres once again into zealous, commandist efforts to mobilize peasant labor or resources.[23]

Beset by these worries, the new secretary also met noisy opposition from lower-ranking cadres embedded in their basic units and bearing obvious loyalties to his predecessor. In particular, he encountered the illiterate, albeit famous labor model Ch'en, who loudly opposed the new policies and appeared willing to collude with other cadres against his leadership. Ch'en engineered contacts with higher Party representatives through personal channels outside the vertical Party structure. To the Party secretary, Ch'en may have appeared a self-righteous but dangerous pest, who, with significant prestige as a labor model and uncertain informal connections to the higher levels, was, after all, low in the Party organization—only one of at least 400 brigade secretaries with whom the county secretary had to deal. Right or wrong, Ch'en promised to be a continuing annoyance, a threat to the smooth functioning of the county office. This situation was aggravated especially by his tendency to make alliances outside the hierarchy along horizontal lines and find points of informal communication with "old boy" neighbors. As political lines began to be drawn more sharply in each subsequent year after 1961, maintaining control over local political or administrative areas like the county must have looked more urgent to high-level incumbents. The Hsiyang secretary's intention to exert control over an important political figure like Ch'en Yung-kuei was likely to have appeared an organizational good in this context.

Structurally, we may see the Party's county secretary as occupying the pinnacle of a local political realm, seeking to insulate his position vis-à-vis the exigencies of mass-level activity, as well as attempting to relate to the demands and pressures of his superiors. In so doing, he would try to maximize his control, constantly viewing the local base of many lower-level units as an entity demanding regulation subject to vertical coordination through his office.

Opposition from below, from free-thinking leaderships such as the Tachai Party branch committee, horizontally linked groups of subordinates with roots in their native communities and years of local revolutionary experience, and especially prestigious local figures like Ch'en, would all pose threats to his ability to control the bureaucratic environment.

In a geographically harsh environment, with poor communication links between dispersed residential clusters, the ability of the county secretary to link contacts and centralize information through his office would naturally be an asset to the command of power. The ability of the aforementioned groups to forge channels that bypassed that center would be an even more significant counter to his control. If things began to go wrong in his sphere, it would expose him to his superior's criticism and threaten his political and professional well-being.[24] Reaction to this dilemma may serve to explain in part the severity of countermeasures taken by the county secretary against dissident local cadres. These efforts came to a head during the Four Clean-ups phase of the Socialist Education movement in late 1964.

The Four Clean-ups Campaign: Resistance and Solidarity at the Intersection of Two Structural Levels

In the fall of 1964, work teams altogether numbering up to 5,000 individuals, including 3,800 persons from outside the county, were dispersed among the collective units of Hsiyang County to carry out the latest phase of the Four Clean-ups campaign, then under the general aegis of a Central Committee Document (the "Later Revised Ten Points") believed to have been drafted by Liu Shao-ch'i. The document suggested that the large numbers of basic-level cadres involved in economic and political corruption could only be caught and corrected by vigorous investigative methods.

Such methods were used in units throughout Hsiyang County. It was said that in Tachai a work team unit under high-level supervision made special efforts to find instances of corruption and certifiable misdemeanors by brigade leaders. The teams followed a common pattern in their work in Tachai and elsewhere, suspending local cadres from office and substituting team members in supervisory positions within the unit while investigation was proceeding. They isolated the cadres under suspicion and attempted to obtain corroboration from members of the collective to substantiate rumors, secret charges, or wrongdoing, as well as seeking to obtain admissions of guilt from the suspect cadres.

In Tachai, a scattergun pattern of charges was made alleging economic and administrative snafus, false claims of land size and output, and serious political errors. Among these was the noteworthy charge, if Ch'en's recollection is a reliable guide, that there was "too much unity" among the Tachai leadership. "Our people asked them," Ch'en stated, " 'What's wrong with unity? Unity is strength isn't it?' Useless. We were guilty of another 'crime'."[25]

Important to Tachai's response to work team activities was the degree of internal solidarity in the face of opposition to the team. The cadres in Tachai stuck together and secured the loyalty of brigade members who refused to indict any of their leadership.[26] Because of the work team method of performing the cadres' duties while the investigation was in progress and isolating cadres from contacts within their units, irregular channels for contact among local cadres became invaluable to local resistance or to cadres' self-protection against charges made during struggle sessions. Several official sources refer to secret meetings in which Tachai's cadres met in out-of-the-way places to discuss the situation. They also refer to other lines of communication with noncadre members of the brigade. Thus, the Tachai cadres stayed abreast of work team activities and enhanced brigade solidarity during the work team's residence.[27] Links within the brigade community were maintained at all costs, and informational networks provided the basis of planning for responses to work team attempts to implicate one or another brigade cadre in corrupt practices.

Tachai's internal solidarity played a part in bucking the work team's determined search for witnesses against the Party branch leadership. In a number of other brigades, local leaders endured severe pressures because of real and alleged crimes, and some apparently did not survive.[28]

The significance of potential horizontal linkages among local units during a time of conflict was illustrated by events in the Houchuang brigade. When a work team had suspended twenty-four of the brigade's twenty-seven cadres and used methods of isolation and intimidation bordering on the third degree to ferret out information or confessions, enforcing a news blackout on the village, the brigade secretary Wang Tung-chou told of how his older daughter was able to contact Ch'en Yung-kuei, an old friend. Ch'en encouraged him to stand up to the accusations. Later, Ch'en was able to visit Wang in Houchuang when he was undergoing intense struggle. Ch'en told him explicitly not to commit suicide.[29] Ch'en told of another time at the height of the struggle when he was taken to district Party committee headquarters in an effort to get him to testify against other cadres from Hsiyang accused of "four unclean" crimes. Ch'en refused.[30]

Structurally, the Four Clean-ups movement at its most intense moment placed Tachai at the intersection of two levels of conflict—one local, the other national in scope. This discussion has emphasized the local level, in which struggles for influence and control within a local arena were apparently entangled with resources that emerged in the context of intense political conflict within the central elite. The character of the conflict surrounding Tachai and other units in Hsiyang County evolved from a pattern of local alliances and hostilities. Around this time Mao Tse-tung and other top national leaders debated appropriate agricultural development models as well as methods of political rectification for deviance in basic-level administration. There is no question that the Tachai episode was settled ultimately (or cooled down), by intervention on the side of the Tachai brigade locally and the Tachai "model" nationally by Chou En-lai and Mao.

The pattern of communication and political links in a case like this, involving very low-level though symbolically important individuals such as Ch'en Yung-kuei and members of the top-level central leadership, remains to be explored. While not attempting to dismiss this vital connection, I would like to use the Tachai experience simply to suggest the possibility of investigating the conceivable appearance of similar patterns in other local conflict situations. In such cases, local cadres like Ch'en Yung-kuei might appeal to personal prestige, acquaintance networks, or other types of loyalties and commitments to forge horizontal channels for communication and political alliance in order to counter hierarchical dispositions of power and information control during periods of significant political conflict.

In this regard, several elements in the Tachai case stand out. Ch'en's prestige as a local notable may be matched by other local labor heroes, as might his long residence in the area and his involvement within a relatively fluid network of acquaintances built in pre-Liberation political and military activities.[31] The carryover of such historical ties to instances of political conflict in later periods is a plausible working hypothesis for future investigation. On the other hand, Ch'en Yung-kuei's particular national-level connections and support were, to say the least, a highly unusual factor, though analogous ties between prestigious local figures and moderately high-status officials might be common enough to be studied comparatively.

Of all factors in the Tachai experience, in my judgment the most profound was the Tachai brigade's internal solidarity. Brigade identity and mass-cadre loyalty were nourished and took their particular forms in the course of Tachai's specific development. For Tachai at least, leadership behavior during the conflictual early and mid-1960s might be considered a genuine case of horizontal mobilization of the brigade community. The actions of the brigade's leadership in the face of vertically structured centralizing pressures can be seen as representing a politically viable agreement of the bulk of the community. Cadres from other units in Hsiyang also collaborated in opposition to aspects of county Party leadership. Whether these associations of cadres indicate congruent patterns of solidarity within their own units, however, is open to question and awaits the acquisition of historical data.

Fuller understanding of the behavior and resources for action of local cadres in conflictual situations depends upon the nature of leader-mass relations at basic levels. The latter can be clarified by more historical and developmental analyses of particular cases whenever such data become available. From the Tachai experience so far, we can simply suggest it as a logical construct. The analysis of leader-mass relations within local units and their implications for the actions of basic-level

239

cadres in relation to each other and to higher-level authorities add a significant new dimension to our understanding of conflicting incentives and bureaucratic structures. From the earlier experience of Tachai, it seems such horizontal linkages can stand for community solidarities rather than cliquish associations of cadres representing essentially themselves.[32]

Epilogue

This brief statement is intended to take account of some of the dramatic changes involving Tachai and the Tachai movement since the above analysis was prepared. In the short interval between the death of Mao and the ascendancy of the Teng Hsiao-p'ing reform group, the Tachai development model reached its greatest prominence. The Second National Conference on Learning from Tachai in Agriculture, held in December 1976, suggested that the Hsiyang County experience in learning from Tachai since 1967 would remain the preeminent model for agricultural development in the post-Mao period and would be extended by aggressive political intervention at the county level and below.[33] But the rehabilitation of Teng in 1977 and the critical Third Plenum of the Eleventh Central Committee of the Chinese Communist Party in December 1978 soon set the stage for a dramatic reversal and ended the political fortunes of those who had promoted the Tachai phenomenon in Shansi Province and on a national scale. When Ch'en Yung-kuei lost his stellar position at the political center in 1980, he had already (in December 1979) been removed from the top Party post in Hsiyang County. And in December 1980, when a new Tachai Party branch committee of seven members was elected, Ch'en was not among them.[34]

During the year following the Third Plenum, sweeping reforms in agrarian policy not only eliminated the sway of the Tachai model but also caught up in their net the practices of the Tachai brigade and Hsiyang County. Remarkably, even the famous Tachai workpoint system was eliminated and private plots restored, among others of the most vaunted institutions of radical Tachai-style collectivism.[35] In addition to opposing the radical thrust of the Tachai model, the assault included a series of scandalous revelations involving economic mistakes, boondoggles and frauds, and charges of serious political leadership misfeasance, especially those committed by Ch'en Yung-kuei as head of the Hsiyang County Party organization.

Most embarrassingly, it was reported that Ch'en had engineered the deliberate misrepresentation of Hsiyang County grain yield figures between 1973 and 1977, overstating the total yield for that period by 272 million catties or 24 percent.[36] The exaggeration was worst in 1973, when 90 million catties were added on to the real figure of 149 million.[37] It appears that in early 1973, the second year of serious drought in Hsiyang

240

County and elsewhere, Ch'en had made optimistic but untenable predictions of future agricultural performance in Hsiyang in order to boost the prestige of the Tachai model. When the actual yield fell well below the promise, the false figures were reported in order to maintain Tachai's national reputation. As a leader and policymaker, Ch'en fell into the same trap as did those political officials he had excoriated and resisted during the Great Leap Forward when he refused to exaggerate Tachai grain statistics and join in the ongoing emulation campaign.

Other instances of economic waste have been publicized. An enormously costly and misguided attempt, apparently inspired by Ch'en Yung-kuei with little attention to technical realities, was made to divert the course of the Hsiao River from West to East in order to water five communes in Hsiyang County and open up new land. This attempt was ultimately abandoned in 1980. An unproductive and unprofitable Hsiyang County hand tractor factory is said to have been kept in operation by heavy state subsidies. It should be noted that none of the recent attacks have called into question the record of the Tachai brigade before the Cultural Revolution, including the often-doubted claim to essential self-reliance in financing its development from the 1940s onward. In fact, most of the serious charges of economic waste and mismanagement as well as costly outside subsidies involve the period of 1973 and afterward. Up to that point, Tachai and Hsiyang seemed to be able to repay outside aid by investments that achieved a sufficient return.

Serious charges have been leveled at Ch'en Yung-kuei and associated cadres, many of whom have lost their positions, involving corruption of political leadership and cadre workstyle. Although these have on the whole gained less attention from outside observers, the subject bears directly on the analysis presented in the main body of this chapter. This study sketches out the structural dimensions of political association and political conflict in the local arena in China, from which an informal political opposition emerged within the county milieu on the basis of personal, face-to-face contacts along horizontal lines of communication. Such informal associations of basic-level cadres might in the ordinary course of events have coexisted with the vertical structure of party and state administration, or even generated the kind of limits on the effectiveness of outside state cadres, as Victor Nee has described in his field study of a county in Canton.[38] But in Hsiyang County in the early 1960s polarization occurred and the loose group of horizontally linked cadres became a significant political opposition to the regular bureaucratic hierarchy. Having the leadership of a "local notable" labor model with informal ties to supporters at much higher levels, this group was able to cohere, protect itself, and ultimately triumph when the rules of the game shifted during the Cultural Revolution.

Recent criticism reveals that horizontal political alliances persisted after the Cultural Revolution—if anything they expanded. But they were transformed from the informal groups of local associates into networks of personal and policy allies holding official positions within the vertical state hierarchy. A greater force could perhaps be wielded by this kind of structure based on both the vertical links associated with the Party apparatus and state power, and the continuance of personal ties, welded together by a shared radical ideology.

Chen and his allies occupied many official positions in the Hsiyang County leadership after 1967. According to an article in the *People's Daily*, 491 cadres originally from Hsiyang (many from the grassroots level) had been promoted to other parts of the province between 1966 and the end of 1979. Of these, 38 had occupied positions of deputy-secretary or revolutionary committee vice-chairperson or higher.[39]

The weapons that could be wielded by this group in power in Hsiyang and in Shansi were substantial—interestingly, the kinds of measures that Ch'en and his associates are now accused of are very similar to those to which they themselves were subjected before the Cultural Revolution. The current criticism against Ch'en, incidentally, tends to substantiate the much more fragmentary data concerning political conflict in the early 1960s. As examples tending to corroborate the earlier enmity, it was reported in 1981 that the Hsiyang County Party secretary from 1962–1964, Chang Chun-huai, was jailed for two years after the Cultural Revolution, and Yueh Yao-hsien, the Party secretary from 1964–1966, died as a result of struggle. It is alleged that in the ten years after the beginning of the Cultural Revolution, 141 persons in Hsiyang, 90 percent of them peasants, died or committed suicide after political struggle, and that Ch'en Yung-kuei had approved of these harsh measures and resisted rehabilitating old enemies even long after policies had changed.[40] Ch'en is said to have used his influence to organize a special investigation committee at the prefecture level to attack nine prefecture cadres who had written reports critical of him between 1967 and 1969. Apparently harassment of these cadres continued for years. One was sentenced to five years in prison and another was said to have died as a result of the persecution.[41]

Other charges involved corruption such as nepotism and the like. Ch'en was accused of having misused his power, prestige, and personal affiliations to obtain several high positions in the Hsiyang Party committee for his irresponsible son, Ch'en Ming-chu, and to obtain exoneration and rehabilitation for a convicted rapist in 1973 or 1974. The alleged criminal happened to be the former husband of Ch'en's second wife. When the case was reinvestigated shortly after the Third Plenum in 1978, Ch'en successfully used personal contacts in Hsiyang County to cover up the matter, prevailing upon the rape victims to remain silent. Only after he fell from power did they speak up and help to reconvict the rapist.[42]

Such abuses of power can be blamed on the specific politics of the

Cultural Revolution and the developments that flowed from it. Under the particular conditions of the Cultural Revolution, which drew cadre militants like Ch'en Yung-kuei into high position and influence, such an informal horizontally linked opposition group could become extended and regularized as part of the vertical bureaucratic hierarchy of the Chinese state. This kind of power structure, fused by an ideology for development made credible by real, earlier experience, had access to a range of power to confer benefits and coerce opposition. Apparently lacking the broad experience and vision necessary for understanding problems beyond the immediate purview and moderating their ambitions, they could use their new-found power for development but also for much more mundane and personal motives.

The group of grassroots cadres who had congregated at an earlier stage around Ch'en's informal leadership in opposition to official programs and practices can be said to have represented, initially, a kind of quasi-democratic opposition representing one version of local interests. The Cultural Revolution gave them official power, but provided no innovative structures for enhancing any such continuing tendencies in the years that followed. Instead the new leaders came to behave in ways just like their predecessors. The picture presented here highlights a central failing of the Cultural Revolution. The mobilization of popular forces was often based on networks of people at the grass roots linked through horizontal channels around informal, popular, and ambitious leaders, and arrayed against a Party and state establishment. But it could not create, in and around state power, a less arbitrary type of political force, or one more representative of validly competing policies. The current emphasis on socialist legality and the protection of individuals from arbitrary use of authority may interrupt the constant repetition of these old patterns. But whether the political reforms sought by the present Chinese leadership, including the emphasis on recruiting technical specialists to political office, can generate the kind of grassroots character and vitality originally expected of people like the Tachai group, and involve them meaningfully in political activity, remains to be seen.

NOTES

1. On the concept of "stateness" see J. P. Nettl, "The State as a Conceptual Variable," *World Politics* 20 (1968):559–592.

2. Vivienne Shue, "Local Views, Central Visions: Some Preliminary Thoughts on Localism in Contemporary Chinese Politics," unpublished manuscript, p. 15.

3. The institutional and economic ramifications of the extension of Tachai brigade experiences to Hsiyang County as a whole, the establishment of the so-called "first Tachai-type County," have been explored in two consecutive articles by Tang Tsou, Marc Blecher, and Mitch Meisner: "Organization, Growth, and Equality in Xiyang County: A Survey of Fourteen Brigades in Seven Communes," Part I, *Modern China* 5 (1979):3–39; Part II, *Modern China* 5 (1979):139–185.

4. The primary sources of interpretation are several interviews with Ch'en Yung-kuei, Chia Ch'eng-jang, Sung Li-ying, and other Tachai personalities in the fall of 1971 by members of an American group who were visiting Tachai for one month. Carl Parris has kindly allowed me access to his notes of these meetings and interviews. Data on both Party membership in the early days and specific information on membership of the mutual aid teams are obscure. The specific reference cited comes from an interview with Sung Li-ying. It appears that Ch'en Yung-kuei, although an early Tachai militant and activist in land reform, became a Party member in a second wave of recruitment of six persons after 1948, an earlier group of five having constituted in 1947 the original Party branch in the village. *Tachai Hungch'i P'iao* [Tachai's Red Flag Waves] (Peking: Nung-yeh ch'u-ban she, 1965), p. 81.

   Nonetheless, by 1949, Ch'en was vice-secretary in the Party branch. It appears that original members of the Party were in all probability of the Chia lineage (with the possible exception of Chao Ta-ho, whom Pairault dates back to Party membership by 1945 and to original membership in the Old and Young Team, though I have seen no clear evidence for the latter). See Thierry Pairault, "Tachai 1945–1975: Un Village Modele Vu de l'Interieur," *Mondes Asiatiques* 11 (Automne 1977):162–195 (pp. 175–177). Another exception is Sung Li-ying, Party member in 1947; but she was married to Chia Chin-ts'ai. This suggests that one of the factors significant in Ch'en's rise to leadership, done first through the medium of the mutual aid process, was an opening up of the Party leadership to individuals outside the Chia clan, implying a broadening of intravillage ties beyond the traditional lineage group connections and thus moving from vertical to horizontal patterns of mobilization in the village.

5. *Tachai Hungch'i* [Tachai's Red Flag] (Taiyuan: Shansi jen-min ch'u-pan she, 1974), p. 241.

6. William Hinton, "Two Ways to Read the 'Red Book'," *New China* (Summer 1977):19–30.

7. Ibid., p. 27. Emphasis added.

8. Ibid., p. 28.

9. In a spatial sense also, communication links were modified in the village during these years. As Ch'en Yung-kuei became recognized as a leader in the practical, daily economic endeavors, his colleagues and "disciples" used to gather with him to eat and talk about problems and daily events in the shade of an old willow tree in the village

commons, a site that once had seen much grimmer proceedings when landlords used it for exemplary beatings of peasants accused of defaulting on obligations. It now became a new kind of public space that furthered the contacts growing around the beginnings of collective work and the controversies (many occurring partly on the level of gossip, apparently) that this entailed.

10. See Mitch Meisner, "Dazhai: The Mass Line in Practice," *Modern China* 4 (1978):27–62 (pp. 44–45).

11. *Tachai's Red Flag*, pp. 240–241.

12. A Chinese catty (*chin*) is about one-half kilogram. A *mou* is a unit of area equivalent to one-fifteenth hectare. Catty/*mou* denotes catty per *mou*.

13. William Hinton, "Bucking the 'Exaggeration Wind'," *New China* (Winter 1977), p. 52.

14. Ibid.

15. Ibid.

16. Ibid.

17. Ibid.

18. Meisner, "Dazhai," p. 46. My source is material in the Parris notes from interviews in Tachai brigade, October 1971.

19. The following section is based on material from the Tachai-Hsiyang interviews contained in the Parris notes.

20. Many official accounts state that Hsiyang County entered a period of decline after 1960 in grain output and per-unit productivity in foodcrop production. Tsou, Blecher, and Meisner, "Organization, Growth, and Equality," (Part II) have attempted to analyze a number of the factors in the economic troubles of that period, centering around a problem of outflow of labor power from the collective agrarian economy. The arrest and reversal of this trend and the reconcentration of labor in agriculture (and local agro-industry) were instrumental in the economic success of Hsiyang after 1967.

21. Gerald Tannebaum, "The Real Spirit of Tachai," *Eastern Horizon* 10 (1971) (p.27). Parris notes.

22. Interview with the vice-chairperson, Hsiyang County revolutionary committee, fall 1971. Parris notes.

23. Policy pronouncements in 1978 once again emphasized the theme of warning against efforts by collective leadership—at brigade levels and above—to overaccumulate investment funds relative to distribution and to command development efforts at the expense of improvements in the standard of living and control of indigenous resources by commune members. For example, Ching Hua, "How to Speed Up China's Agricultural Development," *Peking Review*, no. 42 (20 October 1978):8–12, where Ching speaks of an "urgent task" to "reduce the peasants' burden by every means, including stopping theft, corruption, waste and excesses in the communes and brigades, curtailing expenses, decreasing the number of non-productive personnel, and barring any use of the production teams' labour force and materials without pay" (p. 9).

24. This formulation is developed in a section of my dissertation dealing with Tachai's political history during this period. Mitch Meisner, "In Agriculture Learn from Tachai: Theory and Practice in Chinese Rural Development" (Ph.D. dissertation, University of Chicago, 1977), pp. 232–233.

25. The patterns of internal solidarity and resistance in Tachai are detailed in ibid., pp. 209–215.

26. Ibid.

27. Deirdre Hunter and Neale Hunter, "Our Man in Tachai," *Monthly Review* (May 1972):32.

28. Wang Tung-chou interview.

29. Ch'en Yung-kuei interview, 28 October 1978. Parris notes.

30. Ed Friedman has documented Tachai's experience in a later period when "Tachai had become a counter [among others] in an ultimate reckoning among groups contesting at the center of state power" in 1976. He suggests that Tachai's leadership, despite considerable antipathy, was forced to compromise with the Chiang Ch'ing group for a time and attack Teng Hsiao-p'ing. Friedman draws the harsh judgment that at this time, without any significant top-level support (unlike 1964), in light of its high but for that reason vulnerable position in the national limelight, "To remain a national model of virtue, Tachai virtually had to prostitute itself." Edward Friedman, "The Politics of Local Models, Social Transformation and State Power Struggles in The People's Republic of China: Tachai and Teng Hsiao-p'ing." *China Quarterly* 76 (1978): 873–890, (p. 885). Unlike 1964, in this instance, the power of top-level political actors was unmediated by middle- or local-level structures in its impact on the Tachai brigade. In such an instance, the oppositional weight of horizontal solidarity would be much less. Perhaps, after all this time at the top, stakes in survival as a model unit as such were more strongly incorporated in the Tachai outlook—a corruption of sorts, one could argue.

31. Existing analogues to the pre-Liberation partisan experience must be considered as time moves along.

32. Several other questions prompted by this material remain to be investigated or analyzed. One involves the degree to which basic-level cadres, especially brigade Party secretaries, may validly be understood as "horizontal mobilizers," since they occupy a place in both the administrative hierarchy and in the democratic-centralist discipline structure of the Communist Party. A second question is the extent to which the patterns of behavior displayed in Tachai or by Ch'en Yung-kuei or other Tachai leaders during periods of conflict have been meaningfully communicated to other localities during the dissemination of the Tachai model on a national scale at different periods. Has the experience of Tachai acted as a model for horizontal mobilization in other units? Aspects of the Tachai experience have appeared in a number of official articles and books, but their impact on other similar units in the nation is unknown.

33. For an exegesis of the implications of the Tachai-Hsiyang development model, especially its relation to county-level leadership, see Mitch Meisner and Marc Blecher, "Rural Development, Agrarian Structure, and the County in China," *Bulletin of Concerned Asian Scholars* 13 (April–June 1981):16–31.

34. These facts, and basic material contained in the epilogue, are borrowed from a detailed report on the contemporary fate of Tachai and Hsiyang based on invaluable fieldwork conducted in Tachai and Hsiyang in 1977 and 1980 by Professor Tang Tsou of the University of Chicago. For an extensive narrative and analysis documenting the highlights of change discussed, see Tang Tsou, Marc Blecher, and Mitch Meisner, "Policy Change at the National Summit and Institutional Transformation at the Local Level: The Case of Tachai and Hsiyang County in the Post-Mao Era," in Tang Tsou, ed., *Select Papers from the Center for Far Eastern Studies*, no. 4 (Chicago: University of Chicago, 1981), pp. 241–392. Almost all in-depth research on Tachai has suffered from some bias in its sources, relying on what might be termed "views from the winner's circle"—Professor Tsou's interviews in the field, in particular those of 1980 concerning current political shifts affecting Tachai and Hsiyang most nearly attain an objective level in terms of the candor and balance of views expressed of what happened and why, despite the relative political interests of the particular informants.

35. These are documented and analyzed in Tsou, Blecher, and Meisner, "Organization, Growth, and Equality."

36. *People's Daily*, 7 July 1980, p. 1.

37. Tsou, Blecher, and Meisner, "Policy Change," p. 315.

38. See Victor Nee, "Post-Mao Changes in a South China Production Brigade," *Bulletin of Concerned Asian Scholars* 13 (April–June 1981):38–39.

39. *People's Daily*, 8 November 1980, p. 3.

40. Tsou, Blecher, and Meisner, "Policy Change," p. 306, based on interviews in 1980 and some published material.

41. Ibid., pp. 306–307; *People's Daily*, 1 August 1980, p. 2.

42. Tsou, Blecher, and Meisner, "Policy Change," pp. 307–309.

V. Epilogue

Important changes that have taken place in China since the purge of the Gang of Four in October 1976 reflect more on policy modifications than on basic social structure and the fundamental integrative processes. The chapters in this volume thus have more than a historical interest; they provide a necessary perspective within which to view the recent changes. In this sense, they are part of the current reality.

In this epilogue, rather than summarizing the findings already presented, Godwin Chu and Francis Hsu examine some the the major changes since 1976 and discuss them in context of what existed previously. The foundation of societal integration in China is still in the local communities, which have gained greater vitality following the removal of some of the previous restrictive measures. The communication channels linking the peripheries with the center—the Central Documents, the work teams, and the mass media—have remained much the same. The policy modifications, however, have revealed some systemic flaws inherent in the Party organization, which appears to be lagging behind its new tasks of Four Modernizations. Measures have been put into effect to streamline Party organization. During this period of adjustment, the mass media are assuming a growing role of two-way communication to make up for the structural imbalance. In the long run, the policy shift from ideological rectification to pragmatic development can be expected to invigorate and sustain the processes of societal integration.

10

Integration in China: The Post-Mao Years

Godwin C. Chu
Francis L.K. Hsu

What are the integrative forces that have been holding Chinese society together during the decades of turbulence and change since 1949?

Just as in the past, a major element is the local communities, now embodied in the communes, subdivided into production brigades and production teams. These communities, while maintaining some degree of local autonomy, are organized into a national entity through two major linkages—the administrative channels that are built around the core of the Party structure, and the mass media, which provide channels of two-way communication between the center and the peripheries.

In this chapter, using mass media materials from China, we shall trace the continuities in the basic structural features that link the local communities with the national system, and discuss the significant changes that have taken place in the local communities since the downfall of the Gang of Four. Finally, we shall note some of the problems in the cadre system, which must play a key role in China's national coordination and integration. We shall focus our attention primarily on rural China, where the roots of Chinese society are.

Continuities in Systemic Organization

The basic unit in which task-oriented cooperation and competition take place in rural China is the production team, generally a natural village or part of one. The production team collectively owns its land and other resources, and organizes its members, both men and women, into small groups for various kinds of activities. Families in the team are assigned private plots, which can be used to grow vegetables, raise poultry, and the like. Members of the team elect from among themselves several cadres, including a leader, an accountant, a cashier, a warehouse keeper, and a workpoint recorder, who serve a term of one year, and may be reelected. Usually they are peasants experienced in production and trusted by the villagers.

Several production teams make up a production brigade, and several brigades make up a commune.[1] The commune-brigade-team structure, introduced since 1958, has remained largely intact following its initial readjustments. The production team, as the basic accounting unit, is where food and other crops are produced and distributed among members after deducting expenses and reserves and selling a portion to the state. The team leader and other cadres generally work along with other peasants in the field in addition to their administrative duties. Brigade and team cadres draw no salaries, although they may receive more workpoints than other peasants. Cadres in the communes hold salaried positions and as a rule do not perform manual work. Under state planning, production quotas are assigned to the communes from above and are further allocated to the brigades and teams. Experiments have been proceeding since 1980 to modify the commune system in order to allow commune members more autonomy, as we shall discuss later.

Communication Linkages

The communes, and the brigades and teams under them, are linked with the central government through an intermediary administrative structure consisting of counties, districts, and provinces. Administrative directives of a routine nature travel down from the central government through this administrative structure to reach the communes, and from there proceed to the brigades and teams (see Figure 2). More intensive

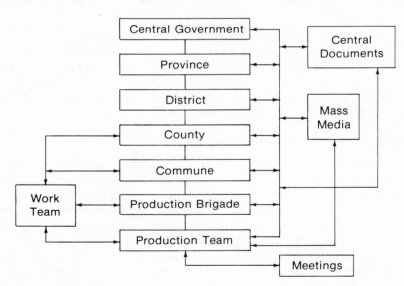

Figure 2
Communication Channels in China

communication occurs in the administrative structure when action programs are to be carried out. An example is the agricultural mechanization which Steven Butler has analyzed.[2] What distinguishes the present system from its predecessors most vividly is the two-way communication along three new channels. Two of the channels are embedded in the administrative structure. One is the dissemination of central documents, which Kenneth Lieberthal has described.[3] The other is the work team, the structure and functions of which have been examined by John Burns.[4] The third is the mass media, including the *tatzupao*.[5]

Central Committee Documents. The Central Committee Documents are a major means by which the leadership in Peking regularly reaches beyond bureaucratic confines to communicate directly with the mass of the people, including the peasants, to inform them about major decisions and to enlist their support. These documents, code-named *chung-fa* in Chinese, may cover a wide range of subject matter, from a new government policy to a production campaign, generally on matters which the people should know about but public dissemination of which is considered either inappropriate or premature. Lieberthal has shown how the abortive coup of Lin Piao was explained to the people in this manner without having to expose the whole case through the media. After the resolution on accelerating agricultural development was officially announced on 6 October 1979,[6] it was revealed that a preliminary draft had been adopted ten months earlier and disseminated as a Central Committee Document to the grassroots levels for study and discussion.[7] Some of the new measures were tried out on an experimental basis in selected areas. Responses were sought from rural cadres and peasants before a final decision was made. Comments were found to be highly favorable: "This is the best document we have seen in years," or "It is like a timely rainfall during a drought," or "This is what the people want."[8] The Central Documents not only serve informative functions, as in the Lin Piao case, but can also facilitate input into the decision-making process to garner a broader base of popular support. These roles have assumed new significance in the nation's current drive toward modernization.

The Work Team. The work team as a social institution dates back to the early years of the Chinese Communist revolution. During the Land Reform of 1950–1952, numerous teams of cadres were sent to the villages to organize the peasants in a class struggle against the landlords.[9] Over the years, work teams have played a role in almost every major campaign, whether it was to investigate local corruption, as in the Four Clean-ups movement,[10] or to promote production, as in the Learn from Tachai movement. In either case, work teams perform concrete linkage functions for the government and the local communities, sometimes fulfilling interest articulation functions as Burns has illustrated in Chapter 7.

Since 1976, work teams continue to be in use, but their functions have come under considerable scrutiny. Doubts have been raised as to whether the dysfunctions may outweigh the benefits, particularly when the work teams are used for production promotion. A county cadre in Anhui Province did an investigation in February 1979 by surveying the 308 production brigades in Tang-tu County, where he worked.[11] During the period from 1970 to 1977, 178 brigades had been assigned work teams to help the peasants learn from the Tachai experience. The remaining 130 brigades did not have work teams sent to them. During that period, while the brigades that had work teams increased their production by 37.3 percent, those that did not increased their production by 42.8 percent, or 5.5 percent more.

"The work teams did a lot of work in the villages. Why were the practical effects not satisfactory?" the report asked. Three explanations were given. First, the work team members were mostly cadres at the county level sent to the villages in rotation, and inexperienced in agriculture. When the number of county cadres was insufficient for village assignment, they were joined by schoolteachers, accountants, factory workers, store clerks, and even cooks. They did not understand the nature of farm work, and sometimes made hasty and disruptive personnel changes in the production brigades and teams.

Second, the work teams in that county were organized into three shifts, each staying in the villages for one year, with no continuity in the work from one shift to another. Each work team was concerned with production increase only in one particular year, without any long-range planning. Some work teams brought in loans for the purchase of machinery and fertilizer in order to increase production, but at the end of the year they walked away, leaving behind unfinished tasks and unpaid loans.

Third, coordination between the work teams and the commune was not clearly defined. Ideally, the two should have worked together through the Party organization to which both belonged. In reality, some work teams functioned under the commune, while others acted as superiors from higher-ups. Even when the two coordinated as equals, lengthy meetings took up much time, with much confusion and inefficiency as a result.

The report reaffirmed the positive role of the work team but warned against its misuse. When to send work teams, of what membership composition, for what purposes, for how long—these are practical questions that can only be answered by analyzing the actual needs.

The Mass Media. The mass media are another important linkage in China's overall communication system. Other than reports on policy announcements, major speeches, official visits, and foreign news, the media play a catalytic role in focusing public attention on the key issues the Party leadership wants to promote, generally in the form of a campaign. The *People's Daily*, for instance, has been giving extensive

254

coverage since mid-1977 to practical problems in the current Four Modernizations campaign. On 9 February 1979, the day Vice Premier Teng Hsiao-ping returned from his visit to the United States, the *People's Daily* had an editorial urging the Chinese to push the Four Modernizations wholeheartedly.[12] It ran a special column in 1979 and 1980 entitled "Contribute Your Wisdom and Strength to Four Modernizations." Successful experiences of factories and communes in different regions in improving production and raising income are regularly reported. Mistakes by cadres at various levels are brought up for criticism. Letters to the editor are published to spotlight problems that have otherwise escaped attention.

One problem concerning the media is credibility. It has now been admitted that much of the domestic coverage during the 1970s, when the radical group was in power, was false. This was revealed by the *Ta Kung Daily*, a Hong Kong newspaper that generally reflects Peking's official thinking.[13] Quoting an editorial in the *Liberation Army Daily* of 14 November 1977, the report said that most Chinese newspapers during the reign of the Gang of Four were filled with empty words. Since then, according to the *Ta Kung Daily*, a movement has been afoot to reform China's newspapers and to restore the spirit that Chairman Mao encouraged during the Yenan days.

In July 1979, nearly three years after the purge of the Gang of Four, the *People's Daily* made an unusually candid assessment in an editorial entitled "Defend Truthfulness, Oppose False Reporting."[14] Since the arrest of the Gang, the editorial said, many newspapers had made an effort to correct false reporting, but in practice, reports that were untrue or only partly true still appeared now and then. Other cases showed selective omission. For instance, said the editorial, a factory had been completed, but due to insufficient power supply and lack of raw materials, production had yet to begin. The news report mentioned the successful completion without a word about the problems that held up production. Sometimes a report was essentially true, but because of the use of hyperbole, suffered from a lack of credibility.[15]

"These practices of false reporting and exaggeration," said the editorial, "have caused serious damage to the enterprises of our Party. They corrupt the Party's workstyle, and affect the Party's reputation. . . . We have suffered a great deal because of this." Part of the problem, the *People's Daily* said, lay with some of the leadership cadres, who liked to cover up their mistakes and gave the reporters only the bright side of a situation. Even when an incorrect report had been exposed by readers, they did not want to cooperate with the investigation team from the newspaper, and refused to make corrections.[16]

Other changes are also noteworthy. Instead of giving concentrated publicity to a few stereotypes, such as the Tachai brigade, the *People's Daily* now publishes reports on cases of production improvement and income increase from many diverse units and even individual peasants. One gets the impression of a growing concern with factual reporting and pragmatism, especially since 1979. The integrative functions of the mass media will be discussed more fully later.

Local Changes since 1976

Changes in the Commune

In the countryside, where the roots of the Chinese system lie, important changes have begun to take place since the purge of the Gang. The commune system was established in 1958 on a pattern of localized collective production and distribution. The radical policies pursued during the reign of the Gang of Four, however, had the effect of smothering the individual work incentive of the peasants without the full benefit of collective productivity. One factor was the rigid restrictions imposed on family-based productive activities that were likely to boost the peasants' cash income, which we shall discuss later. Another was the tendency of administrators at the commune level to draft labor and funds away from the production teams, thus depleting resources for production at the grassroots. An example of such practices was revealed in a special report published in the *People's Daily* on 31 March 1978.[17] Based on a fact-finding investigation conducted around Tientsin by a correspondent of the *People's Daily*, the following conditions were revealed: (1) commune enterprises used production team labor without compensation, up to 238 laborers in one particular commune at one time; (2) in the name of dike construction, the same commune employed laborers from the production teams for work in the commune. The wages of these laborers were charged to their respective production teams; (3) the same commune used public funds, up to 100,000 yuan in 1977, for nonproductive construction. These funds were originally intended for aiding the poorer production teams in the commune. These excessive demands on the production teams were described as "killing the hen for the eggs." The Chinese peasants, in a word, were living below a standard which they could have attained had it not been for the restrictive policies during the 1960s and 1970s.

A major objective of the current government is, therefore, to develop the potential of the peasants for improving their livelihood. The new policy is: The peasants must get rich fast.[18] The urgency of restoring rural prosperity was emphasized at a meeting of agricultural experts in September 1979. China's rural communities, in their assessment, were at a historic turning point.[19] Either agricultural modernization would succeed, or rural China would slide back further into poverty.

The new leadership has pursued two policy changes. One is to restore local autonomy by removing some of the centralized controls enforced by the radical groups during the previous decade. The production brigades and teams in the communes are no longer required to follow rigidly the production quotas handed down from the central government. Nor are they bound by the previous policy, which concentrated on food production at the expense of other more profitable cash crops. Now the local units are encouraged to use their resources in the most productive manner as long as the overall production guidelines are followed. Interference from higher levels is discouraged.

The other policy change is to allow the peasants more room for material incentives by pursuing family sideline activities within the general framework of local collective production.

A symbolically significant step to accentuate the new policy is the revamping of Chairman Mao's "In Agriculture, Learn from Tachai" movement. Hsiyang County, home of the Tachai brigade, made a thorough examination of the Tachai model in August 1979 and came up with several recommendations. The private plots, which in Hsiyang used to be allotted to small collective groups under the Tachai model, are now given back to individual families. Family sideline production, previously considered a form of small capitalism, is now encouraged. Trees around the houses are returned to the families. The Tachai model of group evaluation of workpoints is replaced with more specific criteria. In food distribution, those who work more will get more. This now replaces the previous model, known as "eating from a big bowl," wherein each family declared its needs, which were then assessed at group meetings, resulting in more or less even distribution regardless of work input.[20]

We shall illustrate the new policy on material incentive with two examples, both given national publicity in the *People's Daily*. In the Chen-hu brigade outside Shanghai, a commune member, Fan Tsai-keng, cleared a net profit of 5,900 yuan in 1978 from a variety of sideline activities. His family of nine worked together, both before and after commune hours, and became rich. There were criticisms by other members in his brigade because his sideline profit far exceeded his family income of 1,872 yuan from commune work. The *Wen Hui Daily* of Shanghai, however, endorsed Fan's enterprising spirit: "There is absolutely nothing wrong if a peasant can get rich by working hard." In Fan's case, the paper pointed out, he did not exploit anybody, he did not steal or rob, and he did not let his collective assignment suffer.[21]

In the Hsi-shan brigade of Hsin-chang County in Chekiang, commune member Yuan Cheng-hua raised rabbits as a sideline job, feeding them with grass cut from a nearby hill by his children. In one year he made nearly 1,000 yuan. In comparison, the total wages his family earned from the commune that year were some 370 yuan. The *People's Daily* told this story in a positive vein.[22]

By the spring of 1980, the new policy had begun to pay dividends in terms of increased income among peasants. Although no overall statistics were available, we shall cite Kui-hu Commune in Szechuan

Province as an example. Production Team No. 4 in that commune was a relatively better-off village. Before the new policy, the average annual income of that production team was around 70 yuan per capita, not including income from private plots ranging from 5 to 20 yuan per capita depending on individual families. After the new policy came into effect, the average income for 1979 rose to 354 yuan per capita. In addition, the families were earning sideline income ranging from 200 to 400 yuan per person per year.[23]

Under the new policy, the Chinese government recognizes the inevitability that some peasants will get rich faster than others. The point is that not everybody can get rich at the same time, said the *People's Daily*, and this should not prevent some peasants from making the best of their resources within the collective framework.[24]

Degree of Local Autonomy

While the Chinese peasants seem to be catching on fast to the new accent on material incentives, restoring autonomy to the production brigade and team has proven more difficult. There was initial hesitation as to how far local autonomy should go. During the spring planting of 1979, soon after the word of local autonomy got around through the dissemination of Central Documents, some production teams in northern China began adopting practices which at that time were considered a threat to the viability of the commune system. This was revealed in a letter to the *People's Daily* by Chang Hao, a cadre, following his visit to Loyang.[25] Chang learned that many production teams in that area had either already adopted, or were about to adopt, a practice known as *pao-ch'an tao-tsu*. Members of the production teams organized themselves into small "mutual aid teams" totaling about forty to forty-five people, each consisting of six or seven families. Land, farm tools, and cattle that belonged to the production team were divided up and assigned to the mutual aid teams. In some communes, even the reserve grains were distributed to the mutual aid teams, each of which was to work on its portion of land, assume responsibility for its production quota, and keep what was left.

Chang was told that this was only the first step. The next step would be to assign all production means, including land, and production quotas to the individual families. There was apparently pressure from the county to push this new measure, but Chang said some cadres at both the production brigade and the production team levels told him about their reservations. There was concern about the effect on agricultural mechanization, which requires large-scale operation. What was not mentioned in the letter was the implication that if land and other means of production were distributed to the families, then the system would in effect return to the days after the Land Reform in the early 1950s, when individual farmers were given their own land to work on, leaving the local cadres with little to do.

258

This practice of small team operation was apparently not isolated in Honan. In Kirin Province a similar case was reported.[26] In Nan-wei-tzu Commune, one production team had 101 laborers in 85 families working on 1,900 *mou* of land. In early 1979, they divided themselves into three small operating teams each having its own land, farm tools, and cattle. The plan was for each operating team to sell its autumn crops after contributing its share of reserve grains. When the Party secretary of the commune learned about this, he went to that production team and organized the members to study the two Central Documents on agriculture, which he considered to have been misinterpreted. The Central Documents had encouraged the formation of small operating teams as a more flexible and efficient way of using labor, but not as an accounting unit for the distribution of income. The error was corrected in time, the report said.

The *People's Daily* in a special comment praised the Nan-wei-tzu Commune Party secretary for his action. Production teams were encouraged to work out their own utilization of resources, but, said the official daily, "the communes should not hastily change the basic accounting unit under circumstances when the [required] conditions are not present."[27]

Throughout 1979 and 1980, the Party leadership continued to experiment with different forms of agricultural production and income distribution, according to a report released by the official Hsinhua News Agency in May 1981.[28] In the spring and summer of 1980, the Party's leadership cadres in Peking went to villages across the country, from Yunnan in the southwest to Liaoning in the northeast, for on-the-spot investigations. The purpose was to see under what conditions the basic accounting unit could be modified to promote production. The Party's Central Committee and the prime minister's office later commissioned more than 100 rural workers and economists to conduct a two-month survey of villages in ten provinces. Both Prime Minister Chao Tzu-yang and Hu Yao-pang, secretary-general of the Central Committee, made field trips in early 1981. Afterwards a special session was held at the Party's Central Secretariat on 2 March 1981 to review the findings.

A key topic was the feasibility of a practice known as *pao-ch'an tao-hu*, which Liu Shao-ch'i had successfully employed in 1961 to stimulate a recovery of agricultural production following the initial difficulties of the People's Commune movement. The idea was to assign production quotas not to production teams, but to individual families, with the family allowed to retain the extra crops beyond the fulfillment of the quota. In this sense the family, not the collective, would be the basic accounting unit. This practice was tried out by Liu in various locations for a couple of years, with highly encouraging results. It was severely criticized by the radical group during the Cultural Revolution.

In mid-September 1980, the first Party secretaries of all provinces, depend entirely on its own production. After fulfilling its assigned quota major municipalities, and autonomous regions met in Peking to discuss the feasibility of this practice as a means of promoting agricultural production. A Central Document, issued on 27 September 1980, reaffirmed *pao-ch'an tao-hu* as a practice not inconsistent with socialism as long as it is implemented under the supervision of the production team. Vice Chairman Teng Hsiao-p'ing was quoted by Hsinhua as endorsing this practice in principle for economically backward areas where the land is vast and the population is sparse. Some of the survey results presented to Teng showed a doubling of peasant income after this practice was tried out for one year.

Prime Minister Chao, in summarizing his own field trip observations, suggested three alternative ways of organizing agricultural production which appear to be the basis of an emerging new policy. The three alternatives represent different degrees of collectivism in relation to the strength of the local rural economy.

In areas where the foundation of the collective rural economy is solid, and agricultural production and the standard of living have been improving, agricultural production should continue to be assigned to small task subteams (*tzuo-ye-tsu*). This arrangement is similar to the mutual aid team model (*pao-ch'an tao-tsu*) which caused uneasiness among some local cadres when tried out earlier in Loyang. According to the new policy, the subteams are to be organized on a voluntary basis, under the overall planning and supervision of the production team, to perform specific tasks such as rice growing or vegetable production. A task subteam will work and share production responsibility collectively according to a contract signed with the production team, which will coordinate the income distribution. If a subteam exceeds the production quota specified in the contract, it will receive extra income for distribution among its members. If a subteam fails to fulfill the quota, a penalty will be assessed. Of the three alternatives, this one is a form of higher collectivism.

In rural areas where the economy is at an intermediate level, the degree of collective work management will be given more flexibility. People will still work in small subteams, but production responsibilities will be assigned to individual laborers, not to the subteam. Income will be distributed on the basis of individual task fulfillment within the subteam context, with extra income for extra task achievement by the individual. This form allows more individual incentives within a collective framework of resource utilization.

In relatively backward areas, *pao-ch'an tao-hu* can be practiced to allow individual families to be the units of production assignment and income distribution. A family will receive from the production team its share of land to till (not to own), and will work on its own according to a family production quota rather than in a subteam. The family income will in terms of contribution to the state and setting aside reserves for the production team, the family will keep everything for itself. It will also have to absorb losses, if any. Another difference from the two previous alternatives is that cadres in the production team will have to earn their income through labor like everyone else, instead of getting workpoints by performing supervisory duties, since few are required under *pao-ch'an tao-hu*. According to comments from some peasants, this system will get rid of blind commandism from above, and do away with the practice by which cadres take away the fruits of the labor of the peasants. In some areas, after *pao-ch'an tao-hu* had been practiced for one year, rural family income increased considerably. Several families then got together and pooled their resources to buy major farm implements, cattle, and small tractors.

These alternatives, including *pao-ch'an tao-hu*, refer to agricultural work on land collectively owned by the production teams. In addition, rural families have been allowed to work on their private plots and engage in sideline production. The Chinese farmers apparently wanted various forms of production management and diverse sources of production revenues, said the Hsinhua report. The Party's Central Committee was considering making appropriate readjustments in agricultural organization in order to achieve diversification of rural income.

In another policy statement on the eve of the Sixth Plenary Session of the Party's Central Committee in June 1981, Vice Premier Wan Li made the following remarks:[29]

- The People's Commune system had reached a point of change and reform. Although the Chinese peasants had not yet asked to negate the commune system, the extent of collectivism was currently under review. Two basic socialist principles must be upheld. First, there could be no buying or selling of land. Second, there must be no exploitation. Within these contexts, the original concept of combining government administration and production in a single commune organization was being modified. A major problem in the past had been excessive administrative interference with production. One possible solution would be to place agricultural production under the management of a separate joint enterprise, the nature of which was to be specified.

- The degree of collectivism would be relaxed. The size of the private plots (*tzu-liu-ti*), estimated in spring 1981 to be about 5 to 7 percent of all arable land, would be expanded to 15 percent. It was noted that in some areas productivity from private plots had increased as much as four to six times in the previous couple of years. Even on land collectively cultivated, the peasants would be given the autonomous right to change their crops in order to suit the market needs.

- Another major change being considered would allow an unspecified percentage of peasants (*tzu-liu-jen*) to depart from collective labor and work exclusively on private plots.

These changes, when implemented, will in effect move the agricultural production system close to the days of the Mutual Aid movement of the early 1950s after the Agrarian Land Reform.

Reluctance to Innovate

Some local cadres were afraid to pursue any innovative practices for fear that they might be criticized for deviating from the correct ideological line. The *People's Daily* cited the following case as an illustration.[30] During the heavy snow in the spring of 1979, a production brigade in Hopei Province assigned its sheep and lambs to individual families to care for and save them from being starved or frozen to death. Those who took care of the sheep earned workpoints. In the fall of 1979, two production teams proposed to continue this practice on a regular basis. However, when the Party secretary of the brigade stopped them and asked the commune leadership for approval, the commune said no.

A reader who wrote to the *People's Daily* listed all the advantages of individual families caring for sheep. "But because it involved individual families [*hu*]," said the reader, "nobody dared to give his approval." In a brief comment, the *People's Daily* asked:

> Why is it so? . . . We should no longer be bound by the restrictions of the past, but should encourage the mass of people to learn from practical experience. Our policy is to promote production. We should stimulate the enthusiasm of every family to seek ways of production increase. Otherwise, does it mean that we are pursuing socialism if we herd the sheep together and let them freeze and starve, and that we would be pursuing capitalism if we assign the sheep to individual families and let them grow well?[31]

The issue of ideological line, or "direction" (*fang-hsiang*), has apparently been a major stumbling block to agricultural production.

> In the villages, [said the *People's Daily*] we often hear people say: "This practice is fine, and can stimulate the enthusiasm of commune members. We are just afraid that the direction might not be correct." Or: "This is what the people would like to see, and we are sure grain production will increase. But we are afraid of making an error about the direction."[32]

Under the general premise of collective ownership, said the official daily, the correct direction should be to increase production. But because of the overwhelming leftist influence of the past, the term "direction" has taken on many "mysterious interpretations." The *People's Daily* gave a few examples:

- If a family raises two chickens, it is socialism; if a family raises more than two, it becomes capitalism.
- If a family raises pigs and sheep, it is socialism; if a family raises a cow, it becomes capitalism.
- If there is a barren land outside the village and you simply let weeds grow there, it is socialism; if you assign the land to individual commune members for cultivation and food production, it becomes capitalism.

The result was that both cadres and commune members lived in constant suspense, fearing that they might have done something that violated the correct direction. To liberate productivity, said the *People's Daily*, the Chinese must come out of their ideological bondage and smash the arbitrarily concocted standards of false socialism.

Abuse of Authority

Another problem that has impaired local autonomy is the reluctance of cadres at the county and commune levels to relinquish the authority they have become accustomed to exercising for so long. Since 1978, the central government has repeatedly emphasized that production teams must be allowed to work out their own production plans. But such instructions are sometimes ignored.

In Ning-teh, Fukien Province, when winter planting came in early 1979, the district cadres simply did what they had always done before. They took out the old quotas, which were often unrealistic, and sent them to the production brigades and production teams. This time, the peasants began to complain. They called it "the same old style of commandism," and "blind exercise of leadership." In this case, the district cadres quickly corrected themselves. According to the *People's Daily*, the cadres went to the fields to listen to the peasants and revised their production plans.[33]

An incident in Hopei was not resolved so smoothly. Peasants in a production brigade in Liu-chun Commune had planted watermelons and cucumbers, which were not specified in the production plans. Just before the crops were ripe, the cadres in the commune found out and ordered the peasants to pull up the melons and cucumbers and destroy them. Furthermore, the commune cadres punished the brigade with an additional assessment of 5,000 catties of grain for that year.[34]

Within a week of the first report on this case, many readers wrote to the *People's Daily* to condemn what they considered to be "rotten behavior of blind leadership" and the serious bureaucratism that some cadres still manifested. Even though two Central Documents from Peking have encouraged family sideline production and allowed the production teams flexible wage guidelines under the new policy of local autonomy, one reader said, these directives were ignored by commune cadres in some places.[35]

The destruction of melons in Liu-chun Commune was apparently not the only case of its kind. A similar case, it was revealed, happened in Shangtung in 1975 when the radical group was still in power. A production team had planted fifteen *mou* of melons. Upon learning this, the commune cadres sent a team to destroy all the melons and dismissed the production leader. Even though the commune cadres later realized their error, they considered it beneath their status to admit their wrongdoings in front of the peasants.[36]

The *People's Daily* condemned the latest melon case in a special commentary. "What is serious is not the loss of some 10,000 yuan's worth of melons at Liu-chun Commune but rather, the obnoxious attitudes of a small number of commune cadres toward the people and their benefits," said the official paper. What the Liu-chun Commune cadres destroyed was more than tens of acres of melons: "They destroyed the normal relations between our Party and the people."[37]

The Liu-chun Commune incident, the *People's Daily* said, has revealed that some cadres like to act like "officials sitting on the heads of the people." The ills of the old feudalistic mentality still prevail. The melon incident, said the *People's Daily*, sounded a bell of alarm, demonstrating the necessity and urgency of a healthy democratic system.[38] The paper cited an official government report:

> Our country has a long history of feudalism. Our economic civilization is relatively backward. And we have not properly propagated and implemented democracy in the past. Our system is not adequate. Under those circumstances, autocracy, bureaucratism, special privileges, and head of family style have readily spread. . . . [Therefore] the various leadership cadres in the communes should in the future be elected by the mass of the people. . . .[39]

The Shih-chia-chuang District Office, which has supervisory responsibility over Liu-chun Commune, took the following measures:

1. It directed the county secretary to send a senior level cadre to Liu-chun Commune to help its cadres correct their attitudes. The particular production brigade that had suffered a loss due to the destruction

of melons was encouraged to engage in a variety of productions so that it could increase its income and make up for the loss. No other compensations were mentioned.

2. It distributed the Liu-chun melon case to all units in the district for discussion and criticism.

3. It organized a campaign to study the two Central Committee Documents on the new agricultural policy that were violated by the Liu-chun Commune cadres.[40]

The serious dislocation between the policy guidelines of the new government and the implementation at the local level is underscored by another case that came to light in the midst of the melon incident. On 3 August 1979, the *People's Daily* published a news release from the official news agency Hsinhua, which shows how following the new agricultural guidelines could be misinterpreted as a rightist deviation.[41] At Yang-chia-ping brigade in Hupei, some peasants had responded to the new guidelines and planted cucumbers and bamboo shoots around the houses. They were scared when told that such practices amounted to capitalism. Even though most of them hastened to destroy the plants overnight, they were subject to group criticism.

What is particularly noteworthy about this case, as an illustration of communication failure, was that the misinterpretation came as a result of four days of meetings by county and commune cadres to study the two Central Documents on agricultural production. What was originally intended to be an encouragement for production increase through local autonomy came out as a criticism of capitalism. The rationale of the cadres was: Since the guidelines did not mention planting cucumbers and vegetables around the house as an acceptable form of production, then anyone doing that must be practicing capitalism.

In an editor's note, Hsinhua said the Yang-chia-ping case must not be missed as a minor issue. It showed how deeply rooted some of the leftist thinking imposed by the Gang of Four was. Serious, continual criticism would be necessary, the editor noted, before things in the villages could be managed well.[42]

Reform of the National Cadre System

Cracks in the System

The key to the current Chinese system is the cadres. They are the links between the Party leadership and the people. They transmit the directives from the central government to the grassroots regions. They have the responsibility of organizing the mass of people for action programs, and of transmitting feedback information to the Party leadership. The flow of communication, horizontal as well as vertical, downward and upward, lies primarily in their hands. They also regulate the distribution of material rewards and recognition.

Revelations made since the purge of the Gang of Four have pointed out many flaws in the cadre system, some of which appear to be inherited from traditional Chinese bureaucracy. Cadres at various levels formed themselves into cliques and factions to protect each other, an old custom known as *kuan-kuan hsiang-hu*.[43] Efficiency and performance were often of little consequence. In many organizations, an official report said, it made no difference whether one did a lot or a little, whether one did a good job or a poor job, or whether one did anything at all. A cadre was employed not because of ability, but because of personal relations.[44]

Part of the problem lies in the tenure base of the cadre system. For instance, in the two and a half weeks following its first report on the melon incident, the *People's Daily* received more than 240 letters from twenty-one provinces and municipalities.[45] Many letters said the reason that cadres of Liu-chun Commune could totally ignore the interests of the peasants was that their jobs were like an "iron rice bowl" (*t'ieh-fan-wan*), that is, indestructible. Whether the peasants in a production team were rich or poor was of no concern to them. Their position was always secure. If the commune cadres were popularly elected, and if the people had the supervisory power and could dismiss them, said the letters, the situation would be different.

In the style of cadre work, six problems were noted in an editorial in the *People's Daily*:[46] First was dragging one's feet. There were many resolutions, but few implementations of the resolutions. Instead of taking action, the cadres always wanted first to make a study, and then refer it to "collective leadership" for decision.

Second was "floating high above." Since they were the officials, they had no concern for the welfare of the people. They did not seriously study the instructions from the Party, and did not care to understand the real difficulties in the units below them. They attended meetings and pushed papers, but did nothing.

Third was laxity. They had neither discipline nor organization. Directives were left unimplemented. During office hours, they whittled away their time. In study sessions, they chitchatted. They argued endlessly over petty issues but ignored big problems.

Fourth was inertia. They relaxed under the status quo, and knew only how to follow routine procedures. They were not interested in new situations and new problems. Whenever they ran into difficulties, they complained. They did not examine their own mistakes, and did not listen to criticisms by others.

Fifth were the abuse power and practice of favoritism. Personal relations were paramount. *Tsou-hou-men* (going through the back door) became routine.

Sixth was being extravagant. They wanted to enjoy life in style. Their

266

residences had to be luxurious, their offices comfortable. They indulged in banquets and exchanged gifts. You gave them limousines, and they wanted more. They padded their expense accounts.

These problems existed in different degrees in some of the government organizations, said the *People's Daily*. "Such undesirable practices have seriously impaired the enterprise of socialist modernization, and destroyed the relation between the Party and the people. Unless they are corrected, not only will our government agencies degenerate into the *yamen* of the past, but even the proletarian dictatorship will be changed and corrupted," the official daily said.[47]

Reeducation of Cadres

To remedy these deficiencies, the Party has been taking several measures. One is a campaign, launched in the summer of 1979, to reeducate the cadres and instill in them a new sense of revolutionary fervor which, the Party said, had been destroyed by the Gang of Four. An editorial in the *People's Daily* on 15 August 1979 stated that even those old cadres who had suffered at the hands of the Gang should not use their past grievances as an excuse for special treatment. Nor should the younger cadres consider themselves a privileged class.[48]

The editorial cited a historical anecdote to teach the cadres a lesson. After the founding emperor of the T'ang Dynasty died, there was an internal succession fight, out of which his second son emerged as Emperor T'aitsung. His minister, Wei Cheng, sensing a trend of arrogance and lassitude, spoke bluntly with the emperor. His advice was to curb desires, suppress arrogance, prevent laxity, invite criticism, resist flattery, and avoid favoritism. Emperor T'aitsung took his advice. "These are provocative thoughts for the leadership cadres of our ruling Party," said the editorial. "Shall we not expect these of our leadership?"

As part of this campaign, the Party encouraged the people to expose the erroneous behavior of their cadres and bring it up for public criticism. Soon after the editorial, the *People's Daily* publicized the case of San-ho County as a negative example to be avoided.

San-ho, in Hopei Province, suffered severe damage during the earthquake of 1976. The situation was aggravated by a flood in 1977 which affected the crops. Some 3,400 commune families were homeless and lived in makeshift tents. The county's Party committee, however, commandeered free labor from the production teams to build a new auditorium. Following this example, seven communes and more than ten county agencies began a spree of building new offices. Someone wrote a letter to the prime minister's office that received the attention of Hua Kuofeng. Hua condemned the San-ho cadres and sent the case to the provincial committee for action. Meanwhile, the Party's Central Committee disseminated the errors of San-ho to all units in the nation as a negative lesson to be learned.

On 23 August 1979, nearly a year and a half after the first exposure of the San-ho case, the official daily reported that the county cadres had accepted the criticisms of the mass of the people and corrected their mistakes. All construction projects not related to production had been stopped. Some 600 laborers drafted from the production teams had been returned to agricultural work. Funds and materials commandeered from the production teams had been paid back. Some of the new houses built by the communes had been given to families in need of help.[49]

In an editorial accompanying the story, the *People's Daily* remarked that the wicked trend demonstrated in San-ho in the past was a symptom of feudalism. Hua's instruction had been: "Criticize this wicked trend." "However," said the official daily, "there are still those cadres who consider themselves always right. In their region or unit they are the king, the lord. Even when they are clearly wrong, they would not listen to the slightest criticism from the people. A tiger's backside must not be touched. They storm into a temper if anyone attempts to criticize them. . . . This is completely wrong."[50]

A New Model

The Party leadership is using a variety of media, including short stories, drama, and television plays, to create a new image of cadres. The official newspaper then gives it endorsement and emphasizes that this is the way the cadres should behave. We shall cite one short story, "Director Ch'iao Returns to His Job," as an example.[51]

Director Ch'iao Kuang-pu exemplifies the ideal cadre for the Four Modernizations now being pursued by the Party. A Party member of long standing, Ch'iao suffered from persecution during the reign of Lin Piao and the Gang of Four, at one time even being sent to live in the "cowshed," a Chinese terminology for exile and labor reform. His wife lost her life under ambiguous circumstances. His own body is covered with scars. But Ch'iao does not indulge in self-pity. Now that he is back in his old post as director of a heavy-duty generator factory, he will not let anything stand in the way of production increase. In the factory he faces all kinds of bizarre obstacles, but he is not to be stopped. He is determined to run his factory in a pragmatic and scientific manner despite the opposition and complaints of some of his subordinates.

In contrast, the first Party secretary at the factory, Chi Seng, is portrayed as an opportunist who typifies a trend know as *feng p'ai*, that is, following whatever direction the wind is currently blowing. Chi, also an old cadre, likes to brag about how he was persecuted by the Gang of Four. He has no real ability but is good at sensing his superiors' preferences, and smooth in personal relations. He constantly surveys his environment, even relying on rumors and alley news (*hsiao-tao hsiao-hsi*) to determine how he can best adapt and survive.

While clearly condemning the first Party secretary, the story has more sympathy than blame for another senior cadre, Shih Kan. Formerly Party secretary at the factory, Shih used to work with Director Ch'iao closely twenty years before, when both were young. But the many purges during the days of Lin Piao and the Gang of Four have left him exhausted and disillusioned. He has learned his lesson, so to speak, and now approaches any problem with extreme caution. Sometimes he even pretends not to see a problem.

The official paper praised Director Ch'iao for his courage and pragmatism, and disapproved of the first Party secretary. The tired and dejected Shih Kan was seen as a reflection of many other cadres who could be reeducated and revived.

Evaluation of Cadres

In addition to the education campaign, the Party is looking for concrete ways to evaluate the cadres. In his 1979 administrative report on the work of the government, Hua said: "We must establish an adequate system governing the examination, evaluation, supervision, reward and punishment, and dismissal of cadres so that our cadres will not degenerate from public servants into overlords who ride over the heads of the people."[52]

Such a system of evaluation has been made necessary not only because of the many ills of bureaucratism already noted, but also because "the incompatibility between the current cadre system and the Four Modernizations is becoming more and more striking," as the People's Daily put it.[53] The evaluation has been tried out in urban areas and is expected to apply to rural regions later.

The experience at the machine shop in Tsitsihar, Heilungkiang Province, gives some indication of the new evaluation system.[54] The evaluation, which was tried out in the winter of 1978 and the summer of 1979 on some 270 cadres at the section-chief level, used three main categories: qualifications for the job, level of performance, and ideology and workstyle. Of these, level of performance had the greatest weight. For technical staff, this evaluation would examine the output of the section and the cadre's contribution to the work output. For managerial staff, it would rate their performance in organizing production activities. For cadres in the Party organizations, it would evaluate their effectiveness in implementing the policies of the Party and in coordinating relations with the mass of people, as well as ideological work.

The evaluation was based on personal interviews, input from the workers and other units related to the cadre, output statistics, and other results of investigation regarding the cadre's achievements and shortcomings. Each cadre would be evaluated twice a year, and an overall rating would be given after two years. Four ratings would be used: superior, satisfactory, in need of improvement, and underqualified. After a trial for one year, 14 of the 270 cadres were found underqualified and were demoted. Another 12, also underqualified, were retained on probation. Four cadres were found superior and promoted to leadership positions.

The machine shop said its one-year trial evaluation had three major results. First, it enabled the leadership cadres to know their staff more thoroughly, and thus make more efficient use of labor. Second, it provided an incentive for the cadres to strive for efficiency because superior performance was rewarded and inadequate work was punished. Third, it prompted the cadres to seek professional improvement lest they be left behind.

Improving Communication

Besides these measures, the Party has continued to stress better communication between cadres of higher and lower levels, and between the Party and the people. An editorial in the *People's Daily* suggested that all leadership cadres make an effort to talk to their subordinates.[55] Some leadership cadres, said the official paper, are either indifferent or impatient. Lower-level cadres may have something useful to suggest, or questions to ask. But if a leadership cadre is reluctant to see them, good work cannot be done.

Talking to lower-level cadres can have five benefits, the editorial continued. One gains firsthand information, which can counterbalance one's own bias; one can learn something from one's subordinates; the leader can get to know the subordinates; talking to one's subordinates can avoid misunderstanding and promote unity; and above all, it can help overcome bureaucratism.

The *People's Daily* gave some suggestions on how to talk to subordinates: Don't always talk to the same persons; find some new faces to talk to. Treat the subordinates as equals; don't act like a boss. Use rational analysis, not authority, to convince the subordinates. On important matters, don't deviate from the basic principles. Finally, be patient. If one conversation brings no result, try again.

The Party has emphasized again the linkage function of letters and visits from the people. Such direct contacts are considered vital to the campaign against bureaucratism.[56] But there are leadership cadres, said the *People's Daily*, who treat the letters and visits as trivial matters. Letters from the people pile up for a long time and are not given any attention. When people visit their offices, the cadres either refer the complaints elsewhere, or even suppress them. As a result, some people have had to take a long journey to the provincial capital, or even to Peking, to file a petition. The behavior of these cadres is detrimental to the unity and stability of the country, said the official paper.

According to the *People's Daily*, Hua and other leaders in the central government personally read many letters from the people. Hua gave the following instruction in his government report: "The leaders of all government offices and enterprises must pay careful attention to the cries of the people, and be concerned with their ills and woes. They must personally handle the letters and visits."

Even anonymous letters are not necessarily bad, said the *People's Daily*. As long as the motivation is constructive and the contents are factually true, anonymous letters should be welcome. "After all, how a citizen wants to express his opinions and requests is his democratic right. Nobody should interfere."[57]

The Case of Hsiung I-fu

To eradicate the malaise of bureaucratism apparently will take time. On 25 August 1979, soon after the campaign had been initiated, the *People's Daily* published a letter about the case of Hsiung I-fu, a retired veteran who hung himself in the courthouse of Chiang-yu County, Szechuan Province.[58]

The letter, written by a cadre in a district court in Szechuan, gave the following details: In March 1976, the production team in which Hsiung worked discovered a theft of some 100 catties of ginger. Two commune members were arrested. Under physical punishment, they said Hsiung's wife was one of the accomplices. Even though the two immediately went to the county courthouse to clarify that Hsiung's wife was in fact innocent, the Party secretary in the production brigade put her through torture and examination and forced her to confess. She eventually did. To pay her fine of 480.75 yuan, she had to sell her one-and-a-half-room house, two pigs, and a sewing machine.

Since 1976, Hsiung and his wife had gone to the commune, the county court, the county security bureau, the county Party secretary, the district Party secretary, the district court, and the district security bureau to seek redress. Nobody would accept the case. Finally, in December 1978, the county court reviewed the documents in the commune, but made no further investigation. In April 1979, Hsiung again went to the courthouse to plead his case. While the court cadres were out for a study session, he hung himself.

The *People's Daily* published the letter with a note. "What does the death of Hsiung I-fu tell us? What lessons can we learn from this case? How shall we handle a case like this? Please express your views."[59]

Angry letters descended on the *People's Daily* "like snowflakes." In less than a month, from 25 August to 20 September, the official paper received more than 2,000 letters. The *People's Daily* published four on 22 September 1979. One letter, written by a college teacher and a worker in Peking, said Hsiung was killed by bureaucratism. "We say the Gang of Four killed people; bureaucratism can put people to death too. . . . If we do not resolutely overcome this kind of bureaucratism, there is no guarantee that the tragedy of Hsiung I-fu will not be repeated."[60]

A cadre in the propaganda department of Heng-shui County, Hopei Province, had this to say:

> Why did Hsiung I-fu die in grief? The basic problem is that an ordinary commune member does not have the bare, substantive democratic rights. Why would some of the cadres dare to behave so wantonly? . . . Because the cadres have power and the people have no power. . . . We often say the power of the cadres is given to them by the people. But in reality, what power do ordinary workers and commune members have? They can neither appoint, nor dismiss, and not even accuse or criticize [the cadres]. . . . To solve the many problems [left by the Gang of Four], the basic step is to give people democratic rights. . . . Otherwise, tragic cases like Hsiung I-fu cannot be avoided, and the Four Modernizations will be difficult to realize.[61]

An agricultural cadre in Hupei said Hsiung I-fu was not an isolated case. It was the result of cadre insensitivity to the life or death of the people. "Hsiung's death tells us a lot," the letter said. "He used his own life to give the whole Party a lesson: In the march toward the Four Modernizations, the leaderships at all levels must reform the Party's style to wholeheartedly serve the people."[62]

One month later, the *People's Daily* published a summary of the letters it had received on the death of Hsiung I-fu. The following main points were made. There was serious bureaucratism in some of the Party and government organizations. Both the local cadres and some of the leadership offices were responsible. The traditional style of the Party to serve the people was damaged by Lin Piao and the Gang of Four and had not yet been restored. Under these circumstances, the little people were suffering most. China needed a large contingent of upright judicial personnel who could fight bureaucratism in the way the legendary Pao Kung (Judge Pao) protected the poor and the innocent from the mighty and the powerful. Leadership offices must not turn a deaf ear to letters and visits from the people.[63]

Integrative Forces

Local Solidarity

Given the scope and complexity of the subject matter and the limited nature of our data, we shall refrain from any claim to definitive conclusions on these post-Mao changes in China. The observations that follow, based on the chapters in this volume as well as on our more recent data, are tentative. Even though many important details are still unavailable, the general picture can be sketched with only a marginal degree of ambiguity.

The building block of China's contemporary society is the local village, as it has always been. One fundamental difference between the present and the past is the removal of exploitation, primarily at the hands of the landlords in league with the bureaucrats in the cities, many of whom were landlords themselves. Today in the production teams, which are mostly natural villages, there is a sense of solidarity shared between the peasants and the team cadres, who are themselves peasants elected by their peers. This solidarity, which Marc Blecher calls "communion,"[64] has been built partly on the traditional foundation of kinship-oriented in-group relations that have always existed in Chinese villages. Economically, these relations were reflected in a traditional custom of mutual help known as *hu-t'ung yu-wu*, that is, sharing what you have now with others who will share with you what they have when you are in need someday. This custom has now been institutionalized in collective ownership and distribution in the production teams.

Ideologically, the Chinese peasants have always looked upon their village as the extent of their world. Their political horizons have now been enlarged. Their immediate concern is, however, still with their village, their own production team. The transition from the traditional, landlord-dominated village to the collective production team has been an arduous process. Through trial and error, the Chinese peasants have worked out a system under the Party that combines the collective with the private, in production as well as distribution.

We shall cite two cases to illustrate that this village solidarity, an important cornerstone for social integration, is based on traditional roots of local identity and shared interest. One is the case of the destruction of melons. The reports in the *People's Daily* did not mention how the decision to plant the melons was reached in the production team, but it was apparent that the team cadres were on the side of the peasants and did nothing to stop them. The interference eventually came from cadres in the commune, who were outside the village. The other case involved a major departure from the commune system, when one production team in Nan-wei-tzu Commune started to divide up its land, farm tools, and cattle into small operating teams that would then be allowed to sell their own crops. This action, which was the first step toward revamping the commune system, could not have been taken without the support of the production team cadres. It was the commune secretary, again someone from outside the village, who stopped it.

This communal solidarity, rooted in traditional local identity and shared economic interest, provides the basis for collective task-oriented cooperation in the production teams. It sometimes enables the local groups to fend off administrative encroachment from outside, as the Tachai experience has illustrated.[65] It is this same local solidarity that has enabled the vast rural Chinese population to withstand such spasmodic convulsions as the Cultural Revolution. It kept the Chinese villages beyond the destructive arms of the Red Guards. It provided many local cadres with an umbrella of protection against the wanton deeds of the young rebels. It enabled the villages to survive the restrictive policies of the radical faction. In short, it helped keep China's social fabric intact.

Although this local solidarity grows from traditional roots, its new form has been strengthened by two important developments, one substantive and the other communicative. The substantive development was the land reform programs of the early 1950s that eliminated exploitation by the landlords and put the resources for production into the hands of the Chinese peasants.[66] The communicative development came in the many campaigns during the last three decades. Even though some of the campaigns caused temporary disruptions to village life and production, they have had the latent effect of linking up the villages into a national system of communication. They allow the central government to penetrate the local units and achieve an identification between the ruler and the ruled, as Alan Liu has phrased it.[67] This process has proved to be essential to political socialization. Many Chinese peasants have come a long way from their past ignorance and submissiveness to become articulate and outspoken members of the village community. They participate in the management of their production team in their roles as commune members. There is even a tendency for some of them to speak out on affairs beyond their villages, as indicated by letters published in the official newspaper. They are no longer a "tray of loose sand," as Dr. Sun Yat-sen once lamented.

The melon incident illustrates anew a basic principle regarding social integration in China that has been demonstrated time and again in history. That is, local autonomy is essential to the stability and welfare of Chinese society. The Chinese village fares best when external demands and interference are held to a minimum. This is why rural China was thrown into such chaotic dislocations when the commune system was introduced in 1958 in its initial form.[68] The high degree of collectivism to be controlled by the huge communes would have irretrievably destroyed local village autonomy. The disaster was relatively short-lived because enough members in the Party leadership quickly realized the errors and made necessary adjustments. Much of the local autonomy was soon restored under Liu Shao-ch'i's policy, known as *San-tzu I-pao*.[69] When the radical groups regained power following the Cultural Revolution, which saw the ouster of Liu, they tried again to take away some of the local autonomy. Under rigid centralized control, the result was a slowdown of agricultural productivity. The new leadership in Peking has been working to undo some of the damage caused during the ten years when the Gang of Four was in power. The new policy is to help the peasants get rich by allowing the production team considerable leeway in planning production and managing distribution.

The current policy under which the production team can divide itself up into small subteams already gives the villages more autonomy than they have had since the agricultural cooperative movements in the early 1950s. The manner in which the official *People's Daily* commented on the Nan-wei-tzu Commune case, however, seemed to imply that more changes might be forthcoming. As we may recall, the *People's Daily* said the communes "should not hastily change the basic accounting unit under circumstances when the [required] conditions are not present."[70] This statement left the door ajar for such a change, if and when the as-yet unspecified conditions are present.[71] The new guidelines announced in mid-1981 have indicated the direction of future changes.

National Network

A dual structure of Party branches and government offices links the production teams into a national network under the central government through several intermediary tiers, the brigade, the commune, the county, the district, and the province. At every level there are both a Party unit and an administrative office, with the former directing the latter. The various communication channels we have illustrated give the Party the means to coordinate the goals and means on a national scale and at the same time maintain close touch with the masses.

In short, societal integration in China is achieved at two levels— social integration in the local communities, and political integration at the national level. Both involve relatively intense communication activities such as the group communication in the production teams analyzed by Marc Blecher, the lateral communication at the local level noted by Mitch Meisner, the work team activities described by John Burns, the dissemination of Central Documents examined by Kenneth Lieberthal, and the national campaigns discussed by Charles Cell. Also essential is the county level coordination, as analyzed by Steven Butler.

The effectiveness of these communication channels depends on the prevailing policy, which determines how they are used. There is evidence to suggest that during the rule of the radical group, these channels were not achieving the intended effect. Even though the radical policy has now been altered, the communication channels are only as good as the cadres at the various levels, whose duties are to transmit the directives from the top policymakers and send feedback reactions up from the grass roots. Over the years, the cadre system has manifested bureaucratic flaws in varying degrees of seriousness at one time or another. Victor Falkenheim has noted some of the related problems. One persistent manifestation is commandism, which began to interfere with the Party's programs soon after its military victory in 1949. Partly due to inability or unwillingness to organize the people by education and persuasion, and partly because of the traditional Chinese concept of authority, many cadres simply passed on the directives as orders to be

275

carried out.[72] From the few accounts we have cited from the *People's Daily* in 1979, this phenomenon has not disappeared.

Commandism, or abuse of authority, has been difficult to eradicate despite the Party's repeated rectification campaigns directed at the erring cadres. One reason lies in a common practice inherent in the traditional tendency in China for bureaucrats to cover up for each other, as we noted earlier. This tendency apparently reached unrestrained heights during the ten years from 1966 to 1976, when the radical group was in control. Eager to wrest power away from the Party regulars, the radicals under Chiang Ch'ing placed their followers in many key positions throughout the country. As long as they remained loyal, other errors were considered to be less significant and were generally ignored. As a result, these cadres had almost absolute power in their respective regions, and committed gross mistreatment of the people, which has now begun to receive attention and redress.

Another legacy from the ten years of radicalism following the Cultural Revolution is a huge contingent of cadres who are ill equipped to tackle the problems of the Four Modernizations. The *People's Daily* has noted what it terms a "striking incompatibility" between the cadre system and the requirements of the Four Modernizations. This incompatibility, we think, is partly due to the traditional bureaucratism in new garb, partly related to the past reliance on political campaigns, but primarily a result of the mode of operation of the Chiang Ch'ing group. A cadre's job security, promotion, and indeed survival depended on how well he or she could parrot the ideology of the radical faction. Under a trend known as *ning-tso wu-yu* (rather be left than right), the more radical one acted, the better the chance of recognition. In factories the accent was not on efficient managerial ability, but on skills in organizing mass rallies and criticism sessions. The net result is a large number of young and middle-aged cadres superbly schooled in radical rhetoric but largely lacking in substantive ability to get the job done.

The new leadership gives every indication of being aware of this incompatibility. As reported in the official newspaper, the government is now taking steps to reform the cadre system, particularly to correct the abuse of power and encourage efficient performance. But the ills, partly inherent in traditional Chinese culture, have accumulated for years and are difficult to remedy. Other than the residual influence of the old tradition, one reason is that the purge of the Gang of Four has affected only the top-level supporters. The millions of lower-echelon followers have been allowed to remain, and their enthusiasm for cadre reform is as yet untested. Another reason is that the cultivation of managerial and production abilities takes time.

In the context of a partly enmeshed cadre structure, the mass media as means of two-way communication have assumed an important function of national coordination and integration. We have shown earlier how the official newspapers are used as a forum for exchanging information and experience about practical problems of production. The newspapers are also used as a monitoring device for spotting deviations from the new policies, fulfilling what Harold Lasswell calls the surveillance function of communication.[73]

We shall illustrate another important function of the mass media— reduction of tension and resolution of conflicts—that is essential to societal integration. We are referring to the letters from the people. The Party has encouraged the people to air their problems by writing to the Party secretaries and to the newspapers, particularly the *People's Daily*. Over the years, the Party has made repeated appeals to its cadres to treat the letters as an important bridge between the Party and the people, but these appeals are not always heeded. During the years right after the Cultural Revolution, as the analysis by Godwin Chu and Leonard Chu has shown, letters published in the *People's Daily* became perfunctory echoes of the radical line. By contrast, the letters published since the purge of the Gang of Four have an air of spontaneity and outspokenness. It may be recalled that the *People's Daily* received more than two thousand letters condemning the serious malaise of bureaucracy exposed by the death of Hsiung I-fu. That such letters receive attention from high-level policymakers demonstrates to the people that their grievances can be heard and there is a way to resolve conflicts with local cadres.

New Social Fabric

China's new social fabric is made of strong local fibers closely knit into a central pattern directed from Peking. Instituted in the production teams, the local fibers are as much earthbound as their predecessors.[74] But unlike the villages of the past, the production teams today are securing an increasingly autonomous base in the management of their own affairs. The agrarian land reform of the early 1950s eliminated the pervasive economic and political influences of the landed gentry, removing a perennial source of rural exploitation.[75] In place of the gentry, a new crop of village leaders has risen from the ranks of the peasants. They now manage the use of local resources and work out task-oriented cooperation and the distribution of rewards. Their ascendance to positions of local decision making, as indicated by the composition of production team cadres in Marc Blecher's survey, is an important feature of China's new social fabric. It has opened up avenues of social mobility and altered the relatively fixed social relations that existed in Chinese villages for generations.

While life in traditional rural China was marked by an atmosphere of static harmony and nonaction, the production teams today are charac- terized by incessant action programs of all kinds, each requiring the exposure and subsequent resolution of conflicts. The targets of conflicts have included the landlords in the early 1950s, various cliques in the 1960s and early 1970s, and now bureaucratism. Indeed it is the resolution of such conflicts that gives the production teams a measure of vitality. Through the implementation of action programs by the new village leaders and their team members, a dynamic integration is maintained in the local communities.

Nor does the Chinese village strive for survival in virtually isolated confinement anymore. Not only is there frequent lateral communication with other production teams and brigades in the same commune, but an elaborate communication network, through administrative channels, Central Committee Documents, work teams, and the mass media, often activated in the form of a campaign, links the production teams into an integrated national entity. The flow of communication in the network is primarily downward. But the local units at times are able to send reactions upward, mostly complaints against excessive interference by cadres immediately above them, but also support for government policies such as the one on agricultural development.

Although the Party has stressed the necessity of allowing the people to seek redress by bringing their complaints directly to leadership cadres at higher levels, through either letter writing or personal visits, this policy has not been fully implemented. A more accessible channel, one that is becoming far more effective since the purge of the Gang of Four, is the mass media, particularly the newspapers. Individuals with personal grievances or divergent opinions regarding a local problem can and do write to the People's Daily, and often receive immediate attention. Even major policy issues such as the stigma of individuals' undesirable class identification have been contested through letters, and eventually removed.[76]

Both the People's Daily and the official news agency Hsinhua report on some of the basic issues facing the production teams, such as heavy financial burdens imposed by the communes, or abuse of authority by local cadres. Both the letters and the investigative reporting by the media are significant channels through which the interests and concerns of the common people can be communicated, horizontally as well as upward to the top-level policymakers. We have seen examples of how a letter to the editor touched off a public outcry, followed by actions by the authorities to correct the mistake. The letters column is thus more than a safety valve that prevents the accumulation of tension from reaching an intolerable point. It provides a mechanism for conflict resolution and serves as the instigator of reform in the organizational structure that may eventually lead to its modification.

The mass media as major institutions are among the major structural features that distinguish the current Chinese social system from its traditional predecessors.[77] Because of the nearly total absence of such communication channels in the past, not only was the old Chinese social system never closely integrated,[78] but the imperial court was usually unaware of mounting unrest until it was too late. Traditional China did have its ombudsmen, the *yu shih*, and sometimes specially courageous officials like the legendary Judge Pao with imperial mandate to correct injustice on the spot. But they were too few in number and too sporadic to be effective. In this perspective, the mass media as institutions are of critical importance to societal integration in China, not only because they are powerful instruments for mobilizing and coordinating the national effort, but also because they can be a major mechanism of checks and balances against the abuse of power.

As we pointed out in the introduction, societal integration is a structural process permitting an optimal or minimal fulfillment of systemic functional requisites. In traditional China, the old social structure had its built-in mechanisms in the local communities that enabled the system to meet its minimum needs and to recover from chaos and near disintegration. Its weakness lay in the feeble lines of communication between the center and the peripheries.

China under communism has not only retained and strengthened the integrative features in the local communities, but has built up an extensive communication network to incorporate the local communities into a national entity. The basic structural foundation for this new integration has been laid. While each major rectification campaign in the past twisted or dented the national network, the local communities remained largely unscathed, preventing the system from falling apart despite such turmoil as the Cultural Revolution. The recent shift of policy from ideological indoctrination to pragmatic development has posed new challenges to the Chinese system. Will the national communication network be used in its full capacity to mobilize the Chinese people and meet the requirements of the Four Modernizations? The basic issue, as the melon incident seems to suggest, is: How do Party cadres reorient their thinking and style of operation to carry out the new tasks? The prospects of an invigorated process of societal integration for a higher plateau of national achievement depend on how this issue is resolved.

279

NOTES

1. For a description of the Chinese commune system, see William L. Parish, "Communist Agricultural Organization: China—Team, Brigade, or Commune?" *Problems of Communism* 25 (March–April 1976):51–65. For a model commune in the early 1970s, see Chu Li and Tien Chieh-yun, *Inside a People's Commune* (Peking: Foreign Languages Press, 1974). For an in-depth analysis of the people's commune in the post-Mao era, see Rance L.P. Lee and Siu-Kai Lau, eds., *People's Commune and Rural Development—The Experience of Toushan Commune, Taishan County* (Hong Kong: Chinese University Press, 1981). Brigades and communes are primarily administrative units. In general, cadres at the brigade level are nominated by the production teams and appointed by the commune leadership, while cadres in a commune are appointed by the county. At each level, from the commune down to the production team, Party organization parallels the cadre structure. Not all cadres are Party members, although the more responsible positions, particularly from the brigade level up, are likely to be held by members of the Party.

2. See Steven Butler, Chapter 6 in this volume.

3. See Kenneth Lieberthal, Chapter 5 in this volume.

4. See John P. Burns, Chapter 7 in this volume.

5. The status of *tatzupao* has been in doubt since an announcement in March 1980 that the Party Central Committee will request the amendment of the Constitution to delete the citizenry right of posting *tatzupao*. (See "The Victorious Conclusion of the Fifth Plenary Session," *Jen-min Jih-pao* [People's Daily], 1 March 1980.) A commentary in the *People's Daily* on 10 March 1980 suggested that the *tatzupao*, originally intended to be a forum for democratic public discussion, have been used by some individuals as an instrument for attacking others. Eliminating the right of posting *tatzupao*, said the author of the commentary, would promote national unity. (See "Elimination of the 'Four Big' Meets Popular Sentiments," by Tung Shu-ping, *People's Daily*, 10 March 1980.) Since then the big-character posters have virtually disappeared in China. Posters have been a traditional Chinese means of communication by which official edicts were announced and local grievances were aired. A playmate of Mao Tse-tung, Siao Yu, has described the use of posters in their villages as he witnessed it during his childhood. (See Siao Yu, *Remembering My Boyhood* [Taipei, Taiwan: Yih Wen Chih Monthly Publications, 1969], pp. 77–80.) Posters were very much part of daily life in Yenan, but the term *tatzupao* did not begin to attract wide attention until the Hundred Flowers movement of 1957, when rightist Chinese intellectuals posted many *tatzupao* to criticize some of the Party's policies. The posters gained worldwide recognition during the Cultural Revolution. The 1975 Constitution recognizes *tatzupao* as a basic right of the people to express their views. *Tatzupao* were again headlined in the Western press during the human rights movement in Peking in early 1979. A wall at Hsi Tan off Tien-an-men Square came to be known as the "Democracy Wall" because of the *tatzupao* posted there. In December 1979, the Peking Municipal Government closed the Hsi Tan wall, and designated the walls of Moon Temple further away from the city center for posters. (See "*Tatzupao* to Be Moved from Hsi Tan to Moon Temple," *Takung Pao* [Takung Daily] (Hong Kong), 7 December 1979.) The decision to ban *tatzupao* came three months later. For a brief discussion of the traditional use of posters in China, see Godwin C. Chu, *Radical Change through Communication in Mao's China* (Honolulu: University Press of Hawaii, 1977), pp. 232–238. David Jim-tat Poon has discussed the history and significance of *tatzupao* in contemporary China.

See Poon, "Tatzupao: Its Significance as a Communication Medium," in Godwin C. Chu, ed., *Popular Media in China: Shaping New Cultural Patterns* (Honolulu: University Press of Hawaii, 1978), pp. 184-221. Also see Godwin C. Chu, Philip H. Cheng, and Leonard Chu, *The Roles of Tatzupao in the Cultural Revolution* (Carbondale: Southern Illinois University, 1972).

6. "Resolution of the Chinese Communist Party Central Committee on Certain Issues Related to Accelerating Agricultural Development," *People's Daily*, 6 October 1979.

7. "A Strong Impetus for Accelerating Agricultural Development," editorial, *People's Daily*, 7 October 1979.

8. For example, see "Team Leader Yin Did Right," *People's Daily*, 5 February 1979. This particular document apparently reached down to the peasants; in a number of disputes with leftist-inclined local cadres, said the report, the peasants cited this document as a basis for their demands for greater autonomy. The same report shows how speedily Central Documents are disseminated. Soon after the dissemination of this Central Document on agricultural development, several peasants in Hopei took some fish from a commune fishpond without authorization. When the production team leader asked them for compensation, they refused on the grounds that the Central Document said that wanton deductions and fines should not be imposed on the peasants. In this case, those peasants misread the Central Committee Document to justify their action.

9. See Chu, *Radical Change*, pp. 35-60.

10. See Richard Baum and Frederick C. Teiwes, *Ssu-Ch'ing: The Socialist Education Movement of 1962-1966* (Berkeley: Center for Chinese Studies, University of California, 1968).

11. The following is based on Lu Tao-sheng, "Do Not Misuse Work Teams," *People's Daily*, 5 February 1979.

12. "Wholeheartedly Push the Four Modernizations," editorial, *People's Daily*, 9 February 1979.

13. Chai Chi, "Newspapers in China are Undergoing a Major Reform," Takung Daily (Hong Kong), 7 December 1977.

14. "Defend Truthfulness, Oppose False Reporting," editorial, *People's Daily*, 24 July 1979. Some reports were fabrications, said the editorial. For instance, on 22 February 1979, the *People's Daily* published a correspondent's report on an irrigation project in Anhui, where, it said, "more than 40,000 workers and engineers have been battling a severe snowstorm since last December to construct a permanent irrigation station." As it turned out, the editorial stated, the project had not even been started, not to mention the 40,000 workers who were not yet at the site.

   In another case, the *People's Daily* published on 13 December 1978 a feature story on the death of a revolutionary martyr, Wei Pa-chun, about which it had this to say: "Before his execution, Wei told his wife to have faith in the ultimate victory of the Party, and resolutely carry on the struggle. He took off a button from his clothes and asked his wife to give it to the Party as his last membership fee. Then, his chin firmly up, he walked to the execution ground. . . ." "In fact," the editorial said, "comrade Wei was shot during his illness by a renegade. Such untruthful sensationalism has no place in our news reports."

15. Ibid.

16. Ibid.

17. "Let's See How Many Unreasonable Burdens Are Carried by Production Teams," *People's Daily*, 31 March 1978.

18. "How Can We Make the Peasants Rich as Quickly as Possible," *People's Daily*, 9 August 1979.

19. "Our Nation's Agriculture Has Reached a Historical Turning Point," *People's Daily*, 11 September 1979.

20. "Hsiyang County Discusses the Pragmatic Basis of Truth for the 'Learn from Tachai' Movement," *People's Daily*, 3 October 1979.

21. "Fan Tsai-keng, a Commune Member, Earns Nearly 6,000 Yuan from Family Sideline Production," *People's Daily*, 9 August 1979; also, "A Faultless Income of 6,000 Yuan, *Wen Hui Pao* [Wen Hui Daily] (Shanghai), 6 August 1979, reprinted in *People's Daily*, 9 August 1979.

22. "Yuan Cheng-hua Makes Nearly 1,000 Yuan from Raising Rabbits," *People's Daily*, 25 August 1979.

23. "How Do We View the Increased Income among Some Peasants?" *People's Daily*, 20 April 1980.

24. Ibid.

25. "Stabilize the System of Three-Tiered Ownership, with Production Team as the Foundation," letter by Chang Hao, Bureau of Records, Kansu, *People's Daily*, 15 March 1979.

26. "Nan-wei-tsu Commune Party Secretary Corrects the Error of Using Operation Team as the Accounting Unit," *People's Daily*, 15 March 1979.

27. Editor's note, *People's Daily*, 15 March 1979.

28. The following is based on a special report released by Hsinhua News Agency on 20 May 1981. The report was originally carried by *Liaowang* (Forecast), a magazine published in Peking, in its May 1981 issue, under the title "Constantly Thinking of the 800,000,000 Peasants." It was in a special column reporting on activities of the Party's Central Committee. This particular report covered the 88th regular meeting of the Party's Central Committee Secretariat. It was carried in *Takung Daily* (Hong Kong), 20 May 1981. Also, "A Major Change in Chinese Villages," *Takung Daily*, 16 June 1981.

29. See "Wan Li Discusses Reform in Agriculture and People's Communes," *Takung Daily*, 6 June 1981. What we have provided here are extracts.

30. "How Come Nobody Would Give His Nod to Such a Good Practice?" *People's Daily*, 20 April 1980.

31. Ibid.

32. Nan Lan, "On Direction," *People's Daily*, 28 April 1980.

33. "Abandon Commandism, and Modify Winter Planting Program," *People's Daily*, 10 February 1979.

34. "What Does the Destruction of Melons Case Mean?" *People's Daily*, 27 July 1979. Also, "*Hopei Daily* Comments on Destruction of Melons in Liu-chun Commune," *People's Daily*, 31 July 1979.

35. "Cadres and Commune Members in Hopei Express Anger over Destruction of Melons," *People's Daily*, 1 August 1979; also, "Strong Reactions from Readers in Honan to Destruction of Melons Case," *People's Daily*, 1 August 1979.

36. "Ming-chi Commune Cadres Discuss Destruction of Melons Case," *People's Daily*, 3 August 1979.

37. "On the Incident of Destruction of Melons," *People's Daily*, 3 August 1979.

38. Ibid.

39. Ibid.

40. "Shih-chia-chuang District Office Issues Statement on Destruction of Melons Case," *People's Daily*, 31 July 1979.

41. "A Down-to-Earth Policy Must Not Be Mistaken for Capitalism," *People's Daily*, 3 August 1979.

42. Ibid.

43. "Evaluation of Cadres Must Be Done," editorial, *People's Daily*, 8 August 1979.

44. "The Practice of Using Relatives Must be Avoided," *People's Daily*, 15 August 1979. The official daily revealed some of the practices. For instance, when some leadership cadres are transferred, they bring not only their immediate families, but also secretaries, chauffeurs, and maids, and their family members. Others find ways to transfer to be close to them, not only their grown-up children, but daughters-in-law, sons-in-law, and even their sons' fiancees.

45. "Readers Express Anger, and Ask Provocative Questions on Destruction of Melons Case," *People's Daily*, 20 August 1979.

46. The following is based on "We Must Correct the Workstyle in Government Offices," editorial, *People's Daily*, 21 June 1979.

47. Ibid.

48. "Strict Demands for our Leadership Cadres," editorial, *People's Daily*, 15 August 1979.

49. "Directly Face Mistakes, Courageously Make Corrections—San-ho County Secretary Accepts Criticism," *People's Daily*, 23 August 1979.

50. "The Revelations of San-ho," editorial, *People's Daily*, 23 August 1979.

51. "The Four Modernizations Need Leaders Like Him—Comment on the Short Story 'Director Ch'iao Returns to his Post'," *People's Daily*, 3 September 1979.

52. Quoted in *People's Daily*, "On the Incident of Destruction of Melons," 3 August 1979.

53. "Evaluation of Cadres Must Be Done."

54. "Cadre Evaluation System Tried Out Among Section Chiefs," *People's Daily*, 8 August 1979.

55. The following is based on "Encourage Conversation with Cadres," editorial, *People's Daily*, 11 July 1979.

56. The following is based on "Leadership Cadres Must Personally Handle Letters and Visits from the People," editorial, *People's Daily*, 11 July 1979.

57. "Are Anonymous Letters Necessarily Not Above the Board?" editor's comment, *People's Daily*, 11 July 1979.

58. "What Does the Death of Hsiung I-fu Tell Us?" Teng Ssu-chien, Mien-hsien District Court, Szechuan, *People's Daily*, 25 August 1979.

59. Editor's note, *People's Daily*, 25 August 1979.

60. Pai Hsiao-lang and Kao Chien-ying, "Bureaucratism Kills," *People's Daily*, 22 September 1979.

61. Chiang Hung, "The People Must Have Solid Democratic Rights," *People's Daily*, 22 September 1979.

62. Li Tien-Han, "Reform in Government Offices Must Be Done," *People's Daily*, 22 September 1979.

63. "Lessons We Have Learned from the Death of Hsiung I-fu," *People's Daily*, 27 October 1979.

64. See Marc Blecher, Chapter 4 in this volume.

65. See Mitch Meisner, Chapter 9 in this volume.

66. For analysis of the land reform, see Chu, *Radical Change*, pp. 35–60.

67. By penetration, Liu refers to the process by which the central government reaches regions that hitherto were autonomous. By identification, he refers to the process by which the media gradually diffuse a set of common norms, values, and symbols so that identification can be established vertically between the rulers and the ruled and horizontally among citizens and groups. See Alan P.L. Liu, *Communications and National Integration in Communist China* (Berkeley: University of California Press, 1971), pp. 2–3.

68. The initial chaos in the commune movement has been described in Chu, *Radical Change*, pp. 187–214.

69. Liu Shao-ch'i's *San tzu I-pao* means three *tzu* and one *pao*. These are: *tzu-liu-ti*

284

(private plots), *tzu-yu shih-ch'ang* (rural free markets), *tzu-fu k'uei-ying* (assume loss or profit), *pao-ch'an tao-wu* (production quotas set on families). In other words policy allowed the commune members to retain and cultivate the private plots and to sell the products at rural open markets. Agricultural production quotas were set on the individual families, not on the collective. The production teams in the communes had to pledge to deliver to the state their shares of taxes and grains. Beyond that, they were free to dispose of their profits or assume responsibility for any loss. Liu's policy contributed to the recovery from the three disastrous years in China's agriculture following the Commune Movement of 1958. One major difference between Liu's policy and the current practices is that agricultural production quotas are now set on the production teams, not on individual families. Liu, who was expelled from the Party in the Cultural Revolution, has been posthumously rehabilitated by the Party Central Committee since March 1980. An important treatise authored by Liu on the duty of the Party and its members, dated 1 July 1940, was republished in the *People's Daily* in March 1980. See Liu Shao-ch'i, "How to Be a Good Party Member, How to Build a Good Party," *People's Daily*, 12 March 1980.

70. See editor's note on "Nan-wei-tzu Commune Party Secretary Corrects the Error of Using Operation Team as the Accounting Unit," *People's Daily*, 15 March 1979.

71. The basic accounting unit is important because it determines the nature of the economic system. The smallest basic accounting unit is the individual, which is practiced in the United States when husband and wife file income tax returns separately. In rural China today, as far as the private plot is concerned, the basic accounting unit is the nuclear family, as the family members usually work together and presumably share the income from the private plot. We have had accounts in the official paper suggesting how high family productivity from the private plots can be. It seems that moving the basic accounting unit from the production team level to the small operating teams, each consisting of several families, could increase productivity because small units could mean greater material incentives. The eagerness with which such deviations from the official policy were being pursued by some production teams, for instance those in Loyang as reported in the *People's Daily*, suggests this possible benefit. The question is whether such a move may end up in a rush back to the family as the exclusive accounting unit for both private plots and agricultural production in general. It would seem that if such a rush could be prevented, the current Party leadership may not be averse to a modification of its commune structure which would make the small operating team the basic accounting unit instead of the production team. The former would be a cluster of families while the latter is a village.

72. The practice of "commandism" among cadres in the early 1950s, and the Party's attempt to correct this tendency have been analyzed in Chu, *Radical Change*, pp. 61–87. For the Chinese concept of authority, see Francis L.K. Hsu, *Under the Ancestors' Shadow* (Stanford, CA: Stanford University Press, 1971).

73. Harold D. Lasswell, "The Structure and Function of Communication in Society," in Lyman Bryson, ed., *The Communication of Ideas* (New York: Institute for Religious and Social Studies, 1948); also in Wilbur Schramm, ed., *Mass Communications*, 2nd ed. (Urbana: University of Illinois Press, 1960), pp. 117–130.

74. For analysis of village life in traditional China, see Fei Hsiao-tung, *Peasant Life in China* (London: G. Routledge & Sons, 1939); Fei Hsiao-tung and Chang Chih-I, *Earthbound China* (Chicago: University of Chicago Press, 1945); and Martin C. Yang, *A Chinese Village, Taitou, Shantung Province* (New York: Columbia University Press, 1945). Life in a rural town has been analyzed by Francis Hsu in *Under the Ancestors' Shadow*.

285

75. See C. K. Yang, *A Chinese Village in Early Communist Transition* (Cambridge, MA: MIT Press, 1959).

76. See Chapter 8 in this volume, "Mass Media and Conflict Resolution," by Godwin C. Chu and Leonard L. Chu.

77. Deutsch has made the general observation that the mass media as well as other types of communication are essential to the development of a national community. See Karl W. Deutsch, *Nationalism and Social Communication: An Enquiry into the Foundation of Nationality*, 2nd ed. (Cambridge, MA: MIT Press, 1966), pp. 86-106. Allen argues that mass communication is identical and basic to the meaning of mass society. See Irving L. Allen, "Social Integration as an Organizing Principle," in George Gerbner, ed., *Mass Media Policies in Changing Cultures* (New York: John Wiley & Sons, 1977), pp. 235-248.

78. Francis Hsu, for instance, suggests that a near void existed between the central government and the local communities in traditional China. See Francis L.K. Hsu, *Americans and Chinese: Reflections on Two Cultures and Their People*, 2nd ed. (New York: Doubleday, 1970), pp. 375-379.

CONTRIBUTORS

Marc Blecher received his doctorate in political science from the University of Chicago, and is associate professor of government at Oberlin College. He is the author of several articles on economic distribution and growth, political participation and institutional change in rural China, and, with Gordon White, of *Micropolitics in Contemporary China: A Technical Unit during and after the Cultural Revolution*. He is the general editor and a contributing author of a forthcoming volume on county government, economic development, and urban-rural relations in Shulu County, Hebei, and is beginning a new research project on labor movement between city and countryside in contemporary China.

John P. Burns is a lecturer in the Department of Political Science at the University of Hong Kong, where he teaches public administration and Chinese politics. He completed his Ph.D. at Columbia University, and has contributed to several journals on the topic of political participation in rural China. He is now completing for publication a manuscript entitled, "Village Politics in Rural China."

Steven B. Butler received his Ph.D. in political science from Columbia University and is currently a visiting professor of government at Cornell University. He has been a postdoctoral research scholar at the Center for Chinese Studies at the University of Michigan. In 1980 he spent six months in a commune in northern China conducting field research supported by a grant from the Committee on Scholarly Communications with the People's Republic of China.

Charles P. Cell is associate professor in the Department of Sociology at the University of Wisconsin. Author of *Revolution at Work: Mobilization Campaigns in China*, he received his Ph.D. in sociology from the University of Michigan.

Godwin C. Chu is a research associate of the Communication Institute, East-West Center. A Ph.D. in communication research from Stanford, he has taught at Stanford University, University of Victoria, and Southern Illinois University. Among his publications are *Radical Change through Communication in Mao's China*; *Popular Media in China*; *Shaping New Cultural Patterns*; and, with Francis L.K. Hsu, *Moving a Mountain: Cultural Change in China*.

Leonard L. Chu is a lecturer in the Department of Journalism and Communication at the Chinese University of Hong Kong. He received his Ph.D. from Southern Illinois University. He has published extensively on mass media and communication in China, including *Planned Birth Campaigns in China*. He is associate editor of *Asia Messenger*.

Victor C. Falkenheim is associate professor in the Department of Political Economy at the University of Toronto. A Ph.D. in political science from Columbia University, he has done fieldwork in Taiwan and Hong Kong, and has published in *China Quarterly*, *Asian Survey*, and *Problems of Communism*.

Francis L.K. Hsu, formerly professor and chairman of the Department of Anthropology at Northwestern University, is now professor of anthropology and director of the Center for Cultural Studies in Education at the University of San Francisco. He has been president of the American Anthropological Association, and is the author of numerous articles and books, including *Under the Ancestors' Shadow: Kinship, Personality and Social Mobility in China*; *Clan, Caste and Club*; *China Day by Day*; *Americans and Chinese: Passage to Differences*; and *Moving a Mountain: Cultural Change in China*. He received his Ph.D. in anthropology from the University of London.

Kenneth G. Lieberthal is associate professor of political science at Swarthmore College, with his Ph.D. from Columbia University. He is the author of *Central Documents and Politburo Politics in China* and *Revolution and Tradition in Tientsin*. He has been a consultant to the Department of State and the Rand Corporation, and has published extensively on Chinese foreign policy.

Mitch Meisner, a Ph.D. in political science from the University of Chicago, has taught at Michigan State University, University of Chicago, Iowa State University, Western Washington State University, and the University of California at Santa Cruz. His research articles have been published in *Politics and Society*, *Modern China*, and *China Quarterly*.

INDEX

Agriculture
    bank loans, 125–126, 130–131
    controlled market, 138–139
    grain yield, 123–124, 126–127, 128
    local autonomy in, 129, 137–138
    mechanization of, 119–120, 121, 123,
        130–135, 136–138
    policies since 1979, 253, 261–262
    production, 126–127, 261–262
    Sixty Articles on, 129, 137
Authority, abuse of, in traditional China,
    10, 14, 20 n13

Basic accounting unit, 251, 252, 259–262,
    274–275, 285 n71
Baum, Richard, 13, 36
Big-character posters (*tatzupao*), 29, 35,
    51, 52, 178, 280 n5
    as communication channel, 253,
        280 n5
Britain, Opium War, 9
Bureaucratism, 12, 78, 129–130, 145, 216,
    270, 271–272, 275–276, 278

Cadres
    authority, abuse of, 76–79, 242–243,
        263–265, 271–272, 276, 278
    as communication channel, 53–54,
        65–66, 265–266, 270
    corruption, 147, 149–155
    criticism of, 51, 52, 55, 136, 266–267,
        283 n44
    evaluation of, 269–270
    income, 69, 145, 252
    leadership, 37, 65–69
    local reluctance to innovate, 18, 55,
        262–263
    new image, 268–269
    production role of, 71–72, 123, 124,
        128–129, 131–132, 133, 134,
        137–138
    reeducation of, 267–268
    transmitters of Central Committee
        Documents, 95–96, 97, 100
Campaigns
    communicative techniques of, 27–34,
        42

    as communication channel, 15, 17,
        275
    display in, 27–28, 29, 33
    goals, 25–26, 42, 51, 119, 145–146,
        169 n20, 170 n25
    mass participation in, 29–34
    mobilization process of, 36–42
    process of communication during,
        34–36
    stages of, 34–36
    work teams during, 146–155
    See also by specific name
Catty/*mou* measurement, 231, 245 n12
CD(74)21. *See* Criticizing Lin Piao and
    Confucius campaign
Central Committee Documents (*Chung-*
    fa), 14, 89–90, 112 n4(table), 237
    as communication channel, 253,
        281 n8
    dissemination techniques of, 97–101,
        114–115 n42(table)
    distortion of, 101–105
    numbering of, 112 n7
    and *People's Daily* editorials, 105–111
    transmission process of, 90–97,
        101–105, 110–111, 113 n25,
        114 n32, 117 n77, n78
CDs. *See* Central Committee Documents
Central Documents. *See* Central
    Committee Documents
Chung-fa. See Central Committee
    Documents
Centralization, 50
Chang Chun-huai, 242
Chang Hao, 258
Chang Hsien-chung, 4, 7
Chaos and order (*i-chih i-luan*) pattern, 7
Chao Tzu-yang, 259, 260
Ch'en Ming-chu, 242
Chen Sheng, 3
Ch'en Yung-kuei, 226, 227, 228–231, 234,
    237, 244 n4, 244–245 n9
    as communication channel, 239,
        246 n32
    corruption of, 227, 240–243, 246 n30
    as honest cadre, 231–233, 235, 238,
        239
    as radical, 235, 236
Chiang Ch'ing. *See* Gang of Four

Note: "n" indicates the note number on the page.

Ch'iao Kuang-pu, 268, 269
Ch'in Dynasty, 3, 6
Chinese Communist Party, 10, 251
    agriculture policies, 129, 137, 261–262
    Central Committee, 12, 40, 89–90, 91,
        98, 259
    goals, 25, 43 n5, 48, 58, 121–135, 136,
        137–138
    leadership, 11, 14, 16–18, 25, 43 n5, 53,
        63, 72, 83 n1
    policymaking since 1976, 57–58,
        259–262, 274–275, 276
    Sixth Plenary Session, 13, 18
Ch'ing Dynasty, 4, 7–9
Ching, Emperor, 7, 11
Chi Seng, 268
Chi Teng-k'uei, 125, 129
Chou Dynasty, 6
Chou Hsing, 94, 113 n19
Cleaning Up Class Ranks campaign, 145,
    169 n20, 170 n25
Collectivism, 12, 260–261, 274
Commandism. See Cadres, abuse of
    authority and Bureaucratism
Communes (jen-min kung-she)
    cadres in, 67, 69–72, 73–74, 84 n16,
        252
    changes since 1976, 256–258
    mechanization in, 131–135, 138
    original concept of, 64, 274
    organization of, 64, 65, 83 n6, 168 n4,
        280 n1
    resources, control and allocation of,
        130–134
    reforms of, 12, 16, 18
    sideline activities in, 123–124
    work teams in, 145, 146, 148, 149, 154,
        157, 160
Communication channels, 14, 17–18, 27,
        43 n9, 47–48, 51, 72, 233–234,
        252(figure), 253
    coordination, 119–120, 135, 136–139
    effectiveness of, 275
    hsia fang system, 29–30
    meetings, 28–29, 30–32, 52, 56, 89
    in traditional China, 9, 10, 278–279
    See also big character posters,
        campaigns, Central Committee
        Documents, letters to the editor,
        mass media
Conflict, 175
Confucius, 6, 169 n20
    See also Criticizing Lin Piao and
        Confucius campaign

Coser, Lewis, 175
Criticizing Lin Piao and Confucius
        campaign, 95, 98–99, 108–109,
        169 n20
    CD(74)21, 98–99, 101–105
    work teams during, 145
Cultural Revolution, 29, 34–35, 51, 76–77,
        93, 169 n20, 259
    and Central Committee Documents,
        91, 109
    disillusionment with, 17, 51, 79,
        242–243
    effects of, 56, 57, 67–68
    radicalism of, 15, 177
    work teams during, 145, 146,

Dittmer, Lowell, 145
Downs, Anthony, 143

Five Antis (Wu Fan) movement, 12, 15
Five bad elements, 97, 114 n33, 149,
        171 n38, 198
Four Clean-ups campaign (Ssu-ch'ing),
        13, 36, 135–136, 141 n39, 170 n35
    work teams during, 143, 145, 147, 148,
        149–150, 153, 164–165, 168 n8
    See also Socialist Education
        campaign
Four Modernizations campaign, 3, 53, 177
    problems in, 254–255, 269, 276
    ideal cadre for, 268, 269

Gang of Four, 17–18, 57, 177, 259
    media manipulation by, 109, 110, 255,
        277
    radicalism of, 51, 76–77, 256, 275, 276
Great Britain, exploitation by, 9
Great Leap Forward, exaggerated
        productivity of, 231

Hammond, Edward, 79, 82
Han Dynasty, 7, 11
Hinton, William, 31, 36, 39, 40, 230
Hong Kong, 64, 84 n16, 123, 255
Ho Shen, 8
Hsiung I-fu, 271–272, 277
Hsiyang County, 226, 245 n20
    political conflicts in, 234–236,
        241–242
    work teams in, 227, 237

Hsun-yi County, negative example of, 51, 64, 76–79
Hua Kuo-feng, 49, 111, 210
  on cadre evaluation, 269–271
Huang Lao, rule of, 7, 11, 19 n5
Hung Hsiu-ch'uan, 4
Hu Yao-pang, 259

Inkeles, Alex, 176
Investigation teams (*tiao-ch'a tui*), 144, 168–169 n9

Japan, invasion by, 9, 10, 228

Kiangsu, 101

Landlords, 13, 36, 37–38, 253, 277–278
  exploitation by, 33, 273, 274
Land Reform. *See* Rural Land Reform of 1950–1952
Lasswell, Harold D., 277
Leader-mass relationships, 68, 69–70, 74–75, 76–82
Letters to the editor, 15, 51, 52
  analysis of, 177–178, 213–214, 217–218 n13
  by categories, 188, 189–201
  characteristics of, 178, 179(table), 180–181(table), 182–183(table), 184–185
  as communication channel, 277
  conflict resolution, institution for, 175–176, 214–216, 278
  by contents, 205, 206(table), 207–209
  by groups, 185, 186–187(table), 188–189
  by modes, 201–205
  processing of, 209–213
Li Hsien-nien, 122
Lin Piao, 5l, 92–93, 169 n20
  and CD(74)4, 90–91, 92–95, 112–113 n8
  See also Criticizing Lin Piao and Confucius campaign
Li Ta-chang, 96
Li Tzu-ch'eng, 4, 7
Liu, Alan, 13, 25, 274
Liu-chun Commune. *See* Melon incident, Liu-chun Commune
Liu Shao-ch'i
  author of Central Committee Documents, 106, 117 n77, 237

downfall of, 34–35
  production policies, 259, 274, 284–285 n69
  on work teams, 145
Local autonomy
  degree of, 258–262
  restoration of, 256, 258–261, 274, 284–285 n69
Local solidarity, 16, 272–275
Long Bow village, 30, 31, 36–37, 38, 40, 41
Lung Chi-jui, 8–9

Malraux, Andre, 63
Mao Tse-tung, 9, 11, 34–35, 40
  author of Central Committee Documents, 106
  on cadres, 54, 98
  and campaigns, 34–35
  on conflict, 15
  disillusionment with, 12, 13, 14, 17
  on Great Leap Forward, 49
  on leadership, 144–145
  on mass line, 49–50, 63, 146
  on Tachai brigade, 238–239
  on transformation, 39
  on work models, 32–33
  on work teams, 145
Mass line, theory of, 47, 48–50, 57, 58, 63–65
  as communication channel, 79–82
  post-Mao reform, 78–79
Mass media
  and campaigns, 27, 29, 35
  as communication channel, 251, 254–256, 276–277, 278
  credibility, 255–256, 281 n14
  selective reporting, 101
Meetings. *See* Communication channels
Melon incident, Liu-chun Commune, 263–265, 266, 273, 274
Merton, Robert, 129
Ming Dynasty, 4
Mou measurement, 158, 172 n61
Mutual Aid Teams (*pao-ch'an tao-tsu*), 40
  See also Tachai brigade, mutual aid in

Nee, Victor, 241

One-Hit Three-Oppose campaign, 147, 170 n25

Pao, Judge (Pao Kung), 216, 272, 279

Peasants, 12–13, 256
    and cadre contact, 65–66, 69–72,
      79–82
    and campaigns, 36–41
    and Central Committee Documents,
      97–98
    historical uprisings of, 3–4, 7
    and meetings, 30–31
    political participation of, 51–57, 274
    production workpoints, 135, 136,
      142 n41
People's Daily, 175–176, 254–256
    editorials, role of, 35, 105–111,
      107(table), 117 n83,
      117–118 n84(table)
    letters column, 176–177, 213, 217 n12,
      270–271
    See also Letters to the editor
Political integration, 6–9
Personalized rule (*jen-chih*), 10, 216
Population, growth of, 9
Production brigades, (*sheng-ch'an ta tui*),
    140 n14, 168 n4
    cadres in, 67–72, 73–74, 84 n16
    income, 145, 257–258
    mechanization in, 132, 138
    organization of, 64, 65, 83 n6, 251,
      280 n1
    sideline activities in, 123–124,
      156–157, 257–258
    solidarity, 225–226
    workpoint system, 153
    work teams in, 145–160 passim,
      170 n36, 254
Production teams (*sheng-ch'an hsiao-*
    tui), 125, 140 n14, 168 n4
    autonomy of, 55, 137–138, 274–275
    basic accounting unit of, 251–252,
      259, 275, 285 n71
    cadres in, 67–72, 73–74, 84 n16,
      135–136, 141 n39
    conflict resolution in, 278
    coordination indicators in, 129–130
    income, 122–124, 129, 145, 258
    organization of, 65, 83 n6, 251, 280 n1
    sideline activities in, 123–124, 127,
      128, 258
    solidarity, 273
    workpoint system in, 159–160
    work teams in, 145–160 passim,
      170 n36

Radicals. *See* Gang of Four

Rectify and Rebuild the Party campaign,
    145, 169 n20
Red Eyebrows (*Ch'ih-mei*) movement, 3
Red Flag, 35, 50, 215
Red Guards, 15, 29, 35, 273–274
Rural Land Reform of 1950–1952, 11, 12,
    15, 274
Russia. *See* Soviet Union

San-ho County, negative example of,
    267–268
San-tzu I-pao policy, 274, 284–285 n69
Shih Huang Ti, Emperor, 3, 6–7
Shih Kan, 269
Shue, Vivienne, 225
Simmel, George, 175
Snow, Edgar, 40
Socialist Education campaign, 35, 36, 106,
    112 n6, 117 n83, 168 n8, 169 n20
    work teams during, 145–146
    See also Four Clean-ups campaign
Socialist legality, 79
Social system
    allocation in, 4, 11–12
    and communication, 5(figure),
      10, 278–279
    conflict resolution in, 15–16, 25–26,
      47, 48–49, 175
    disintegration in, 3–4, 8–9, 10, 11–12
    goals, 4–5, 18, 25, 43 n5
    modern integration in, 11, 16–17
    roots, 16, 251, 256
    stability, 3, 10
    traditional integration, 6, 9–10, 273
Societal integration, process of, 4, 5, 6, 14,
    19 n3, n4, 47, 279
    achievement of, 50, 275
Soviet Union, coercive mobilization in, 40
Squatting on the spot (*tun tien*), 70, 73–74,
    84 n31, 135, 136, 141 n37
Study Tachai campaign, 54, 128, 145, 157,
    159, 164–165, 169 n20, 257
    See also Tachai brigade
Sun Yat-sen, 9, 274

Tachai brigade, 16
    Four Clean-ups campaign in, 237, 238
    grain yield, 231, 233, 240–241
    mutual aid in, 227–231
    as national model, 226, 229, 238–239,
      246 n30, n32, 257
    solidarity, 237–238, 239–240

work team in, 238
  See also Study Tachai campaign
T'ai-p'ing Rebellion, 4, 8, 9
T'aitsung, Emperor, 267
Tang Dynasty, 267
Tatzupao. See Big-character posters
Teiwes, Frederick C., 13
Teng Hsiao-p'ing, 106, 255, 260
Thompson, James D., 120, 138, 142 n44
Three Antis (*San Fan*) campaign, 13,
      28–29
Three Loyalties campaign, 147, 170 n25
Three Togethers (*san-t'ung*) procedures,
      76, 144, 161, 162, 167, 170 n36
Tien-an-men Square, 33, 53
Tseng Kuo-fan, 8, 14

Union of Soviet Socialist Republics. *See*
      Soviet Union
United States, conflict resolution in, 175
Unity (*t'uan chieh*), 48

Verba, Sidney, 72
Village, role of, 273, 277

Wang Mang, 3
Wang Pi-ch'eng, 93, 95, 97
Wang Tung-chou, 238
Warlords, 9, 10
Warring States period, 6
Wei Cheng, 267
Wen, Emperor, 7, 11
Weng Sen-ho, 103–104
Western invasion, 7–8, 9, 10, 11
Work teams (*kung tso tui*), 14–15, 74–76,
      143–147, 168 n4
  as peasants' communication channel,
      143–144, 161–167, 253
  campaign, 147–155, 157–159, 170 n36,
      170–171 n37
  classification of, 165(table)
  criticism of, 145, 254
  issues investigated by,
      165–166(table)
  noncampaign, 155–157, 159–160
Wu Kuang, 3

Yao Wen-yuan, 109, 110
Yellow Turbans (*Huang-chin*) movement,
      3–4

Yueh Yao-hsien, 242
Yu, Frederick T.C., 13, 176